T0330366

Market Instruments and the Protection of Natural Resources

CRITICAL ISSUES IN ENVIRONMENTAL TAXATION

Series Editors: Larry Kreiser, *Cleveland State University, USA*, Hope Ashiabor, *Macquarie University, Australia* and Janet E. Milne, *Vermont Law School, USA*

The *Critical Issues in Environmental Taxation* series provides insights and analysis on environmental taxation issues on an international basis and explores detailed theories for achieving environmental goals through fiscal policy. Each book in the series contains pioneering and thought-provoking contributions by the world's leading environmental tax scholars who respond to the diverse challenges posed by environmental sustainability.

Previous volumes in the series:

Original book published by CCH Incorporated

Volumes I–IV published by Richmond Law Publishers

Volumes V–VIII published by Oxford University Press

Volume IX onwards published by Edward Elgar Publishing

Recent titles in the series include:

Volume XI   Carbon Pricing, Growth and the Environment
Edited by Larry Kreiser, Ana Yábar Sterling, Pedro Herrera, Janet E. Milne and Hope Ashiabor

Volume XII   Green Taxation and Environmental Sustainability
Edited by Larry Kreiser, Ana Yábar Sterling, Pedro Herrera, Janet E. Milne and Hope Ashiabor

Volume XIII   Market Based Instruments
National Experiences in Environmental Sustainability
Edited by Larry Kreiser, David Duff, Janet E. Milne and Hope Ashiabor

Volume XIV   Environmental Taxation and Green Fiscal Reform
Theory and Impact
Edited by Larry Kreiser, Soocheol Lee, Kazuhiro Ueta, Janet E. Milne and Hope Ashiabor

Volume XV   Carbon Pricing
Design, Experiences and Issues
Edited by Larry Kreiser, Mikael Skou Andersen, Birgitte Egelund Olsen, Stefan Speck, Janet E. Milne and Hope Ashiabor

Volume XVI   Environmental Pricing
Studies in Policy Choices and Interactions
Edited by Larry Kreiser, Mikael Skou Andersen, Birgitte Egelund Olsen, Stefan Speck, Janet E. Milne and Hope Ashiabor

Volume XVII   Green Fiscal Reform for a Sustainable Future
Reform, Innovation and Renewable Energy
Edited by Natalie P. Stoianoff, Larry Kreiser, Bill Butcher, Janet E. Milne and Hope Ashiabor

Volume XVIII   Market Instruments and the Protection of Natural Resources
Edited by Natalie P. Stoianoff, Larry Kreiser, Bill Butcher, Janet E. Milne and Hope Ashiabor

Market Instruments and the Protection of Natural Resources

Edited by

Natalie P. Stoianoff

Professor of Law and Director of the Intellectual Property Program, University of Technology Sydney, Australia

Larry Kreiser

Professor Emeritus of Accounting, Cleveland State University, USA

Bill Butcher

Director of Coursework Programs, Taxation and Business Law, University of New South Wales, Australia

Janet E. Milne

Professor of Law, Vermont Law School, USA

Hope Ashiabor

Associate Professor of Law, Macquarie University, Australia

CRITICAL ISSUES IN ENVIRONMENTAL TAXATION
VOLUME XVIII

Cheltenham, UK • Northampton, MA, USA

Published by
Edward Elgar Publishing Limited
The Lypiatts
15 Lansdown Road
Cheltenham
Glos GL50 2JA
UK

Edward Elgar Publishing, Inc.
William Pratt House
9 Dewey Court
Northampton
Massachusetts 01060
USA

A catalogue record for this book
is available from the British Library

Library of Congress Control Number: 2016938585

This book is available electronically in **Elgar**online
Law subject collection
DOI 10.4337/9781786431219

ISBN 978 1 78643 120 2 (cased)
ISBN 978 1 78643 121 9 (eBook)

Typeset by Servis Filmsetting Ltd, Stockport, Cheshire

Contents

Figures

Tables

Editorial review board

The fourteen chapters in this book have been brought to publication with the help of an editorial review board dedicated to peer review. The 21 members of the board are committed to the field of environmental taxation and are active participants in environmental taxation events around the world.

Chair:

Natalie P. Stoianoff
University of Technology Sydney, Australia

Members:

Mikael Skou Andersen
Aarhus University, Denmark

Hope Ashiabor
Macquarie University, Australia

Celeste Black
University of Sydney, Australia

Nils Axel Braathen
Organisation for Economic Co-operation and Development (OECD), France

Karen Bubna-Litic
University of South Australia, Australia

Bill Butcher
University of New South Wales, Australia

Damien Giurco
University of Technology Sydney, Australia

Wayne Gumley
Monash University, Australia

Ann Hansford
University of Exeter, United Kingdom

Mona L. Hymel
University of Arizona, USA

Larry Kreiser
Cleveland State University, USA

Soocheol Lee
Meijo University, Japan

Roberta Mann
University of Oregon, USA

Janet E. Milne
Vermont Law School, USA

Anna Mortimore
Griffith University, Australia

Sven Rudolph
Kyoto University, Japan

Stefan Speck
European Environment Agency, Denmark

Stefan Weishaar
University of Groningen, The Netherlands

Jian Wu
Renmin University, China

Yan Xu
The Chinese University of Hong Kong, Hong Kong

Contributors

Elena de Lemos Pinto Aydos, University of Newcastle, Australia

Karen Bubna-Litic, University of South Australia, Australia

Bill Butcher, University of New South Wales, Australia

Mary Margaret Callison, Wright State University, USA

Mingde Cao, China University of Political Science and Law, China

Jacqueline Cottrell, Green Budget Europe, Belgium

Marian Dobranschi, Mendel University in Brno, Czech Republic

Ana Carolina Cerqueira Duque, Campos Mello Advogados, Brazil

François Fortier, United Nations Office for Sustainable Development, USA

Wayne Gumley, Monash University, Australia

Mona L. Hymel, University of Arizona, USA

Vanessa Johnston, Monash University, Australia

Claudia Kettner, Austrian Institute of Economic Research (WIFO), Austria

Larry Kreiser, Cleveland State University, USA

Paul Lee, Cleveland State University, USA

Achim Lerch, Hessian University of Cooperative Education, Germany

Danuse Nerudova, Mendel University in Brno, Czech Republic

Stathis Palassis, University of Technology Sydney, Australia

Sven Rudolph, Kyoto University, Japan

Kai Schlegelmilch, Green Budget Germany, Germany

Hans Sprohge, Wright State University, USA

Rahmat Tavallali, Walsh University, USA

Preface

One-third of the world's population face water scarcity; 70 percent of the world's fisheries are depleted or overexploited; soil degradation affects 30 percent of the world's irrigated lands, 40 percent of rain-fed agricultural lands, and 70 percent of rangelands and every year 1.0 million people die prematurely from respiratory illnesses associated with air pollution. (World Bank, *The Climate Change, Environment, and Natural Resources Management*, 2008 at http://go.worldbank.org/ABCDXUZ7B0)

It is well noted that delay in reducing greenhouse gas emissions can and has caused irreparable harm to our natural resources. The Paris United Nations climate conference in December 2015 produced a landmark agreement achieving consensus that all 196 countries attending, rich or poor, will commit to tackling climate change. Only through a concerted global effort to reduce emissions can we achieve a stabilisation of our climate and save our precious natural environment and indeed our future. However, pressures on natural resources come from other directions as well, such as overuse, mismanagement and contamination.

In Volume XVIII of the Critical Issues in Environmental Taxation, environmental experts focus on our natural resources. The use of market and fiscal instruments to protect our natural resources from rural to marine environments is reviewed. Market instruments that are designed to protect the global atmosphere are evaluated. Meanwhile, consideration is given to shifting the tax burden to achieve environmentally responsible outcomes.

We hope readers find these studies of interest and worthy of serious consideration for the development of policies that will achieve a stable global environment.

Natalie P. Stoianoff, Lead Editor
Larry Kreiser, Co-Editor
Bill Butcher, Co-Editor
Janet E. Milne, Co-Editor
Hope Ashiabor, Co-Editor

PART I

Balancing sustainable use and natural resource protection

1. The use of market-based instruments in protecting South Australia's marine protected areas

Karen Bubna-Litic

1. INTRODUCTION

In October 2014, a system of sanctuary zones came into operation in the Australian state of South Australia. The coming into force of these sanctuary zones was the last step in a process designed to protect South Australia's unique marine diversity which began some 15 years previously.[1]

These sanctuary zones are 'no fishing' zones and are part of the marine protected areas of the state.[2] They number 83 and cover approximately 6% of South Australia's marine area. Marine protected areas cover approximately 44% of the state's marine area. The non-sanctuary zoned marine protected areas, which cover 38% of the state's marine areas, allow a variety of fishing (both commercial and recreational) and other recreational activities.[3]

The designation of these 83 sanctuary zones has caused much concern, anxiety and distress to many of South Australia's fishing communities.[4] This paper focuses on the conflict with the commercial fishers and the use of market mechanisms to try to come to a resolution of this conflict. It aims to evaluate the effectiveness of a particular market-based instrument to deal with the concerns of these stakeholders and analyse the outcomes in the establishment and zoning of South Australia's Marine Parks.

Section 2 will look at the background to the protection of marine diversity in South Australia (SA). It will describe the uniqueness of the marine diversity of SA and the process embarked on for its protection. Section 3 will set out the concerns of the fishing industry and what efforts were involved in trying to ameliorate these concerns. Section 4 will evaluate the use of the market based instruments used in this process and Section 5 will discuss the resolution using this mechanism and what lessons can be used and applied in other jurisdictions.

2.   BACKGROUND

a.   SA's Unique Marine Environment

South Australia's marine environment covers approximately 60,000 square kilometres including 5000 kilometres of coastline.[5] Its waters are home to some of the most unique marine diversity in the world. For example, these waters hold more than 720 fish species, including tropical and cold water species; over 1200 species of marine algae; and approximately 80% of the world's total population of Australian sea lions.[6] It hosts the world's largest known breeding aggregation of giant cuttlefish. Its state marine emblem is the amazing Leafy Sea Dragon, found nowhere else in the world. In fact, approximately 80% of known species are endemic;[7] in comparison, the Great Barrier Reef is home to 15–20% endemic species.[8]

This uniqueness of the SA marine environment is the result of three main conditions:

(1)   A long period of geographic isolation, resulting from isolating ocean currents. It is in the middle of the longest south-facing coastline in the world and the ocean currents have isolated marine life in SA for a long period of time.[9] This contrasts with the Great Barrier Reef, which shares most of its marine life with the Pacific Ocean.

(2)   Exposure to severe climatic conditions, leading to more extreme temperatures.[10] This has resulted in plants and animals evolving to survive in these harsh conditions and living nowhere else in the world.

(3)   Living in one of the most nutrient poor parts of the global marine environment.[11] This leads to greater species diversity, as life has to evolve at a much greater rate to cope with the low nutrient conditions.

In addition to these conditions, South Australia has 150 offshore islands with pristine ecosystems. Another unique element of the South Australian environment is that it contains two of only three inverse estuaries in the world, the other one being in California. In these two estuaries, Spencer Gulf and Gulf St Vincent, there is no freshwater input at the top of each gulf, which means that they are much more saline at their tips than at their open ends. This results in a unique aquaculture environment.[12]

b.   Legislative Background to Protecting SA's Marine Environment

Internationally marine parks are recognised as a key tool in protecting and conserving habitats and marine biological diversity.[13] Much like land-based national parks, marine parks play a central role in maintaining ecological processes, protecting areas of natural and cultural heritage, and assisting in adapting to the impacts of climate change.[14] South Australia has a chequered history in protecting marine diversity, even though its marine and estuarine waters represent some of the most unique and biologically diverse waters in the world.[15]

Historically, marine areas in South Australia were protected by the establishment of Aquatic Reserves under the *Fisheries Act 1971* (SA) (now the *Fisheries Management Act 2007* (SA)). This Act provided regulations to restrict and regulate all activities within these Aquatic Reserves.

In 1991, the Commonwealth government announced a 10 year marine conservation programme to ensure the conservation and sustainable use of Australia's marine and estuarine environments, by adopting a bio-geographic/ecosystem approach.[16] The programme was endorsed by states and territories under the Inter-governmental Agreement.[17] However, this approach was not adopted by SA. Instead, SA identified and selected aquatic reserves based on 'perceived social benefits', rather than on an ecosystem approach. This proved to be detrimental to marine biodiversity as many coastal fish and crustacean species reached the 'fully exploited' status.[18]

In 2007, the *Marine Parks* Bill was passed and became law. The aim of the Act is to protect and conserve marine biological diversity and marine habitats by providing for the management of a comprehensive, adequate and representative (CAR) network of marine parks. Through this process, the focus has shifted from fisheries management to conservation.

c. Involving Relevant Stakeholders in the Process

In 2009, South Australia proclaimed a network of 19 Marine Parks, covering 44% of South Australia's waters. Under the *Marine Parks Act 2007* (SA), there is a requirement for community participation in the declaration (outer boundaries process) and management (zoning) of the marine parks.[19]

The outer-boundaries process attracted more than 2000 submissions, but the zoning process proved more controversial, particularly with respect to the establishment of the 83 sanctuary zones in which fishing has been banned. This zoning process took 5 years and attracted more than 8000 submissions through an extensive consultation process.[20] In 2012, Marine Park management plans and zoning regulations were put into place, declaring 83 sanctuary zones to come into force on 1 October 2014.

Community participation was embedded into the process on the basis that the success of the marine parks would ultimately depend on steward-ship by the community. If the government could not get the support of the community at large, then the marine parks would fail. Gaining this support was a challenging task as there were a number of stakeholder groups holding conflicting views. These groups included commercial fishers, recreational fishers, tourism operators, environmental groups, indigenous groups and rural communities. The commercial fishers and those in the surrounding rural regions feared job losses, loss of livelihoods and loss of traditions.[21] The recreational fishers were divided on the issue. Some argued they had a right to fish in the ocean, whereas others understood the importance of preserving the marine life for future generations. In addition to the interest of the fishers, environmental groups and indigenous groups were interested in preservation and concern for future generations.

In order to gain the support of the community, the relevant government department went beyond the requirements under the *Marine Parks Act 2007* (SA) and decided that best practice would be to also involve the public in the zoning process. The Act only required public consultation in the designation of the boundaries of the Marine Parks, not the zoning of these parks. To this end, it embarked on the establishment of 13 Marine Park Local Advisory Groups (MPLAGs), with the intention of facilitating a more robust consultation process. The selection of the members of the MPLAGs was on a volunteer basis and some of these groups ended up with an overrepresentation of certain stakeholder groups, leading to some conflict throughout the process.[22]

One of the goals of the process was that the zoning aimed to minimise the economic impacts and/or displacement of existing fishing activities, so that it would have less than a 5% economic impact.[23] To help ensure this result, a tracking tool called SAMPIT was employed. This tool was deployed to each of the MPLAGs and members of commercial and recreational stakeholder groups were asked to plot, through SAMPIT, their high-value fishing areas.[24] The intention of the government in using this tool was to ensure the least possible overlap between the high-value fishing areas and the establishment of the sanctuary zones. The resulting economic impact was about 1.7% of the state's commercial fishing effort, which was significantly lower than the target of less than a 5% economic impact.[25]

The consultation process has been regarded as a success, on the basis of a number of indicators.[26] The fact that the department went beyond the legislative requirement by setting up 13 MPLAGs to establish the management and zoning plans, the fact that more than 10,000 submissions were received during the process and the fact that 19 marine parks were established by the process are all indicators of an effective participation process. However, there were some limitations in the process.

The two main areas of conflict were in regards to the conservation groups, who withdrew from the MPLAG process owing to the aggressive behaviour of other stakeholders, and the conflict with the commercial fishers.[27] The conservation groups were brought back into the process when the department called a two day meeting of all the peak stakeholder groups to look at the suggested zonings from the MPLAGs and they then issued a draft zoning and management plan for wider public consultation.[28] This process caused concern for members of the MPLAGs, who thought that their final advice to the government would be 'immediately rubber stamped'.[29] The presiding member of the Marine Parks Council, Professor Rob Lewis, believed the government could have better managed the expectations of the MPLAGs, explaining that, in addition to their advice, other factors such as the science and the socio-economics also need to be considered.[30]

The conflict with the commercial fishers is discussed in the remainder of this paper, together with the market mechanisms used to try to resolve this particular conflict.

3. CONFLICT WITH THE COMMERCIAL FISHERS

There were many conflicting values inherent in applying an effective community consultation process in the zoning of Marine Park Areas in SA. Environmental, economic and social values all needed to be considered in this process. Exacerbating this is the fact that South Australians view the marine environment in a number of different ways. Some see it as providing a livelihood and source of income (commercial fishers, industries using shipping, tourist operators, mineral resource companies and aquaculture). Others see it as a source of pleasure and recreational opportunities (boat owners, recreational fishers, divers, sporting groups, holidaymakers). It is also seen as a precious and fragile environment to be protected and conserved. The ways in which people behave in our marine or coastal environments are driven by these views.

Various issues have been identified in the past identification and management of marine protected areas which illustrate these conflicting values. These include over-fishing, disturbed breeding grounds, the need to protect older fish with a high reproduction rate, the impact that marine protected areas have on the fishing industry with smaller areas of water to exploit, resulting in a smaller catch, the loss of value of fishing licences and issues of tourism.[31] Many of the communities also depend on the fishing industry for employment. It is their way of life and it holds their traditional values. There is also the associated fear of job losses and unemployment in the regions. These multiple potential areas of conflict have been described as a 'convergence of conflict',[32] which needs to be managed. However, there are enormous difficulties in reconciling the competing concerns of the environment, the sustainability of the fishing sector of the economy, the effects on recreational fishers and the real or feared effects on livelihoods and communities.

At the end of the consultation process, 83 sanctuary zones were established and all of the stakeholders agreed that the results were something they could live with.[33] The commercial fishing industry had argued that displacement of their livelihoods could be avoided by pragmatic zoning and that any distribution effort needed to take place without impacting ecological or economic sustainability of the fishery.

In the end, the economic impact on the commercial fishing industry was less than 1.7%[34] and the government committed to buying back commercial fishing entitlements to offset this impact.

4.   USE OF MARKET-BASED INSTRUMENTS AND OTHER TOOLS

a.   The Impact of Sanctuary Zones on Commercial Fishing

The value of South Australia's commercial fishing industry is around $400 million,[35] and this industry is managed through a series of fisheries management plans under the *Fisheries Management Act 2007* (SA). For example, the management plan for the SA Commercial Abalone Fishery is a 10 year plan running from 1 September 2012,[36] and the management plan for the Northern Zone Rock Lobster Fishery is a five year plan running from 14 November 2014.[37] The designation of SA's marine parks can be seen as a way to rebuild the sustainability of the fishing industry.[38] In principle, this process needs to ensure that the stakeholders who bear the cost of the rebuilding process will receive some of the benefits and that they recognise and value the long-term benefits of this process.[39]

It has been recognised that the zoning in the marine parks will have some displacement impact on the commercial fishing effort. If this displacement cannot be redistributed, the government will have to remove this effort to ensure sustainability of the impacted fishing stock, in line with the objectives under the *Marine Parks Act 2007* (SA).[40] The SA government set out a four step process, with compulsory acquisition as a last resort.[41]

These four steps were:

(1) avoid displacement by pragmatic zoning;
(2) redistribute effort only where possible without impacting ecological or economic sustainability of the fishery;
(3) market-based buy-back of sufficient effort to avoid impact on the fishery;
(4) compulsory acquisition as a last resort option.

The view of the government was to manage the commercial catch/effort reduction entirely through a voluntary, market-based buy-back of sufficient effort to avoid negative impacts on the fishery. The programme was conducted to mitigate the risk to fish stocks associated with displaced catch and effort on areas of the fishery that remain open to fishing.[42] If the voluntary programme was not successful, the last resort option would be compulsory acquisition under the *Marine Parks Act 2007*.[43] The Voluntary Catch/Effort Reduction Programme, administered by Primary Industries and Regions SA (PIRSA), began in July 2013 to allow for enough time before the no fishing zones came into operation on 1 October 2014.

The impacts vary depending on the nature of the fishery itself. For example, the impacts of specific controls on fishing for migratory or pelagic species (sardines) are very different to those on fishing for sedentary species (abalone).[44]

The following fisheries were examined to see what impact these sanctuary zones would have on their industry—sardine, prawn, abalone, rock lobster, marine scalefish and blue crab fisheries. If the economic impact was greater than the agreed 5%, a buy-back mechanism would be instituted.

The data on sardines showed that the average impact of not harvesting in the designated sanctuary zones from 2000 to 2011 was 1.93%, varying from 0% in 2000 to 11.8% in 2011.[45] PIRSA concluded that this estimated displacement could be sustainably distributed and so no buy-backs were instituted within the sardine industry.[46] There was similar data with prawns and with the blue crab fishery. The data in relation to prawns found that there was a 0.09% impact from Spencer Gulf and 0.56% from Gulf St Vincent, and that this estimated displacement could be sustainably redistributed.[47]

The abalone, rock lobster, marine scalefish fisheries and charter boat fishery all found themselves heavily impacted by the establishment of the sanctuary zones. The average historical catch of abalone displaced over the past 21 years in the sanctuary zones amounts to more than 8% with percentages varying across the different zones and between the different varieties (blacklip and greenlip abalone). To better manage the buy-back process, regions A and B in the Western Zone abalone fishery were amalgamated into a single region.[48] This was to ensure that, after the buy-back, the remaining abalone fisheries were able to fulfil their quotas, by having a larger catch region.

For the rock lobster fisheries, the average historical catch displaced was greater than 6%, with the buy-back target being approximately 260 pots.[49]

The marine scalefish fishery is licensed on the basis of fishing days and it covers fishing by handline, longline, haul net and other gear. The total average historical catch displaced by the sanctuary zones is greater than 5% so the buy-backs for each of these fishing methods are 863 handline fishing days, 225 longline fishing days, 701 haul net fishing days and 672 other fishing days.[50] The calculations have been based on the fishery returns of the licence holders for the last five years, with an average of the best four out of the last five.[51] Government policy is that catch history does not transfer with a licence and that only current holders come within this process. For those holding a licence for less than five years, the lowest catch year will be eliminated and the remaining years averaged.

Charter boat fishing is a major taker of fish in South Australian waters. It is a commercial platform for recreational fishing and is considered as a commercial operation rather than being commercial fishers. Operators are not allowed to sell or trade the fish caught. Their income comes from providing a service to their clients. In 2014/2015, there were 105 licences given, with 61 of these being active in the industry.[52] The five-year average customer trip days from 2007/2008 to 2012/2013 was 21,807[53] and the number of customer days overlapping with the sanctuary zones was 1136 customer days.[54] As the average historical effort displaced was more than 5%, the buy-back programme target was licences amounting to 1136 customer days.

b.   The Buy-back Process

The buy-backs for these fisheries matched the average historical catch displaced by the establishment of the sanctuary zones. The question then becomes how these buy-back targets will be implemented. The process was for the government of South Australia to seek the voluntary surrender of relevant fishing licences or licence entitlements. The alternative to a voluntary buy-back scheme was compulsory acquisition under the *Marine Parks Act 2007* (SA).[55] After the call for offers to voluntarily surrender their entitlements,[56] the Minister for Agriculture, Food and Fisheries or a nominated delegate considered each offer and make a decision to accept or reject the offer. Licence holders had the right to review this decision within 30 days of the decision.[57]

The criteria against which the offers to surrender were assessed were:

(a) whether the offer would reduce catch and effort from the fishery and/
or sanctuary zones;
(b) whether the offer reflected an effective use of public money with
appropriate monetary consideration relevant to recent historic
transactions and current open market prices; and
(c) minimisation of impacts on future fisheries management
arrangements.[58]

The buy-back process was informed by independent economic data
for each of the impacted fisheries.[59] These included the Northern and
Southern Zone Rock Lobster, Abalone, Charter Boat, and Marine Scale
fisheries. For each fishery, the indicators reported annually include the
gross value of production, cost of management, financial performance,
the determination of major cost increases, regional economic impacts and
economic rent. Each particular fishery had different requirements but
there were some common elements. There was a preference to buy back the
quotas in whole licences. This preference for whole licence buy-back meant
that, in some instances, there was quota in excess of the reduction target.
The aim of the government was to extinguish whole licences, so where
there was excess quota, the seller of the licence could either transfer this
excess quota to other fishers or, if the whole licence was surrendered to the
government, the government would find a way of equitably returning the
quota to the fishery.

With abalone and rock lobster, the buy-back process would not consider
an application to surrender if that application would result in the licence
holder breaching the minimum quota/pot holding.[60] With marine scalefish, the historical catch of the different species were taken into account.

5. RESOLUTION

The economic impact of the establishment of the sanctuary zones came
in at around 1.7%, which was substantially less than the 5% target. Even
so, the commercial fishers had some concerns with the buy-backs, with
one of their main concerns being the possibility that, with fewer licensees, the management costs would increase.[61] This did not occur with the
government reducing the management fees of the remaining licensees.[62]

A number of different mechanisms have been used to manage fisheries
in South Australia, over the past 60 years. Taking the Northern Zone Rock
Lobster Fishery as an example, as early as 1966, a winter closure was introduced in order to protect spawning females and conserve egg production.[63]
In 1967, limits were placed on pot and boat numbers in the fishery. In 1968

in recognition of the significant differences in biological, geological and ecological characteristics between the eastern and western borders of the South Australian coast, the South Australian Rock Lobster Fishery was separated into the Northern and Southern Zones.[64] Table 1.1 summarises the major mechanisms used in the commercial lobster industry to manage the sustainability of the industry.[65]

A review of the fishery undertaken by government managers and scientists in 1992 indicated that catches of more than 1100 and 1200 tonnes in 1990 and 1991, respectively, were unsustainable in the long term.[66] This review recommended that effort levels should be reduced to accommodate a catch closer to 850 tonnes. Following this review, government managers and scientists advocated strongly for the introduction of a quota management system in both the Northern Zone and Southern Zone Rock Lobster fisheries to ensure the long-term sustainability and profitability of these fisheries. As a result of this review process, a quota management system was introduced in the Southern Zone Rock Lobster Fishery in 1993 and, in the Northern Zone, 10 years later in 2003.

In summary, between 1966 and 2003, the northern rock lobster fishery was managed through a series of mechanisms, which included closures, limits on pots and boat numbers and increases in the allowable size. In 2003, a quota was introduced with a total allowable commercial catch (TACC) of 625 tonnes. Since the introduction of the quota, the first time the TACC was fully taken was in 2009, at 310 tonnes. This TACC remained for the next two years, to 2012, when it was increased to 345 tonnes (a lot less than the 1200 tonnes in 1991).

In 2013, under the South Australian government's Commercial Fisheries Voluntary Catch/Effort Reduction Programme, four licences from the Northern Zone Rock Lobster Fishery were surrendered voluntarily.[67]

In April 2015, the state's rock lobster fishery launched a temporal and spatial management study to try to maintain this industry in light of climate change impacts and the restrictions placed on it by the establishment of the sanctuary zones. The aim of this study is to increase profitability, while maintaining a strong focus on sustainable fishing practices. This results in fishing less but at a time when prices are at a premium, so as to maintain the profitability and sustainability of the fishery.[68] This is a positive outcome coming arguably from the establishment of the sanctuary zones, which made the industry look at coming to a win–win solution from what looked like a losing situation for the fishery and one of concern to the commercial fishers.

The importance of such a project is that it emphasises the need for a robust monitoring programme to ensure that the smaller catchment areas for rock lobsters do not strain these new areas, and to monitor the

Table 1.1   *Mechanisms used in the commercial lobster industry to manage the sustainability of the industry*

Year	Major management milestones
1978	First major review of fishery
1985	10% pot reduction
	Upper limits of pots increased from 60 to 65
1992	10% pot reduction
	Upper limits of pots decreased from 65 to 60
	Second major review of fishery
1993	One week time closure
1994	Another one week time closure
	Size limit increased from 98.5 to 102 mm
1995	Another one week time closure
1997	First management plan for the fisheries published
	Flexible time closure system introduced
1999	Another 3 days of time closure
2000	Size limit increased from 102 to 105 mm
2001	7% effort reduction introduced (14 days of further time closures)
2002	8% effort reduction introduced (~16 days of further time closures)
	Review of management and scientific programme undertaken
	Upper limit of pots increased from 60 to 70
2003	Quota system introduced with a TACC (total allowable commercial catch) of 625 tonnes
	VMS (Vessel Monitoring System), sealed bins and prior reporting introduced
	Escape gaps introduced
2004	TACC reduced from 625 to 520 tonnes
2005	Upper limit of pots increased from 70 to 100
	Lower pot limit decreased from 25 to 20 pots
2007	Second Management Plan published
2008	TACC reduced to 470 tonnes
2009	TACC reduced to 310 tonnes
	TACC fully taken for the first time since the introduction of quota in 2003
2010	Harvest strategy reviewed and implemented
2011	TACC maintained at 310 tonnes
2012	TACC increased to 345 tonnes consistent with the 2011 harvest strategy
2013	TACC maintained at 345 tonnes
	Introduction of sea lion exclusion devices for pots in water less than 100 m
	Four licences surrendered through a Marine Parks: Commercial Fisheries Voluntary Catch/Effort Reduction Programme

sanctuary zones. The rock lobster fishery is working closely on this project with PIRSA and SARDI,[69] and has attracted funding from Fisheries Research Development Corporation.[70]

The spokesman for the abalone industry is also pleased that the voluntary buy-back was successful. As Abalone Industry Association of South Australia President, Jonas Woolford said, 'If the voluntary process hadn't worked, it would have triggered the Marine Parks Act legislation, and no-one wanted that'.[71] The amounts that licences were bought back for were confidential but the Director of Fisheries said that abalone licences would be worth $5–7 million.[72]

All in all, the voluntary buy-backs were regarded as a successful method to deal with the displaced catch resulting from the establishment of the sanctuary zones. A total of 115 applications[73] were received and the total payout was around $20 million. This included four lobster licences from the northern rock lobster fishery[74] and one licence from the southern rock lobster fishery.[75]

6.   CONCLUSION

The process of declaring South Australia's Marine Parks and determining their zoning took a period of more than 15 years and the consultation process received more than 10,000 submissions. As people's livelihoods were going to be impacted, there was always the expectation that there would be some conflict in the process.

However, it became clear that all affected stakeholder groups could live with the outcome. For example, the peak stakeholder group for recreational fishers, RecFish, told the Parliamentary inquiry into the Marine Parks that they had lost some access to fisheries but had gained some protection for nursery and spawning areas, and noted, 'We didn't get everything we wanted, but life is like that in the real world',[76] and that they believed the zones captured the most important breeding areas.[77]

The Abalone Industry Association of SA were of the view that the government's conservation and ecological aims for the marine environment could be achieved 'without impacting on the sustainability of South Australia's most successful abalone fishery'[78] and the Conservation Council told the inquiry that they did not get all that they wanted, but 'in the end we got a great first step on marine parks, management plants and sanctuary zones'.[79]

A number of tools were used to try to minimise the pain particularly to the commercial fishers whose livelihoods were going to be impacted by the declaration of no-fishing sanctuary zones. Taking away these areas of fishing would increase the pressure on the areas remaining. To alleviate this pressure on the fish, there were four possible options—the least palatable was for the government to compulsorily acquire some of the fishing licences.

The preferred option was the voluntary market-based buy-back through the SA Marine Parks' voluntary catch/effort reduction programme for commercial fisheries.[80] The programme was conducted to mitigate the risk to fish stocks associated with displaced catch and effort on areas of the fishery that remain open to fishing,[81] and as Jonas Woolford said, 'If the voluntary process hadn't worked, it would have triggered the Marine Parks Act legislation, and no-one wanted that'.[82]

This research has identified two important elements needed to ensure the success of a market-based approach to dealing with the impacts of natural resource protection through the establishment of Marine Protected areas. The first of these is to ensure trust in the process. Two principles can help build trust. The first principle is to recognise the value of local knowledge, and capture this local knowledge. A tool such as SAMPIT can capture this knowledge. The second principle is to ensure a robust and long-term monitoring programme, such as the rock lobster fishery's temporal and spatial management study. The second element needed is to have detailed fishing data to be able to determine the economic impact of the displacement.

The impact of this voluntary market-based buy-back programme will be closely monitored by PIRSA. At the present time, the state's rock lobster fishery's temporal and spatial management study[83] is examining the impact of climate change, and the restrictions following the establishment of the sanctuary zones, including the buy-backs. This is a crucial first step in the monitoring process and is most likely to be the model used for all the other fisheries impacted by the buy-back.

NOTES

1. Karen Bubna-Litic, Emma Goreham, Taylor Pope, Kvitka Becker and Alex Craig (2015) 'The effectiveness of the participation principle in protecting Marine Diversity in South Australia', in IUCN Law For Sustainability, p.6, http://www.lawforsustainability.org/case-studies/effectiveness-participation-principle-protecting-marine-diversity-south-australia.
2. National Parks Parks SA, http://www.environment.sa.gov.au/marineparks/About/zones.
3. These include general managed use zones and habitat protection zones, ibid.
4. Karen Bubna-Litic et al., as above, note 1.
5. Geoscience Australia (2010) 'Coastline lengths, Geoscience Australia, Canberra', http://www.ga.gov.au/scientific-topics/national-location-information/dimensions/border-lengths#heading-1.

6. SA Department of Environment, Water and Natural Resources, 'South Australia's Marine Park Network, Explanatory Document', November 2012, p. 4. See also K. Edyvane (1999) 'Conserving Marine Biodiversity in South Australia—Part 2—Identification of areas of high conservation value in South Australia, SARDI and PIRSA, Adelaide, Australia', http://www.ffc.org.au/FFC_files/MPA%20refs/SARDI%20reports%20and%20maps/marine_biodiversity_part2_full_version.pdf.

7. Department for Environment and Heritage (2009) *A Technical Report on the Outer Boundaries of South Australia's Marine Parks Network*. Department for Environment and Heritage, South Australia, p. 25.

8. Ibid.

9. South Australia Government, Department of Marine Parks (2010) 'The Natural Values of South Australia's Marine Environment'.

10. National Climate Change Adaptation Research Facility (2011) 'Climate Change and the Marine Environment: South Australia'. University of Tasmania, Fact Sheet no. 4, http://arnmbr.org/content/images/uploads/Information_Sheet_4.pdf.

11. Department for Environment and Heritage (2009) *A Technical Report on the Outer Boundaries of South Australia's Marine Parks Network*. Department for Environment and Heritage, South Australia, p. 21.

12. Ibid., p. 34.

13. Commonwealth Department of Environment and Heritage (2003) 'The Benefits of Marine Protected Areas', https://www.environment.gov.au/system/files/resources/5eaad4f9-e8e0-45d1-b889-83648c7b2ceb/files/benefits-mpas.pdf.

14. Ibid.

15. K.S. Edyvane, *Conserving Marine Biodiversity in South Australia—Part 1—Background, Status and Review of Approach to Marine Biodiversity Conservation in South Australia* (May 1999), SARDI Aquatic Environment, http://www.sardi.sa.gov.au/__data/assets/pdf_file/0004/94594/marine_biodiversity_part1_full_version.pdf.>.

16. J.L. Baker (2004) *Towards a System of Ecologically Representative Marine Protected Areas in South Australian Marine Bioregions—Technical Report*. Prepared for Coast and Marine Conservation Branch, Department for Environment and Heritage, South Australia.

17. Intergovernmental Agreement on the Environment (IGAE), https://www.environment.gov.au/about-us/esd/publications/intergovernmental-agreement.

18. Karen Bubna-Litic et al., as above, note 1, p. 7.

19. Sections 8, 10, 22 and 29.

20. Karen Bubna-Litic et al., as above, note 1, p. 11.

21. Ibid., p. 7.

22. For a full evaluation of the consultation process, see Karen Bubna-Litic, Emma Goreham, Taylor Pope, Kvitka Becker and Alex Craig (2015) 'The effectiveness of the participation principle in protecting Marine Diversity in South Australia', in IUCN Law For Sustainability, http://www.lawforsustainability.org/case-studies/effectiveness-participation-principle-protecting-marine-diversity-south-australia.

23. Parliament of South Australia, Final Report of the Select Committee on Marine Parks in South Australia, tabled in the Legislative Council on 13 November 2013, p. 8.

24. The final SAMPIT charts for each of the Marine Park Areas can be found at the Marine Parks website, http://www.environment.sa.gov.au/marineparks/About/history/Local_Advisory_Groups/LAG_meetings_and_reports.

25. Parliament of South Australia, Final Report of the Select Committee on Marine Parks in South Australia, tabled in the Legislative Council on 13 November 2013, p. 8.

26. See Karen Bubna-Litic et al., above, note 1.

27. For a full discussion of the effectiveness of the principle of participation in the management and zoning of SA's Marine Parks process, see Bubna-Litic et al., above, note 1.

28. It was in response to this document that more than 8000 public submissions were received. In response, 50 changes were made to the zonings.

29. Parliament of South Australia, Final Report of the Select Committee on Marine Parks in South Australia, tabled in the Legislative Council on 13 November 2013, p. 11.
30. Ibid.
31. Karen Bubna-Litic et al., as above, note 1.
32. Rob Lewis, 'Convergence of Conflict' letters to the editor, SA Life, February 2014.
33. Parliament of South Australia, Final Report of the Select Committee on Marine Parks in South Australia, tabled in the Legislative Council on 13 November 2013.
34. South Australian Research and Development Institute (SARDI) report 'Estimates of historical commercial fishery catches/effort in final sanctuary and habitat protection zones in South Australia's Marine Parks', http://www.pir.sa.gov.au/__data/assets/pdf_file/0004/232258/Habitat_Protection_Zones_in_SA_Marine_Parks_2.pdf.
35. According to the Australian Bureau of Statistics, it was $394,363,000 in 2009–2010, http://www.abs.gov.au/ausstats/abs@.nsf/Lookup/by%20Subject/1301.0~2012~Main%20Features~Fishing~182.
36. Approved pursuant to section 44 of the *Fisheries Management Act 2007*, http://pir.sa.gov.au/__data/assets/pdf_file/0004/12982/Abalone_Fishery_Management_Plan_-_September_2012_.pdf.
37. http://pir.sa.gov.au/__data/assets/pdf_file/0005/57956/NZRFL_Management_Plan_October_2014.pdf.
38. Habitat conservation and enhancement is an important element of rebuilding. See Organisation for Economic Co-operation and Development (2012) *Rebuilding Fisheries: The Way Forward*, p. 12, http://www.keepeek.com/Digital-Asset-Management/oecd/agriculture-and-food/rebuilding-fisheries_9789264176935-en#page1.
39. Ibid.
40. Section 7, *Marine Parks Act 2007 (SA)*.
41. Displaced Commercial Fishing Policy Framework: South Australian Government, April 2011, Appendix 4 in DEWNR, 'South Australia's marine park network: explanatory document', November 2012.
42. PIRSA, 'Management plan for the South Australian Commercial Northern Rock Lobster Fishery', p. 11, http://pir.sa.gov.au/__data/assets/pdf_file/0005/57956/NZRFL_Management_Plan_October_2014.pdf.
43. PIRSA, 'SA Marine Parks: Commercial Fisheries Voluntary Catch/Effort Reduction Program', July 2013.
44. Ibid., p. 4.
45. Ibid., p. 5.
46. Ibid.
47. Ibid.
48. Ibid.
49. Ibid.
50. Ibid., p. 6.
51. Ibid., p. 7.
52. Angelo Tsolos and Melleessa Boyle (2015) 'Non-confidential 2014–2015 data summary of the South Australian Charter Boat Fishery', November 2015, http://pir.sa.gov.au/__data/assets/pdf_file/0010/267499/20151104_NON_Confidential_2014_15_Data_Summary_of_the_South_Australian_Charter_Boat_Fishery_to_PIRSA_Fisheries_and_Aquaculture_-_FINAL.pdf.
53. Ibid., p. 4.
54. PIRSA, 'SA Marine Parks: Commercial Fisheries Voluntary Catch/Effort Reduction Program', July 2013, p. 7.
55. Displaced Commercial Fishing Policy Framework, above, note 41.
56. Be they licences, quota units or pots.
57. PIRSA, 'SA Marine Parks: Commercial Fisheries Voluntary Catch/Effort Reduction Program', July 2013, p. 8.
58. Ibid.
59. EconSearch Pty Ltd, 'Economic indicators for the commercial fisheries of South

        Australia (1998–2015)', http://www.econsearch.com.au/pages/completed-projects/fishing-
        aquaculture/fish10.php.
60. Ibid., p. 12.
61. 'Licence buyback could cut abalone costs', The Fish Site, January 2014, http://www.
        thefishsite.com/fishnews/22233/licence-buyback-could-cut-abalone-costs/.
62. Parliament of South Australia, Final Report of the Select Committee on Marine Parks
        in South Australia, tabled in the Legislative Council on 13 November 2013, p. 6.
63. PIRSA, Management Plan for the South Australian Commercial Northern Rock Lobster
        Fishery, November 2014, p. 8, http://pir.sa.gov.au/__data/assets/pdf_file/0005/57956/
        NZRFL_Management_Plan_October_2014.pdf.
64. Ibid.
65. Ibid., p. 9.
66. Ibid., p. 8.
67. Ibid.
68. Harry Fisher, 'Lobster project to benefit fishery', 2 April 2015, Port Lincoln Times,
        http://www.portlincolntimes.com.au/story/2984978/lobster-project-to-benefit-fishery/.
69. Ibid.
70. Fisheries Research Development Corporation, 'SRL IPA: informing spatial and tem-
        poral management of the South Australian Northern Zone Southern Rock Lobster
        (Jasus edwardsii) fishery', Project Number 2014, p. 702, http://frdc.com.au/research/
        current_research_projects/Pages/default.aspx.
71. 'Licence buyback could cut abalone costs', The Fish Site, 15 January 2014, http://www.
        thefishsite.com/fishnews/22233/licence-buyback-could-cut-abalone-costs/#sthash.
        CRcWKDLE.dpuf.
72. Marine Parks Select Committee Hansard documents.
73. Parliament of South Australia, Final Report of the Select Committee on Marine Parks
        in South Australia, tabled in the Legislative Council on 13 November 2013, p. 17.
74. PIRSA, Management Plan for the South Australian Commercial Northern Rock
        Lobster   Fishery,   http://pir.sa.gov.au/__data/assets/pdf_file/0005/57956/NZRFL_
        Management_Plan_October_2014.pdf.
75. Unfortunately, the data from the other impacted fisheries is not publicly available.
76. Parliament of South Australia, Final Report of the Select Committee on Marine Parks
        in South Australia, tabled in the Legislative Council on 13 November 2013, p. 7 (evi-
        dence given by B. Schahinger).
77. Ibid., evidence from I. Fitzgerald.
78. Ibid., p. 10.
79. Ibid., evidence by Tony Kelly, CEO Conservation Council, p. 13.
80. PIRSA, as above, note 43.
81. PIRSA, Management Plan for the South Australian Commercial Northern Rock
        Lobster Fishery, p. 11, http://pir.sa.gov.au/__data/assets/pdf_file/0005/57956/NZRFL_
        Management_Plan_October_2014.pdf.
82. Jonas Woolford, 'Abalone Industry of South Australia', as quoted in the Port
        Lincoln Times, 14 January 2014, http://www.portlincolntimes.com.au/story/2020325/
        buyback-could-cut-abalone-costs/?cs=1500.
83. Announced in April 2015.

2. A bottom-up approach to developing REDD+ programs in Brazilian states and California

Ana Carolina Cerqueira Duque

1. INTRODUCTION

This paper analyzes the opportunity to develop Reducing Emissions from Deforestation and Forest Degradation (REDD+) programs in Brazilian states through negotiations with the State of California after its recently enacted cap-and-trade program. The proposed discussion is of great importance as the 2015 Paris Agreement recognized the need to implement policies and created incentives for reducing emissions from deforestation and forest degradation. In view of this, a bottom-up approach in which states from different countries join forces to promote reductions in deforestation could be a golden opportunity to motivate other countries to reduce carbon emissions and include similar frameworks in their Intended Nationally Determined Contributions, as foreseen in the Paris Agreement.

To enlighten readers on the current scenario, an overview of recent events and the mechanisms to reduce carbon emissions is included. Owing to the focus on REDD+, California's cap-and-trade program will be described with an emphasis on the sections that pertain to this program. As for Brazil, the current legislation and adopted mitigation solutions, specifically those in the states of Acre and Mato Grosso, will be discussed in order to set the scene for the importance of a REDD+ program in the country.

The paper then analyzes the opportunity for state-level agreements through the current legislation, the negotiations that have been conducted thus far, and the critics of linkage between these states. Finally, the paper evaluates whether the existing legislation in Brazil is sufficient to promote the program, before going on to offer recommendations to guarantee a more transparent and solid framework.

2. OVERVIEW OF CLIMATE CHANGE: CURRENT SCENARIO

Nowadays, climate change is a palpable problem that is mostly felt in developing countries. As described by the Intergovernmental Panel on Climate Change (IPCC),[1] 'warming of the climate system is unequivocal, and since the 1950s, many of the observed changes are unprecedented over decades to millennia. The atmosphere and ocean have warmed, the amounts of snow and ice have diminished, and sea level has risen.'[2] Even though the IPCC declined to define what a safe level of greenhouse gas (GHG) concentration should be, it concluded that the stabilization of carbon dioxide (CO_2) concentration at any level requires a reduction in global GHG emissions.[3] It also highlighted three important consequences if countries do not take action to reduce GHG emissions:[4] (a) an overall loss in global welfare; (b) greater impacts on poor countries that lack the resources necessary to implement adaptation policies; and (c) increased costs for all nations.

In response to this alarming information, governments have been acting to control GHG emissions through vertical regulation, first defining international duties and standards so that nations can later implement their own laws within their respective legal systems.[5] The relevance of a vertical regulatory scheme has been more debated since the enactment of the United Nations Framework Convention on Climate Change (UNFCCC) and, after that, the creation of the Kyoto Protocol in 1997.

The Kyoto Protocol differed from the UNFCCC as it included the economic impacts on developing countries as a concern.[6] It also enacted a cap-and-trade system, which is an environmentally and economically sensible approach to controlling GHG emissions.[7] This scheme helps companies innovate in order to meet, or even come in under, their allocated limits, making it an important tool for reducing GHG as it incentivizes creativity, energy conservation and investments in cleaner technology.[8]

In the same way as the cap-and-trade system, the REDD+ program was also created with a 'top-down' approach when it was introduced to climate negotiations at the UNFCCC's Conference of the Parties (COP) 11 in 2005. The program aims to incentivize developing countries to reduce their deforestation rates and, if successful, compensate them financially.[9] Currently, it includes deforestation, degradation, carbon enhancement and engagement of indigenous peoples and local communities.

Although these policies began with international negotiations, the slow progress in expanding them and enforcing compliance made the discussions move outside the international sphere. For instance, cap-and-trade schemes such as the Regional Greenhouse Gas Initiative Inc.[10] and the Western Climate Initiative Inc.[11] were created to operate independently from the Kyoto Protocol. Another example is found in Brazil, where state[12] and municipalities enacted legislation on deforestation prevention and the payment for environmental services.[13] Therefore, the question at hand is whether emissions can be reduced through regulation with commitments defined as 'top-down', meaning via an international treaty, or 'bottom-up', with local legislation influencing other nations.[14]

After COP 21 in December 2016, and the resulting Paris Agreement—which shall be open for signing from 22 April 2016 in New York—the answer to achieving the goal of keeping global temperatures from rising more than 2°C (3.6°F) by 2100[15] is a combination of these approaches. Thus, it is a top-down approach when setting the goals for reducing GHG emissions (among other obligations), and a bottom-up approach when allowing each nation to submit its own plan to reduce GHG emissions rather than trying to agree on a one-size-fits-all strategy.[16]

According to the agreement, in order to achieve this goal, the parties shall prepare, communicate and maintain successive 'intended nationally determined contributions' in which they convey ambitious efforts to reduce GHG.[17] Within these efforts, the parties are encouraged to take action to implement and support—including through result-based payments—policies and activities relating to reducing emissions from deforestation, forest degradation, conservation, sustainable management of forests and the enhancement of forest carbon stocks in developing countries.[18]

As such, the Paris Agreement not only foresaw the need to develop REDD+ as a means of reducing GHG emissions, but also encouraged countries to take action locally or through cooperation agreements between the signatory parties. As we shall see below, such cooperation seems to be the path California and the Brazilian states of Acre and Mato Grosso should follow.

3. CALIFORNIA'S INITIATIVE

California has long been known for its bold policies. Its pioneering measures on promoting renewable energy sources, energy efficiency and mitigation of transport emissions were the starting point for cutting GHG.[19] On 27 September 2006 the state adopted the Global Warming Solution Act of 2006, Assembly Bill 32 (AB 32), which intended to reduce GHG emissions to 1990 levels by 2020.

AB 32 is considered by many experts to be of particular importance as it could lead other American states to take similar action.[20] Although federal legislation would have been the most adequate solution, the US Senate failed to pass the Waxman–Markey bill, which would have established a variant of national emissions trading. As a result, federal legislation on the matter is restricted to the Clean Air Act and regulations issued by the Environmental Protection Agency.[21]

Notwithstanding the importance of the existing regulation, the AB 32 program was innovative in several ways, mixing direct regulation on GHG with a cap-and-trade program that was implemented by its regulatory body, the California Air Resources Board (CARB), in 2013. Given the purpose of this paper, only some aspects of the cap-and-trade program shall be analyzed, leaving out other relevant aspects of AB 32.[22]

AB 32's cap-and-trade program defined that allowances are to be distributed by the state to regulated businesses, either given for free or sold at auction.[23] At the end of each compliance period, companies surrender sufficient allowances back to the government to cover their compliance obligations, which are based on their emissions.[24] The less they emit, the less they pay. As a result, a powerful financial incentive is created for those companies that can clean up more cheaply and sell their permits to those with higher treatment costs.

If they fail to meet their compliance requirements, CARB may apply a $25,000 fine per missing allowance.[25] To reduce emissions over time, the number of available allowances decreases every year, similar to the cap.[26] On the other hand, for companies to have more flexibility, they can purchase additional allowances or invest in emission reduction projects that leave them with extra allowances that can then be sold.

The program also incentivizes emission reductions beyond regulated pollution sources through the use of *offset credits*, which are verified emission reductions achieved through projects that reduce GHG in the short or long term.[27] Its main purpose is to constrain costs of GHG reduction by increasing the supply of low-price compliance options.[28] Nonetheless, they are not freely emitted and GHG reduction or GHG removal enhancement must be real, additional, quantifiable, permanent, verifiable and enforceable.[29] This means that such reductions must be accounted for permanently and would not have occurred in a business-as-usual scenario, nor be required by any other law, regulation or legally binding mandate. Additionally, the reduction projects must be located in the USA and its territories, Canada or Mexico. In addition to this territorial constraint, facilities may use no more than 8% of their allowed emissions.[30]

The statute also foresees *sector-based offset credits* that do not have a geographic limitation. According to Section 95991, sector-based offsets allow developing countries or subnational jurisdictions within those countries to receive credits generated from REDD+.[31] The idea is that, if overall degradation or deforestation is reduced in a large geographical area through plans that ensure that leakage and fraud are avoided, credits will be granted. Its use is even stricter, as facilities may only use up to 4% of their allowed emissions.[32]

For the sector-based program to be eligible, public notice and comment should be given in accordance to the Administrative Procedure Act.[33] In addition, Section 95994 imposes several eligibility requirements, such as being additional, permanent and verifiable.[34] Taking into account that both natural and human-induced reversal can occur, forest owners are required to identify and quantify the risk of reversal from different agents based on project-specific circumstances. These risks determine the quantity of offset credits that the project will generate.[35]

Another important part of AB 32 for the purpose of this article is the possibility of *linkage*, which means the approval of compliance instruments from other jurisdictions and the enforcement of California's compliance instruments in such jurisdictions.[36] Therefore, the statute allows California to link with other jurisdictions so long as there is notice and a comment proposition in which the governor provides a series of findings.[37] Once approved, allowances or sector-based offsets issued in other linking jurisdictions through REDD+ projects can be purchased by companies in California.[38] Thus far, the first and only jurisdiction to link with California's cap-and-trade system is the Canadian province of Quebec.[39]

4.   BRAZILIAN FEDERAL LEGISLATION ON REDUCING GHG

Brazil's emissions profile is different from that of the USA and other developed countries, where emissions come from fossil fuel combustion.[40] According to the Brazilian Second National Communication to UNFCCC, CO_2 emissions from land-use changes and the forestry sector represent 77% of total emissions.[41] This makes the government inclined to enact command-and-control regulation for deforestation rather than adopting a cap-and-trade program for industry.

From an international standpoint, Brazil is a signatory of the UNFCCC and the Kyoto Protocol, having committed to reducing GHG emissions as part of its common but differentiated responsibilities.[42] It is safe to say that Brazil has exceeded its mere 'due diligence' responsibility of updating national inventories of anthropogenic emissions[43] and has been undertaking voluntary commitments for the reduction of GHG.[44]

In 2009, Brazil enacted its National Policy on Climate Change after the country's president announced voluntary mitigation goals[45] at COP 15. Despite criticism owing to the broad language of the policy, the law implemented several instruments to fund and monitor climate change programs, while also adopting a national voluntary commitment to reduce projected emissions by up to 38.9% by 2020.[46]

In addition to these efforts, the Plan for Prevention and Control of Deforestation in the Legal Amazon[47] (PPCDAm) was incorporated into the National Policy on Climate Change. The plan's main focus is to promote rural and land planning, while also fostering sustainable production.[48] According to the Brazilian National Institute of Space Research, which monitors Brazilian forests via satellite, deforestation rates have dropped considerably since the implementation of PPCDAm.[49] However, in 2013 a notable increase in deforestation was reported by non-governmental organizations (NGO).[50] Therefore, Brazil still faces many challenges before its voluntary goals must be met in 2020.

4.1 Brazilian Federal Legislation on REDD+

Brazil's main challenge in reducing GHG is keeping its forests intact. This is not an easy task owing to the size of the Amazon forest and the economic situation of the states that comprise it. In these states development is needed for the growing population and forest conservation seems to go against agricultural interests, which presumably increase economic growth and employment.[51] To change this scenario and preserve the existing forest, as the Brazilian Constitution dictates,[52] projects to capture GHG and payment for environmental services are key.

However, no federal legislation has been enacted in this regard thus far. In fact, little action has been taken at the federal level at all, with the exception of the government supporting REDD+ by launching a website with information on the matter and the discussion of bills of law by the House of Representatives.[53] Thus, similar to the California example, regulation of REDD+ programs has been led by states, especially Mato Grosso and Acre.[54]

4.2 Mato Grosso and Acre's REDD+ Initiatives

Although Mato Grosso and Acre are both located within the Legal Amazon, they are very different in size, economy and deforestation levels. Mato Grosso was ranked second with 1508 km^2 of deforested land from 2014 to 2015 in comparison with the other nine states that compose the Legal Amazon, as described by the Brazilian satellite monitoring system. It is the second largest state in Brazil and has an economy based on agriculture—mainly the production of soy and livestock—which puts pressure on protected areas.

In 2013, Mato Grosso enacted Law 9878/2013, which created a basic framework for a REDD+ program that will be further detailed through regulation. The law established the following institutions: (a) a technical panel; (b) a managing counsel; (c) the state environmental protection agency; and (d) the state climate change forum. These governmental bodies shall address important regulatory aspects of REDD+, such as leakage, registration and monitoring of deforestation.[55] Additionally, the law is innovative in its requirement for compliance with international standards that Brazil had previously agreed to, as well as allowing for the establishment of cooperation agreements with public and private institutions from other countries.[56]

Acre, on the other hand, is small and the least densely populated state in the country. Its economy is based on the exploitation of natural resources such as rubber and Brazil nuts.[57] It was ranked sixth in terms of deforestation in the Legal Amazon[58] from 2014 to 2015.

Despite the legislative advances in Mato Grosso, Acre is considered the leading state in terms of REDD+ regulation. In 2010, Acre enacted landmark legislation on the matter through Law 2.308/2010, creating the State System of Incentives for Environmental Services (SISA), which provided an innovative, jurisdiction-wide approach to low-carbon rural development.

SISA established a set of principles, policies, institutions and instruments for building an effective program to achieve environmental sustainability through ecosystem service incentives.[59] It was designed to promote public–private initiatives to achieve the state's goals with respect to ecosystem services. The law also created the following bodies that shall manage, control and further regulate its REDD+ program: (a) a regulation, registry and control institute; (b) a validation and managing commission; (c) a technical committee; and (d) an ombudsman.

Moreover, it encouraged strengthened cooperation and alignment at the international, national, subnational and local levels, as did the law recently enacted in Mato Grosso. One example is the continuing talks with the State of Chiapas in Mexico and the State of California in the USA in order to strengthen REDD+ programs across these jurisdictions.

5. IS THERE AN OPPORTUNITY FOR AGREEMENTS BETWEEN BRAZILIAN STATES AND CALIFORNIA?

As previously stated, AB 32 permits linkage with other jurisdictions through the purchase of sector-based offset credits by companies in California as long as administrative procedures have been undertaken to verify if the governor's findings are present within the REDD+ program in question, and if the offsets generated in the jurisdiction are considered additional, verifiable and so forth.[60]

Hence, for Acre and Mato Grosso's REDD+ projects to be linked to California, their legislation should be drafted in accordance with those specifications. Given the increase in deforestation in the Legal Amazon[61] and the possibility of encouraging programs that may reduce the use of Brazil's natural resources, an analysis of the existing legislation is required to better understand the possibility of linkage.

Acre has an advantageous position in this regard, as it has been negotiating with Chiapas and California since 2010, when the three states signed a Memorandum of Understanding as part of a collaborative effort to reduce emissions from global deforestation and forest degradation. This cooperation has a technical, legal and institutional design focus as part of the effort to link their state REDD+ programs with California's cap-and-trade program, bypassing the UNFCCC gridlock.[62]

In the continuing efforts to promote linkage between these states, the REDD+ Offsets Working Group (ROW) was created to provide stakeholder input and recommendations regarding the design of compliance-grade jurisdictional REDD+ programs as well as options for linking such programs.[63]

This initiative has a jurisdictional approach rather than a project-level approach, as it seeks to ensure the environmental integrity of offsets that might enter California's cap-and-trade system, as will be discussed further.[64] It is also of great importance as it can cast a light on the development of other projects in different American states and greatly increase the global impact of AB 32. Linkage would send a positive message that political leadership in mitigating climate change can lead to opportunities for programs that aim to alleviate poverty and restore natural ecosystems together.[65]

Furthermore, linkage with programs in different jurisdictions is perceived as the future of climate agreements, which means developing a bottom set of regulations for states and municipalities within countries to further incentivize an international framework or a hybrid system.[66] The importance of this is even greater considering the recently negotiated Paris Agreement, which incentivized this approach to reducing GHG emissions. That said, it is critical for California's cap-and-trade system to allow linkage with credible programs in other jurisdictions, which means having a transparent and efficient set of rules and guidelines that create safe and rigorous monitoring of the programs.[67]

Given this scenario, it is important to evaluate whether the existing legislation in Brazil is sufficient to be considered credible, transparent and in accordance with the requirements of AB 32, as occurred with the Province of Quebec in January 2014.

5.1   ROW's Recommendations and Existing State Legislation in Brazil

As mentioned above, negotiations for linking with California's cap-and-trade system are more advanced with the state governments of Chiapas and Acre. According to ROW, these states are key players for linkage owing to Acre's advanced legislation on REDD+ programs and Chiapas's rich rainforest biodiversity. However, there was no language in the report that could preclude Mato Grosso from attempting to link its REDD+ program with that of California. Considering the set of recommendations drafted by ROW and the current legislation in the two states, further analysis of the legislation in the Brazilian states shall be conducted.

The *first recommendation* by ROW was to limit the scope of a jurisdiction's program to only account for emissions from deforestation and forest degradation. Any enhancement of carbon stocks (e.g. through forest restoration) in degraded forests or previously forested areas should only be included after a robust monitoring system has been developed. This would put the program in a 'trial phase'. If successful, the program could be amplified to incorporate reforestation.

The laws in both Brazilian states foresee the possibility of accounting for recovering degraded areas and have created specific bodies for evaluation and monitoring of the system.[68] Nevertheless, only time will tell if the creation and implementation of these laws shall be conducted as expected. Therefore, the cautious limitations recommended by ROW were an incentive for the jurisdictions to act in good faith and ensure that their laws are effectively implemented.

As for the *second recommendation*, reference levels must be defined in order to better assess additionality, while the states should also demonstrate their 'own effort' in achieving part of these reductions.[69] ROW considers reference levels to be key in better estimating future forest carbon emissions in the absence of the program. In this regard, it suggested a 10-year period of analysis between 1995 and 2010 so long as it is supported by empirical evidence.[70]

Complying with this requirement should not be a problem for Acre or Mato Grosso considering the existing satellite data on deforestation that is available online and shows that deforestation levels have been drastically reduced in the Legal Amazon since the enactment of PPCDAm.

The *third recommendation* referred to the required elements needed for the jurisdiction to generate emission reductions capable of being recognized by AB 32. Thus, a clear and thorough framework should develop:

(a) crediting for REDD+ offsets, defining responsibilities for how and to whom those credits will be issued, registered and tracked; (b) a database for carbon accounting and registry systems for project details and descriptions used to verify whether regulated entities are in compliance with AB 32; (c) state-level accounting to avoid leakage, reversals and double counting with federal efforts; and finally (d) a safeguard system that ensures the protection and enhancement of local, forest-dependent communities (including indigenous peoples). In short, it is key that states provide transparency in the programs that will be recognized by California.[71]

To meet such requirements, Acre aims to create three specific and independent governmental bodies that are composed of an equal number of members from governmental agencies and the community. Currently, only one of the governmental bodies has been created, the Validation and Monitoring Commission. This commission is composed of two NGOs,[72] the Workers Association and the Wood and Management Industries Association. It is also noteworthy that Acre's law states that independent audits shall be periodically completed to assess the impacts of the program and its instruments.

Therefore, Acre's law is in compliance with ROW's recommendations for participation of local communities, transparency and monitoring. Nonetheless, only with the creation of all the governmental bodies and the analysis of their regulations will it be safe to affirm compliance with all the requirements. For now, the State Environmental Protection Agency is in charge of regulating, controlling and registering the REDD+ project, eliminating the independence intended by the law.

As for Mato Grosso, registry, management and transparency of the REDD+ program is solely conducted by the State Environmental Protection Agency. The law has direct language on the need to maintain the traceability of transactions in order to avoid double crediting and expressly touches on the registration scheme needed to provide transparency to the program, sufficiently meeting ROW's requirements in this regard.[73] As does the law in Acre, Mato Grosso created a Managing Counsel that will approve regulations for REDD+ and analyze the results of periodically executed independent audits. This counsel is composed of 12 participants, of which half are members of the community.[74] Thus, the law proposes broader participation by the civil community than does that of Acre.

As a result, both state laws touch on the concerns presented by ROW. However, Mato Grosso has a more detailed piece of legislation. It also innovates via the creation of a fallback system to be allocated to the REDD+ program in case any deforestation occurs owing to force majeure. This provision is similar to insurance, as it guarantees that emissions will be achieved even in adverse scenarios.[75] It is an interesting approach to avoiding reversals, as required by AB 32 and encouraged by ROW.[76]

ROW's *fourth* and last *recommendation* pertains to the linking option between states. It recommends that the linkage should not operate as a 'binding' treaty-like agreement as dictated by public international law, as it would not be enforceable, as required in the governor's findings.[77] Because Brazil is a federation, states cannot sign treaties with other countries. As in the USA,[78] only the president is vested with the power to sign treaties.

According to AB 32, not only the partner jurisdiction will need to design its program accordingly, but the State of California should also be able to enforce the provisions of its cap-and-trade program and related laws on any entity located within the linking jurisdiction to the maximum extent permitted under the USA and California constitutions. Thus, a treaty as described above would not be applicable.

Nonetheless, treaties are not the only solution, as international cooperation agreements can also be binding and recognized as decentralized public diplomatic negotiations entered into by states and municipalities.[79] Mato Grosso's law, for example, already foresees the possibility of the state establishing a cooperation agreement with federal, state and municipal governments within Brazil, as well as with private and public institutions internationally.[80] Acre, however, has no provision in this regard.

5.2   Problems with Linkage and Risk Mitigation

In addition to ROW's recommendations, two criticisms over linkage must be addressed. The first relates to public participation, while the second deals with corruption in the linked jurisdictions.

Public participation in REDD+ has always been a central concern for its development. Some suspect that the program might only benefit a select few, notably polluters and investors, leaving very little for those who need it most.[81] This was also one of ROW's main concerns, leading to the requirements for transparency during the entire issuance process of REDD+ credits and the participation of forest communities.

For this reason, Brazilian legislators have acted in order to mitigate this risk by providing access to information, first as ensured in the Brazilian constitution, and second in Federal Law 10.650/2003, which guarantees access to environmental information to any interested party. More recently, Federal Law 12.527/2011 was enacted, requiring all governmental bodies to provide any and all information to their citizens.

All these provisions can be applied to REDD+ programs, in addition to Acre and Mato Grosso's state legislations, which are clear in their intent to promote transparency and propose broader discussion with impacted communities. As shown above, Mato Grosso further broadened the discussion of REDD+ projects, as half of the representatives that compose the Validation and Monitoring Commission come from the community, while Acre preferred to guarantee the participation through NGOs. Thus, their intent to promote participation ensures that the rights described on paper are exercised within each program.

The second concern relates to possible corruption at any stage in the certification and crediting of the offsets. Corruption is a huge problem in Brazil, as is widely known by the international community from the current scandals involving public and private companies.[82] According to the U4 Anti-Corruption Resource Center,[83] the financial rewards associated with the program generate incentives for dishonest measures, such as reporting false reforestation achievements or incentivizing projects that have no additionality. Although the existing satellite monitoring in Brazil could aid in combating corruption, the main issue is the interpretation of the data and the potential conflicts of interest that may arise in the verification of offsets.[84] From the organization's view, it is possible that beneficiaries of REDD+ payments may attempt to exert undue influence or offer illicit financial payments to agencies responsible for data production and analysis.

To mitigate such risk, many actions have been taken by Acre and Mato Grosso within their respective REDD+ programs. The first is having transparency as a main objective of the project, as previously mentioned. The second is the fact that both states include recommendations from a scientific/technical body in their decision-making processes, making it less political. The third is having the participation of a variety of community members on their monitoring counsels, as they can report any corruption. The fourth action pertains to the legal obligation to hire independent auditors to assess their programs, with the findings being reviewed by the monitoring counsel. To ensure transparency, it is advisable that these reports are published. Lastly, complaints can be filed by any citizen through the REDD+ system's ombudsmen or directly to the state prosecutor's office.

Despite these important provisions, Mato Grosso's law did not create a financially independent body, as Acre's will once all the SISA bodies have been created. Therefore, critics may still affirm that corruption risks are not fully mitigated owing to political interference.

6.   CONCLUSION

AB 32 is in the spotlight for being a possible model for the development of a national cap-and-trade program in the USA. This makes it internationally relevant owing to the impacts of climate change throughout the world. As experts have put it, California's system cannot be *perceived* to be a failure.[85]

As foreseen in AB 32, linkage between jurisdictions is possible and has been developing quickly between Acre and Chiapas. In fact, this bottom-up approach that aims to link emerging GHG mitigation efforts throughout the world, especially in California and Brazil, represents an important path forward in achieving a truly global approach to the problem of climate change.[86] With the Paris Agreement, it is now even more important considering the goal of keeping global temperatures from rising more than 2°C.

Mato Grosso could be an example of the program's expansion, especially considering its set of rules that directly comply with ROW's recommendations, while also bringing innovative insights. Therefore, the linkage between the California and Brazilian state governments will not only guarantee financial benefits for these poor states to promote reductions in forest degradation, but also cut the costs of reducing GHG for companies in California.

Nonetheless, these states must still enact clear, detailed and consistent regulations to avoid double crediting, leakage and reversals, while guaranteeing transparency and active participation of the community in their programs. While Mato Grosso should provide more autonomy to the governmental body as a means of preventing corruption, Acre could benefit from updating its law to foresee a reserve system in case any deforestation occurs owing to force majeure. Surprisingly, the states' laws are complementary and could benefit from having more cohesive frameworks.

It is time again for Brazil to take groundbreaking action—this time through Acre and Mato Grosso—and push for further negotiations with California in order to develop a strong REDD+ program.

NOTES

1. Information available at http://www.ipcc.ch/organization/organization.shtml (accessed April 23, 2015).
2. Intergovernmental Panel on Climate Change's Fifth Assessment Report (Synthesis Report), 2014, available at: http://www.ipcc.ch/pdf/assessment-report/ar5/syr/SYR_AR5_FINAL_full_wcover.pdf (accessed February 8, 2016).
3. Farhana Yamin, *Climate Change and Carbon Markets: A Handbook of Emission Reduction Mechanisms*, Earthscan, London, 2008.
4. Eric A. Posner and David Weisbach, *Climate Change Justice*, Princeton University Press, Princeton, NJ, 2010, p. 20.
5. Erkki J. Hollo, Kati Kulovesi and Michael Mehling (Eds), *Climate Change and the Law*, Springer, Berlin, 2010, p. 43.

6.   Kyoto Protocol, article 2 item 3.
7.   *How Cap and Trade Works, Environmental Defense Fund*, available at: http://www.edf. org/climate/how-cap-and-trade-works (accessed April 23, 2015).
8.   Id., p. 7.
9.   United Nations REDD Framework, available at: http://www.un-redd.org/Portals/15/ documents/publications/UN-REDD_FrameworkDocument.pdf (accessed April 27, 2015).
10. GGI is a cooperative effort among nine states to reduce GHG emissions, available at: http://www.rggi.org/rggi (accessed April 28, 2015).
11. WCI Inc. is a non-profit corporation that provides services to state and provincial greenhouse gas emission trading programs, available at: http://www.wci-inc.org (accessed April 28, 2015).
12. For example, Mato Grosso State Law no. 9.878/ 2013.
13. See Instituto Socioambiental and Forest Trends, *Avoided Deforestation (REDD) and Indigenous Peoples: Experiences, Challenges and Opportunities in the Amazon Context*, ISA, Sao Paulo, 2010, p. 133.
14. Erkki J. Hollo, Kati Kulovesi and Michael Mehling (Eds), *Climate Change and the Law*, Springer, Berlin, 2010, p. 44.
15. Paris Agreement, article 2, available at: http://unfccc.int/resource/docs/2015/cop21/eng/ l09r01.pdf (accessed January 5, 2016).
16. Justin Worland, *What to Know About the Historic 'Paris Agreement' on Climate Change*, available at: http://time.com/4146764/paris-agreement-climate-cop-21/ (accessed January 5, 2016).
17. Id. 15, article 2.
18. Id. 15, article 5.
19. Id. 14, at 481.
20. Robert N. Stavins, *Economics and Politics in California: Cap-and-Trade Allowance Allocation and Trade Exposure*, 2013, available at: http://www.robertstavinsblog. org/2013/08/16/economics-and-politics-in-california-cap-and-trade-allowance-allocation-and-trade-exposure/ (accessed April 27, 2015).
21. The authority of the US Environmental Protection Agency (EPA) to regulate and impose restrictions on GHG emissions is highly controversial, as perceivable from the last Supreme Court decision in Utility Air Regulatory Group v. EPA, available at: http://www.epa.gov/climatechange/EPAactivities/regulatory-initiatives.html (accessed June 15, 2015).
22. Deborah Lambe and Daniel Farber, *California's Cap-and-Trade Auction Proceeds: Taxes, Fees, or Something Else?* (May 2012), available at: https://www.law.berkeley.edu/ centers/clee/resources/publications/ (accessed May 20, 2014).
23. Katherine Hsia-Kiung, Emily Reyna and Timothy O'Connor, *California Carbon Market Watch: A Comprehensive Analysis of the Golden State's Cap-and-Trade Program/ Year One 2012–2013*, available at: edf.org/california-cap-and-trade-updates (accessed April 27, 2015).
24. Id. 23.
25. See Cal. Code Regs tit. 17, Section § 96014 (2013).
26. Katherine Hsia-Kiung, Emily Reyna and Timothy O'Connor, *California Carbon Market Watch: A Comprehensive Analysis of the Golden State's Cap-and-Trade Program/ Year One 2012–2013*, footnote 16, at 3, available at: edf.org/california-cap-and-trade-updates.
27. Id. 28, § 95802(a)(12) (2013).
28. Chicara Onda and James Fine, *Cost Containment through Offsets in the Cap-and-Trade Program under California's Global Warming Solutions Act*, 2011, available at: http:// www.edf.org/sites/default/files/EDF%20AB%2032offsetsmodelingmemo%20final2_ updated_3Jan2012_v2.pdf (accessed April 27, 2015).
29. Id. 28, § 95994, (a) (2013).
30. Id. 28, § 95854. (2013).
31. Id. 28, § 95802 (b): (33) (2013).

32. Id. 28, § 95854(c) (2013).
33. Id. 28, § 95992 (2013).
34. Id. 32.
35. California/US Forestry Offset Projects, available at: http://theredddesk.org/markets-standards/california-us-forestry-offset-projects-ab-32. (accessed April 1, 2015).
36. Id. 28, § 95802 (a) (152).
37. Id. 28, §95991(2013).
38. Id. 28, § 95942 (a) (2013).
39. Linkage Readiness Report, available at: http://www.arb.ca.gov/cc/capandtrade/linkage/linkage.htm (accessed May 10, 2015).
40. Id. 21, at 649.
41. Brazil's Second National Communication, available at: http://www.mct.gov.br/index.php/content/view/326984.html (accessed April 29, 2015).
42. United Nations Framework Convention on Climate Change, article 4.1.
43. Id. 21, at 640.
44. State of Paraíba Law 9.336/2011 created a reduction commitment of 36.1% until 2020.
45. Law 12.187/2009 dictates a reduction of 36–39% of GHG until 2020 based on a 'business as usual' scenario.
46. Law 12.187/ 2009, article 6.
47. The Legal Amazon was created by Law 1806/1953 and includes the Amazon Forest within the states of Acre, Amapá, Amazonas, Pará, Rondônia and Roraima and a portion of the states of Mato Grosso, Tocantins and Maranhão.
48. Action Plan for Prevention and Control of Deforestation in the Legal Amazon, available at: http://www.mma.gov.br/images/arquivo/80120/PPCDAm/_FINAL_PPCDAM.PDF (accessed May 1, 2015).
49. Id.
50. According to information provided by Imazon, a Brazilian NGO, deforestation from March 2014 to March 2015 increased 195%, available at: http://imazon.org.br/PDFimazon/Portugues/transparencia_florestal/amazonia_legal/SAD-Janeiro2015.pdf (accessed June 10, 2015).
51. Carlos Eduardo Frickmann Young, *Deforestation and Rural Unemployment in the Atlantic Forest*, 2006, available at: http://www.floram.org/files/v13n2/v13n2a7.pdf (accessed May 23, 2015).
52. Brazilian Constitution, article 225, paragraph 4.
53. The bills proposed in 2009 and 2010 have been shelved, only Bill 225/2015 is still being discussed by the legislature.
54. The Amazonas State Law, for example, mentions REDD+; however, it did not implement a framework to develop it.
55. Law 9878/2013, article 5.
56. Law 9878/2013, article 32. 'The State of Mato Grosso may establish cooperative agreements with counties, other states and the federal governments, as well as public and private institutions in other countries'.
57. See *Encyclopaedia Britannica*, do Brasil Publicações, São Paulo, 1998, vol. 1, at 58.
58. See data published by the NGO Imazon, available at: http://imazon.org.br/PDFimazon/Portugues/transparencia_florestal/amazonia_legal/SAD-Janeiro2015.pdf (accessed June 10, 2015).
59. Law 2.308/2010, article 2.
60. Id. 39, at See Cal. Code Regs tit. 17, § 95994 (3) (2013).
61. Id. 55.
62. Chris Cosslet, *California Leads the Way towards REDD+ Carbon Markets*, available at: http://redd-plus.com/drupal/california-climate-change-AB32-and-redd-plus-carbon-markets (accessed April 1, 2015).
63. ROW is composed of state representatives and technical experts who serve in their personal capacities.
64. See Green Technology Leadership Group, California, Acre and Chiapas, available at:

http://greentechleadership.org/documents/2013/07/row-final-recommendations-2.pdf (accessed April 30, 2015).

65. Id. 66.
66. Robert Stavins, Academic expert, in Katherine Hsia-Kiung, Emily Reyna and Timothy O'Connor, *California Carbon Market Watch: A Comprehensive Analysis of the Golden State's Cap-and-Trade Program/Year One 2012–2013*, available at: edf.org/california-cap-and-trade-updates (accessed April 30, 2015), at 30.
67. Id.
68. Law 9878/2013, article 4 and Law 2.308/2010, article 2.
69. Id. 92 at 4.
70. Id. 92 at 21.
71. ROW recommends that California should not issue credits directly to REDD+ partner jurisdictions, but instead recognize credits issued by partner jurisdictions or approved third-party programs that meet California's requirements, as California would not have the means to effectively control the issuance of such credits.
72. The participants are World Wildlife Fund and the Amazonian Work Group, a Brazilian NGO in defense of forest-dependent communities.
73. In article 26 of the State Law 9878/2013.
74. The counsel is composed of three representatives from forest-dependent communities, one representative of indigenous peoples, one representative of an NGO and one representative of an association related to REDD+ programs.
75. State Law 9878/2013, article 27.
76. Id. 77 at 38.
77. Id. 57.
78. United States v Curtiss-Wright Export Corp. Supreme Court of the United States, 1936.
79. Marcela Garcia Fonseca, *Os entes federativos brasileiros frente ao Direito Internacional*, Universidade de São Paulo, São Paulo, 2013.
80. Id. 81.
81. S. Butt, J. Parson and T. Stephens, *Brazil and Indonesia: REaDD+y or not? Law, Tropical Forests and Carbon. The case of REDD+*, Chapter 1, Cambridge University Press, Cambridge, 2011, at 262.
82. See Capping Brazil's Corruption Gusher, available at: http://www.bloombergview.com/articles/2014-11-28/capping-brazils-corruption-gusher (accessed May 20, 2015).
83. U4 Anti Corruption Resource Center, *Corruption and REDD+ Identifying Risks Amid Complexity*, 2–3, 2012, available at: http://www.u4.no/publications/corruption-and-redd-identifying-risks-amid-complexity.
84. See Alan Ramo and W.-N.W. Hastings, The California offset game: who wins and who loses?, *J. Env. L. & Pol'y* 109 (2014), at 147.
85. Id. 93, at 31.
86. Robert Stavins, Academic expert, in Katherine Hsia-Kiung, Emily Reyna and Timothy O'Connor, *California Carbon Market Watch: A Comprehensive Analysis of the Golden State's Cap-and-Trade Program/Year One 2012–2013*, at 30, available at: edf.org/california-cap-and-trade-updates.

3. Sowing the seed of change: Why Australia's land sector needs a carbon price to encourage mitigation of GHG emissions and promote sustainable land use

Vanessa Johnston

1. INTRODUCTION

According to Australia's most recent National Greenhouse Gas Inventory, greenhouse gas ('GHG') emissions arising from agricultural activities, forestry and land use change ('land sector') accounted for almost 15% of Australia's GHG emissions in 2013, being the third largest contribution of any economic sector.[1] More than half of Australia's total land area is used for agricultural or forestry purposes.[2] In light of the legal obligations that Australia has under the Kyoto Protocol to mitigate GHG emissions by 2% below 2000 levels by 2020,[3] it is important that entities in Australia's land sector are encouraged to mitigate GHG emissions that arise from their activities. The 'Emissions Reduction Fund' ('ERF') is intended to encourage mitigation of GHG emissions in all economic sectors, as the flagship measure of Australia's current climate change policy, the 'Direct Action Plan'.[4] Projects that mitigate land sector GHG emissions may also promote sustainable land use practices that reduce human-induced degradation or disturbance of land in relation to water, soil, biodiversity, native vegetation, invasive species or diseases.[5] As far as possible, land sector entities should be encouraged to implement emissions mitigation projects that also improve the sustainability of land use.

Between 1 July 2014 and 30 June 2017, the Government will distribute approximately $2.55 billion from the ERF as grants paid to entities that voluntarily undertake eligible GHG emissions mitigation projects.[6] More specifically, these grants are paid to entities in exchange for GHG emissions 'savings', each tonne of which is represented by an Australian

Carbon Credit Unit ('carbon credit'). To date, the Australian Government has paid an average of $13.10 for each carbon credit purchased from GHG emitters.[7] The process of creating and exchanging carbon credits is governed by the *Carbon Credits (Carbon Farming Initiative) Act 2011* (Cth) ('Carbon Credits Act').[8]

Attributing a value to GHG emissions, or 'carbon price', provides a financial incentive for consumers to change their behaviour to avoid emissions-intensive activities, favour low-emissions alternatives or specifically mitigate GHG emissions.[9] Grants paid to entities from the ERF are forms of financial assistance provided directly to entities by a government to incentivise mitigation or avoidance of GHG emissions. A grant is a form of indirect carbon price; while it will affect the overall cost of specific activities that lead to GHG emissions, it does not impose a specific price on GHG emissions *per se*. In effect, polluters are paid from the ERF to voluntarily mitigate or avoid GHG emissions.[10] Alternatively, a tax or tradeable emissions permit system can be imposed on GHG emissions so that polluters are obliged to pay the environmental and social costs of activities that lead to GHG emissions.[11] These instruments are direct carbon pricing instruments as they specifically increase the cost of an activity based on GHG emissions.

In Australia's land sector the ERF may not be the most appropriate instrument to encourage mitigation of GHG emissions. In practice, whether the ERF can encourage entities in Australia's land sector to implement GHG emissions mitigation projects that simultaneously promote sustainable land use practices depends on how it accommodates the characteristics of relevant entities and land-based activities. If the ERF neither penalises land sector entities that emit GHGs, nor obliges entities to implement sustainable land use practices, then the ERF merely maintains the status quo in this sector.

This chapter considers whether the ERF can encourage both GHG emissions mitigation and greater sustainable land use in Australia, and whether prospects for achieving both of these objectives are improved by a carbon price. Section 2 examines the provisions of the ERF, and considers how land sector entities have participated in the scheme to date, including aspects of the scheme that may limit ongoing or future participation by these entities. Section 3 then considers why it is better to establish a carbon price, rather than use the ERF, to encourage mitigation of GHG emissions and sustainable land use. Ultimately, this chapter argues that a carbon price is central to encouraging activities in the land sector that achieve both objectives.

2. HOW DOES AUSTRALIA'S ERF OPERATE IN RELATION TO LAND SECTOR ENTITIES?

Entities that voluntarily agree to undertake GHG emissions mitigation projects will be eligible to receive financial assistance from the ERF once they satisfy the two-stage process set out in the Carbon Credits Act. Stage one concludes with eligible projects being issued with carbon credits by the Clean Energy Regulator in relation to expected GHG emissions savings. As a result of stage two, entities are paid from the ERF to sell their carbon credits to the Australian Government.

The Clean Energy Regulator is responsible for issuing a 'certificate of entitlement' to land sector entities in respect of proposed GHG emissions mitigation projects. A certificate of entitlement sets out the total number of carbon credits that will be issued to the relevant entity, one carbon credit being equivalent to each tonne of mitigated or avoided GHG emissions. However, the Clean Energy Regulator may only issue the certificate once it is satisfied that the project meets the prescribed eligibility criteria,[12] including various conditions set out in s 27(4), such as:

(a)   the project is, or is to be, carried on in Australia; and
(b)   the project is covered by a methodology determination; and
(c)   the project meets such requirements as are set out in the methodology determination in accordance with paragraph 106(1)(b); and
(d)   the project meets the additionality requirements set out in subsection (4A) of this section; and
. . .
(g)   if the project is a sequestration offsets project—the project area, or each project area, meets the requirements set out in subsection (5) of this section; and
. . .
(l)   the project meets the eligibility requirements (if any) specified in the regulations or the legislative rules; and
(m)   the project is not an excluded offsets project.

While projects undertaken in the land sector can be standard 'emissions-offset' projects, they can also be a 'sequestration offsets project', which is a project designed to mitigate GHG emissions by sequestering GHG emissions in biomass (e.g. trees) or soil, or avoiding GHG emissions being released from these sources.[13] While this provides entities in the land sector with a wide variety of possible GHG emissions mitigation projects, sequestration projects must meet specific eligibility requirements. These include, for example, permanence rules that oblige entities to guarantee that GHG emissions saved from eligible projects will not be emitted back into the atmosphere for either 25 or 100 years.[14]

Once the Clean Energy Regulator is satisfied that the project meets each of these criteria, and has issued the entity with carbon credits, the entity has an opportunity to sell those credits to the Australian Government at a reverse auction.[15] The price paid for carbon credits by the Australian Government is limited by a 'benchmark' price[16] that is set to promote 'least-cost' mitigation of GHG emissions.[17] The benchmark price is set prior to each auction, according to factors such as the previous value of carbon credits and the quantity of GHG emissions savings needed for Australia to achieve agreed GHG emissions mitigation targets.[18] The Australian Government enters into a contract of sale with each successful entity, where carbon credits are delivered (and paid for) over an average period of 7 years.[19]

(a)   How have Land Sector Entities Fared under ERF Auctions?

The results of auctions held pursuant to the Carbon Credits Act reveal how, and by what means, entities in the land sector are participating in the ERF. Results of the first two auctions, held in April and November 2015 respectively, indicate that entities in the land sector have so far been willing and successful participants. At the first auction approximately 60% of the carbon credits purchased (equivalent to 28.8 out of 47 million tonnes of saved GHG emissions) were issued in respect of projects in the land sector, including trees or soil carbon sequestration projects (28 million tonnes),[20] strategic early dry season fire management projects in savannah areas (0.5 million tonnes) and piggery methane gas capture projects (0.3 million tonnes).[21] The average price paid for carbon credits at the first auction was $13.95 per credit/tonne.[22]

At the second auction, the Australian Government purchased a further 45.5 million carbon credits/GHG emissions savings, at a lower average price of $12.25 per credit/tonne.[23] Almost 80% of credits purchased at the second auction were attributable to the land sector, generated from reforestation, avoided deforestation, regrowth 'vegetation' projects (25.6 million tonnes),[24] savannah burning projects (6.6 million tonnes), and agricultural activities such as piggeries, cattle/dairy, cotton and soil sequestration (4 million tonnes).[25]

While these results indicate that land sector entities have been relatively successful at ERF auctions to date, ongoing success of this kind may not be sustainable given the nature and variety of the successful projects. Consequently, the ERF may have limited potential to encourage GHG emissions mitigation in this sector in the long term.

(b)   Pitfalls of the ERF for Entities in Australia's Land Sector

Stemming from the 'least-cost' emphasis of the Direct Action Plan and current average price of carbon credits, the long-term potential of the ERF to encourage mitigation of GHG emissions and promote sustainable land use practices in Australia is restricted by the:

- limited availability of 'least cost' abatement opportunities;
- minimal reward for projects based on existing 'climate resilient' or 'sustainable land use' practices; and
- risk of perverse outcomes.

(i)   Limited availability of 'least-cost' abatement opportunities

There is unlikely to be a large number of GHG emissions mitigation projects in the land sector that are viable at the current carbon credit price. For example, 75% of carbon credits purchased for sequestration projects at the first auction in April 2015 will arise from 'native forest protection projects',[26] which involve protection of 'native forests' that have been approved for clearing to create cropland or grassland.[27] As these projects involve avoiding future clearing, they can be implemented and managed at little cost. However, they are a limited source of GHG emissions savings because of certain provisions of the Carbon Credits Act.

Pursuant to s 27(4)(d), projects must meet additionality requirements to ensure that entities are only rewarded for real, measurable and long-term emissions savings that would not otherwise be achieved in the normal course of business.[28] More specifically, the Carbon Credits Act requires that projects must meet 'regulatory', and 'government program' additionality requirements to be issued with carbon credits by the Clean Energy Regulator.[29] A project will fail to meet these requirements if the project could be carried out: by a State, Territory, or Commonwealth authority; under a State, Territory, or Commonwealth law; or under another Government scheme or programme. According to Government data, more than 70% of Australia's native forest (representing 88,000 of 123,000 hectares) is located on Crown land.[30] As public ownership increases the likelihood that the Government could undertake the proposed project instead of a private entity, it is likely that projects that propose to protect native forest located on Crown land will not meet additionality requirements, and be ineligible for funding under the ERF. The area of native forest that can be protected under the ERF is also restricted by s 27(4)(m), which excludes projects to protect native forests that have clearing approval for fire protection purposes, or where clearing would improve the environmental quality of the land.[31] These requirements limit the areas of forest whose protection could be eligible for funding under the ERF, and are therefore unlikely to provide a sustained source of carbon credits for land sector entities.

This argument is further supported by the results of the second ERF auction, at which most emissions savings have been purchased from entities involved in forest regeneration projects.[32] In this case, forest regeneration is unlikely to provide an ongoing source of carbon credits because the estimated cost of forest regeneration varies widely across Australia depending on land type. These results support industry expectations that revegetation of agricultural land, for example, may be commercially viable at a 'modest' price per hectare.[33] However, the costs associated with revegetating other kinds of land are far higher—exceeding $60,000 per hectare in tropical areas.[34]

Both native forest protection and regeneration projects have been successful in recent ERF auctions as an accessible form of 'least-cost' abatement in Australia's land sector. Their success indicates the nature of projects that land sector entities are willing to undertake for financial assistance of $13 per carbon credit/tonne of saved GHG emissions. However, the greater concern is that these kinds of projects are limited, and that the ERF cannot incentivise more expensive projects that are needed to encourage land use change or encourage the growth of sustainable land use practices, revegetation of tropical areas (as above), permanent environmental plantings,[35] soil grazing systems or changes to agricultural processes. Economic models indicate that there is little potential for land use change to occur on agricultural land where carbon prices remain below $65 per tonne,[36] which far exceeds the current average price under the ERF. Importantly, the cost of ongoing compliance with ERF requirements (such as verification and auditing costs over the contract term) is not included in this price.[37] Consequently, the price of carbon credits is already influencing the kinds of projects that entities are willing to implement to mitigate GHG emissions from activities in the land sector.

(ii)   Minimal reward for projects based on existing 'climate resilient' or sustainable land use practices

As indicated by the additionality requirements discussed above, the ERF focuses on securing additional GHG emissions savings.[38] This means that projects must also be 'new', having not already commenced at the time application is made for carbon credits.[39] This requirement may exclude projects from the ERF that are based on existing 'climate resilient' or sustainable land use practices that farmers have already adopted. Alternatively, land sector entities could be encouraged to undertake cheaper projects that satisfy ERF requirements, rather than developing or expanding on existing climate resilient or sustainable land use practices that are not supported by the scheme. Industry commentators argue that the additionality requirements of the Carbon Credits Act will specifically disadvantage farmers who have been 'early adopters' of these kinds of land use practices.[40]

Furthermore, the additionality requirements of the ERF could encourage farmers to alter the design of their existing sustainable land use practices to obtain a benefit from the ERF, i.e. to decide whether projects will be designed to satisfy funding criteria of the ERF or a non-ERF mechanism. For example, the *Income Tax Assessment Act 1997* (Cth) provides favourable treatment to taxpayers who enter into a 'conservation covenant', or undertake 'Landcare' projects on their land.[41] Tax deductions and offsets paid under these programmes between 1 July 2014 and 30 June 2017 are expected to exceed $5 million.[42] This indicates that entities in the land sector will need to decide whether to satisfy eligibility criteria to receive tax concessions, at the expense of funding from the ERF. In this case, the potential GHG emissions savings arising from those projects may not be maximised.

(iii) Risk of perverse outcomes

There is a risk that the ERF could lead to perverse outcomes, including risks associated with leakage and permanence of emissions savings,[43] or the decision that land owners and managers make about land use. Competition for land is increasing, not only between possible uses within the land-sector, but also between land and other sectors of the economy.[44] There is a risk that entities in the land sector may choose to allow their land to be sold, leased or used for activities based on profitability, and at the expense of GHG emissions savings and sustainable land use practices. While it is far too soon to determine whether this will occur in Australia's land sector, there is already evidence that companies are considering how best to use land to carry out their business with the support of the ERF in other sectors. For example, it may be more profitable to allow agricultural/ forestry land to be used for energy purposes (whether fossil fuel for renewable), or for other commercial use. In this regard, experiences in Europe indicate that Australia will have to re-evaluate the demands that renewable energy production places on land use in Australia.[45] Rather than change the use of land overall, entities should consider how GHG emissions mitigation projects could be implemented on different parts of their land, without changing the overall use.[46] On this basis, the design of the ERF may lead to perverse outcomes in the land sector, neither encouraging the mitigation of land sector GHG emissions nor promoting sustainable land use practices.

Land sector entities face numerous challenges in obtaining funding from the ERF, which arise from the design of the Carbon Credits Act and the way that the price of carbon credits is determined pursuant to this Act. The above discussion has illustrated that the value of financial assistance provided to entities in the land sector is a fundamental reason why the ERF is unlikely to provide ongoing encouragement to land sector entities to mitigate GHG emissions over a longer term. On this basis, a carbon price could better encourage land sector entities to mitigate GHG emissions in ways that also promote sustainable land use.

3.   CARBON PRICING OPTIONS IN AUSTRALIA'S LAND SECTOR

As previously noted, laws that implement an emissions trading scheme or tax can be designed to price carbon directly, because they increase the cost of activities based on the resulting GHG emissions. Increasing the price of activities that lead to GHG emissions encourages entities to reduce or avoid those activities for financial reasons.[47]

Between 1 July 2012 and 30 June 2014, the Australian Government used a carbon price, in conjunction with other measures, to encourage mitigation of GHG emissions, including those arising from the land sector. More specifically, during this time a superseded version of the now current Carbon Credits Act created the 'Carbon Farming Initiative' ('CFI'). The CFI had a similar design to the current ERF, except that it applied primarily to entities in the land sector.[48] This narrower CFI was linked to a 'carbon tax' imposed by the former *Clean Energy Act 2011* (Cth): carbon credits issued under the CFI could be purchased by entities to satisfy their obligations under that legislation.[49] In December 2014, the Climate Change Authority issued a report on the CFI, which analysed its environmental performance in relation to mitigating GHG emissions.[50] According to this report, the performances of the CFI and ERF to date are generally comparable. During its three years of operation, the Clean Energy Regulator issued 10.6 million carbon credits to 178 projects in accordance with 26 Method Statements under the CFI.[51] The Climate Change Authority reported that the CFI resulted in GHG emissions savings of 10 million tonnes, an average reduction of 2.5 million tonnes per annum.[52] This is comparable to achievements proposed at the first ERF auction, where the combined commitment of successful land sector entities was an average GHG emissions mitigation of 2.8 million tonnes over the next 10 years.[53]

Given that the results of the CFI and the expected results of the ERF are similar, why should a carbon price be reinstated in Australia's land sector? A carbon price can not only minimise the challenges posed to land sector entities by the ERF identified above, but also encourage greater sustainable land use practices in the long term. As a result, whether a carbon price complements or replaces the ERF, it is a tool that can help to achieve the dual objectives of GHG emissions mitigation and sustainable land use practices in Australia's land sector. Ultimately, Australia's political and economic circumstances will determine whether a carbon price is implemented.[54]

Historical experience indicates that governments are hesitant to subject land-based activities to a carbon price. For example, the Australian Government considered whether agricultural and reforestation projects could be covered by an emissions trading scheme proposed under the 2008 'Carbon Pollution Reduction Scheme' policy.[55] Based on stakeholder feedback the proposal proceeded on the basis that agricultural emissions would be excluded during the initial years of operation, and that reforestation activities would only be covered on a voluntary basis.[56] In these years, the Australian Government intended to rely on financial assistance measures and regulatory standards to encourage mitigation of GHG emissions until the emissions trading scheme could be expanded to cover relevant activities. This approach follows that adopted under the European Union emissions trading scheme, where the agricultural sector is excluded from the regulation scheme, but subject to specific GHG emissions mitigation targets and complementary regulatory standards.[57] Furthermore, not all land-based activities are well suited to direct carbon pricing, such as sequestration projects that increase carbon sinks that naturally remove GHG emissions from the atmosphere rather than reduce GHG emissions from existing practices. Although it may be difficult to design a carbon price that applies to these kinds of activities, a carbon price can be imposed in the land sector in other ways. When compared with the current ERF, a carbon price can increase the range of projects that are made viable in this sector by higher carbon prices, rewarding existing sustainable or climate resilient land use practices.

First, a carbon price can broaden the scope of GHG emissions mitigation opportunities in the land sector based on price. This occurs because an economy-wide carbon price is likely to be higher than the current value of carbon credits. Australian Treasury models that preceded the proposed 'Carbon Pollution Reduction Scheme' in 2008, and the 'carbon tax' in 2011, valued one tonne of GHG emissions at $40 and $23, respectively, in the year commencing 1 July 2012.[58] As discussed above, a higher carbon price should encourage more expensive regeneration, permanent planting or sequestration projects to become financially viable.

Second, a carbon price can broaden the scope of GHG emissions mitigation opportunities in the land sector based on covered activities. While the ERF encourages land sector entities to undertake specific GHG emissions mitigation projects, a carbon price can be applied more generally to activities that lead to GHG emissions. For example, a carbon price can influence the decisions that land sector entities make in relation to vehicle or machinery purchase, selection of transport fuels or electricity use.[59] It is vital that land sector entities are encouraged to mitigate GHG emissions from these products. For example, there is substantial opportunity to mitigate GHG emissions from transport fuel, as almost 13% of all diesel consumed in 2009–2010 was consumed in the agriculture and forestry sectors.[60] While the land sector makes a much smaller contribution to electricity consumption (1%), this does mean that energy efficiency improvements cannot contribute to overall GHG emissions savings in the sector.[61]

Importantly, a carbon price can reward entities that save GHG emissions in relation to these products, regardless of the quantity of GHG emissions saved. It is more difficult for a similar reward to be provided under the ERF,[62] because the Clean Energy Regulator is prohibited by auction rules from accepting bids for less than 2000 carbon credits from each participating entity.[63] This threshold is problematic for entities that make changes in respect of a small number of vehicles or machinery, or implement small-scale energy efficiency projects. A carbon price has no such minimum threshold, thereby rewarding entities for saving emissions that fall below the minimum ERF bid size. The broad scope of a carbon price will also benefit entities that GHG emissions because of existing sustainable land use or climate-resilient practices. As discussed above, entities cannot benefit from existing projects under the ERF because of complex additionality requirements. Entities are also penalised where alternative incentive schemes are available (conservation covenants, Landcare, etc.). Under a carbon price entities will not have to choose between incentive schemes, and will be able to benefit from emissions savings generated from existing schemes for as long as those savings continue.

4. CONCLUSION

The Australian Government has designed the ERF to encourage mitigation of GHG emissions from all economic sectors, based on the CFI incentive scheme that once only applied to the land sector. The design of the ERF, as it has been amended to apply to all economic sectors, creates challenges for the land sector, as it encourages a limited variety of abatement opportunities owing to the low value of carbon credits, provides minimal reward for existing sustainable and climate resilient practices, and risks perverse outcomes in relation to future land use. A carbon price re-focuses the task of mitigating GHG emissions on polluters and is a vital component of the measures applied to Australia's land sector for this purpose. This chapter has identified how a carbon price can minimise specific challenges posed by the ERF for entities in this sector, as it can encourage more expensive projects to be implemented, while still rewarding entities for existing sustainable and climate resilient practices.

While a carbon price might lead to comparable GHG emissions savings to the ERF in the short-term, it is a vital component in measures intended to achieve these savings in the long term. Importantly, a carbon price encourages polluters to change patterns of consumption to favour low-emissions activities and to invest in those activities for the future. This is vital for the ongoing viability of Australia's land sector in a carbon-constrained economy.

NOTES

1. Commonwealth of Australia, *Australian National Greenhouse Accounts: National Inventory Report 2014, The Australian Government Submission to the United Nations Framework Convention on Climate Change* (2015), Vol. 1, 242; Vol. 2, 1.
2. Australian Bureau of Statistics, 'Agricultural Environment', *Yearbook Australia* (no. 1301.1, 24 May 2012); Department of Agriculture and Water Resources, *Australia's Forests* (25 February 2015), http://www.agriculture.gov.au/forestry/australias-forests.
3. *Kyoto Protocol to the Framework Convention on Climate Change*, opened for signature 16 March 1998, 2303 UNTS 148 (entered into force 16 February 2005), annex B, as amended by Conference of the Parties, United Nations Framework Convention on Climate Change, Agreed Outcome Pursuant to the Bali Action Plan UN Doc. FCCC/CMP/2012/13/Add.1 (28 February 2013), Decision 1/CMP.8. Note that this target is smaller than the target committed to under Australia's 'Direct Action Plan', below n 4.
4. Liberal Party of Australia, *The Coalition's Direct Action Plan* (2011).
5. Justin Healy, *Sustainable Land Management* (Issues in Society no. 331, Balmain, NSW, 2014), 1.
6. Australian Government, *Emissions Reduction Fund: White Paper* (2014), 8; see also Australian Government, 'Emissions Reduction Fund: Green Paper' (Report, 2013).
7. The median value of the average carbon credit price paid at the first and second ERF auctions ($13.95 and $12.25, respectively).
8. See further, Department of Environment, *Legislation* (2015) Emissions Reduction Fund, http://www.environment.gov.au/climate-change/emissions-reduction-fund/about/legislation.
9. Sir Nicholas Stern, *The Economics of Climate Change* (Cambridge University Press, Cambridge, 2007), chapter 17. In addition to carbon pricing, Stern argues that a mix of instruments is required to promote 'responsible behaviour'.
10. Zada Lipman and Gerry Bates, 'Economic Instruments in Australian Pollution Control' in *Pollution Law in Australia* (LexisNexis, Chatswood, 2002), 81–82; Direct financial assistance measures have low compatibility with the polluter pays principle, see OECD, *Economic Instruments for Environment Protection* (OCDE-OECD, Paris, 1989), 117.
11. *Report of the United Nations Conference on Environment and Development Annex 1: Rio*

Declaration on Environment and Development A/CONF.151/26 (Vol. 1), principle 16; Philippe Sands, *Principles of International Environmental Law* (Cambridge University Press, Cambridge, 2nd edn, 2003), 279, 24–25; Ross Garnaut, *The Garnaut Climate Change Review* (Cambridge University Press, Melbourne, 2008), [13.1.1].

12. Carbon Credits Act ss 15, 27. Note the applicant responsible for a project must also meet certain criteria, for example see s 60.

13. Carbon Credits Act s 54.

14. Carbon Credits Act ss 27(3)(e) and (f), 87.

15. Carbon Credits Act s 20F. Two auctions have occurred to date, on 14–15 April 2015 and 4–5 November 2015. See Australian Government, *Auction Results* (November 2015) Emissions Reduction Fund, http://www.cleanenergyregulator.gov.au/ERF/Auctions-results.

16. Clean Energy Regulator, 'Emissions Reduction Fund: Auction Guidelines' (February 2015), http://www.cleanenergyregulator.gov.au/DocumentAssets/Documents/ERF%20auction%20guidelines%20-%20archived.pdf.

17. Carbon Credits Act s 20G; Australian Government, *Emissions Reduction Fund: White Paper* (2014).

18. Australian Government, *Emissions Reduction Fund: White Paper* (2014), 44.

19. Carbon Credits Act s 69(3).

20. See definition in Carbon Credits Act s 54.

21. Clean Energy Regulator, 'Auction Results Factsheet: April 2015' (May 2015).

22. Clean Energy Regulator, 'Auction Results: April 2015' (Media Release, 25 May 2015).

23. Clean Energy Regulator, 'Auction Results Factsheet: November 2015' (November 2015).

24. Clean Energy Regulator, *Vegetation Methods* (22 January 2016) Emissions Reduction Fund, http://www.cleanenergyregulator.gov.au/ERF/Choosing-a-project-type/Opportunities-for-the-land-sector/Vegetation-methods.

25. Ibid. Clean Energy Regulator, *Agricultural Methods* (25 September 2015) Emissions Reduction Fund, http://www.cleanenergyregulator.gov.au/ERF/Choosing-a-project-type/Opportunities-for-the-land-sector/Agricultural-methods. See further Carbon Credits Act s 5.

26. Rounded addition of 'volume of abatement committed under contract'; Clean Energy Regulator, *Carbon Abatement Contract Register* (April 2015) Emissions Reduction Fund, http://www.cleanenergyregulator.gov.au/ERF/project-and-contracts-registers/carbon-abatement-contract-register; carbon credits from native forest protection projects accounted for approximately 21 out of 28 million tonnes purchased from 'sequestration' projects generally.

27. Carbon Credits (Carbon Farming Initiative—Avoided Deforestation 1.1) Methodology Determination 2015 (25 March 2015) clause 10.

28. The difficulty of meeting 'additionality' requirements is discussed comprehensively in literature relating to the Clean Development and Joint Implementation mechanisms relating to Kyoto Protocol arts 6 and 12. For example Emma Paulsson, 'A Review of CDM Literature: From Fine-Tuning to Critical Scrutiny?' (2009) 6 *International Environmental Agreements* 63 reviews key issues relating to additionality under the Kyoto Protocol. Further discussion of additionality is outside the scope of this article.

29. Carbon Credits Act ss 27(4A)(b), (c).

30. Land not forming part of 'Private forest' or 'Unresolved tenure' categories, see Department of Agriculture and Forestry, above n 2.

31. Carbon Credits (Carbon Farming Initiative) Regulations 2011 (Cth) r 3.36(g).

32. Clean Energy Regulator, *Carbon Abatement Contract Register* (12 November 2015) Emissions Reduction Fund, http://www.cleanenergyregulator.gov.au/ERF/project-and-contracts-registers/carbon-abatement-contract-register.

33. As discussed in Brett Bryan et al., 'Land Use Efficiency: Anticipating Future Demand for Land-Sector Greenhouse Gas Emissions Abatement and Managing Trade-Offs with

Agriculture, Water, and Biodiversity' (2015) 21 *Global Change Biology* 4098 and associated citations.

34. Penny van Oosterzee, 'Carbon Farming Initiative Will Fail Farmers and Rural Communities' (8 July 2014) *The Conversation*, http://theconversation.com/carbon-farming-initiative-will-fail-farmers-and-rural-communities-28276.
35. Freddy Sharpe, 'Carbon Forestry Opportunities and the CFI' (Carbon Farming Conference, Dubbo, 23 October 2012); van Oosterzee, ibid.
36. As discussed in Bryan et al., above n 33, and associated citations.
37. Sharpe, above n 35. ERF Methodologies establish formulas to help entities to quantify emissions savings from projects to be audited during the contract term.
38. Carbon Credits Act s 27(4A).
39. Carbon Credits Act ss 27(4A)(a).
40. Patrick Francis, 'So Called "Carbon Farming" Fails to Embrace Broadacre Farmers: High Hopes for Soil Carbon Revenue Dashed' (25 March 2015) Moffitts Farm, http://www.moffittsfarm.com.au/2015/03/25/so-called-carbon-farming-fails-to-embrace-broadacre-farmers/.
41. *Income Tax Assessment Act 1997* (Cth) divs 31, 40-G.While land subject to conservation covenants is no longer excluded from the ERF by the recent repeal of Carbon Credits (Carbon Farming Initiative) Regulations 2011 (Cth) r 3.29, there is only limited circumstances in which activities supporting a conservation covenant can also be eligible for the ERF owing to the other additionality requirements, see Clean Energy Regulator, 'Meeting the Requirements of "Regulatory Additionality" with Conservation Covenants', *Sequestration Guidance* (August 2015) Emissions Reduction Fund, http://www.cleanenergyregulator.gov.au/ERF/Pages/Forms%20and%20resources/Regulatory%20Guidance/Sequestration%20guidance/Meeting-the-requirements-of-regulatory-additionality-with-conservation-covenants.aspx.
42. Australian Treasury, *Tax Expenditures Statement 2014* (2014) 55. Pursuant to Item 'B66' (combined with Item 'B69'), the estimated expenditure is $5 million between 1 July 2014 and 30 June 2017.
43. Analogous to problems associated with the 'Clean Development Mechanism' established under Kyoto Protocol, art 12; for example as discussed in Paulsson, above n 28. The Carbon Credits Act contains set out permanence periods relating to sequestration projects, see above n 14 and associated text.
44. As discussed in Bryan et al., above n 33, and associated citations; Reputex Carbon, 'Unlocking Land Sector Abatement: Outlook for the Emissions Reduction Fund' (January 2014) 8.
45. David Howard et al., 'The Impact of Sustainable Energy Production on Land Use in Britain through to 2050' (2009) 26S *Land Use Policy* 284.
46. For example, Australian Wide Research Institute, 'Managing Greenhouse Gas Emissions in Viticulture' (March 2015) considered how sequestration projects could be established in conjunction with use of land for viticulture; T.T.H. Nguyen et al., 'Effect of Farming Practices for Greenhouse Gas Mitigation and Subsequent Alternative Land Use on Environmental Impacts of Beef Cattle Production Systems' (2013) 7 *Animal* 860, identified the potential for forests to be established on 'excess' land in beef cattle farms to offset GHG emissions.
47. Sir Nicholas Stern, *The Economics of Climate Change* (Cambridge University Press, Cambridge, 2007), 24.
48. The Government intended that projects registered under CFI to continue their registration under the ERF, see Climate Change Authority, *Carbon Farming Initiative Review Report* (2014), 8–9, 11. Also note different funding arrangements for each schemes; while polluters paid carbon tax liability from their own funds, taxpayer funds from consolidated revenue are used for the ERF.
49. *Clean Energy Act 2011* (Cth) (repealed) ss 5, 122.
50. Climate Change Authority, *Carbon Farming Initiative Review Report* (2014).
51. Ibid., 16, 18–19.

52. Ibid., 24.
53. Clean Energy Regulator, above n 22; Clean Energy Regulator, above n 26.
54. Janet Milne, 'Environmental Taxation: Why Theory Matters' in Janet Milne et al. (eds) *Critical Issues in Environmental Taxation: Volume 1* (Richmond, UK, 2003).
55. Australian Government, *Carbon Pollution Reduction Scheme: Australia's Low Pollution Future White Paper* (December 2008).
56. Ibid., Policy Positions 6.21–6.22.
57. *Directive 2003/87/EC of the European Parliament and of the Council of 13 October 2003 Establishing a Scheme for Greenhouse Gas Emission Allowances Trading within the Community and amending Council Directive 96/61/EC* [2003] *OJ* L 275/32, annex I.
58. Carbon Pollution Reduction Scheme Bill (2010) s 89 ($40 in the year commencing 1 July 2012); *Clean Energy Act 2011* (Cth) (repealed) s 100 ($23 in the year commencing 1 July 2012).
59. Reputex Carbon, above n 44, 5, identified that reducing these indirect costs were a key driver of carbon farming projects commenced under the former *Clean Energy Act 2011* (Cth).
60. Australian Bureau of Statistics, 'Energy Use' *Yearbook Australia* (no. 1301.1, 24 May 2012), Chart 19.13.
61. Climate Change Authority, 'Analysis of Electricity Consumption, Electricity Generation Emissions Intensity, and Economy-Wide Emissions' (Report, October 2013) [Table 3].
62. Carbon Credits (Carbon Farming Initiative—Land and Sea Transport) Methodology Determination 2015 (13 February 2015).
63. Clean Energy Regulator, 'Emissions Reduction Fund—Guidelines for the Second Auction on 4–5 November 2015' (21 August 2015) 2.

PART II

Protecting water resources

4. Fighting for water: The role of federal market instruments in addressing water issues in the United States

Mona L. Hymel

> The nation behaves well if it treats the natural resources as assets which it must turn over to the next generation increased, and not impaired, in value.[1]

Water probably stands first as the resource requiring national attention and protection. Water has been and continues to be wasted as though the Earth's supply is endless. Yet our usable supplies of water are diminishing and, in some cases, being exhausted. Based on recent climate change data, the United Nations World Meteorological Organization announced that 2015 is the warmest year on record, with the last 5 years being the hottest period.[2] The worst impacts of global warming, such as intensified storms, rising sea levels and bizarre weather, are becoming a reality as the greenhouse gas level exceeds thresholds scientists believe will trigger these events.[3] Policymakers must conquer many moving targets. This article focuses on one of the fastest moving targets—the US water crisis. Water scarcity, water allocation, and water degradation are discussed.

The federal tax system can be part of a national program to address water problems.[4] This article considers whether a federal water trading scheme is an option for the United States and how market instruments, such as tax incentives, can facilitate the creation of such a market. Because water issues tend to be local or regional, creating and implementing a federal water trading program will be a complex task. Determining how the US federal government can feasibly implement a nationwide water trading scheme may require innovative solutions, but tax incentives have successfully created national markets in the past. For example, the creation of a national water trading scheme through the use of federal market instruments can be analogized with the creation of the market for ethanol. None existed before the enactment of federal tax incentives. This article discusses existing mechanisms to deal with water issues and analyzes the potential to implement federal legislation to abate water problems. Ultimately, the solution to the water crisis in the United States will probably stem from many policy alternatives working in tandem. Evaluating a national water trading market and tax incentives designed to mitigate other water issues, however, stand as a critical aspect for addressing water issues in the United States.

I. BACKGROUND ON US WATER ISSUES: EVIDENCE OF DRAMATIC AND GROWING WATER PROBLEMS

The United States faces water problems so serious that they threaten the US economy, security and environment. Among the most critical threats to US water are pollution, scarcity, allocation issues, inefficient water use and ownership rights. As the most disastrous effects of climate change continue to materialize, water catastrophes will be some of the worst. Climate change will be experienced within the water cycle—through droughts, floods, depleted rivers, shrinking reservoirs, dried-out soils, melting glaciers, loss of snowpack and overall shortages of water.[5] The US Southwest and Great Plains are extremely likely to experience 'unprecedented mega-droughts' during this century.[6] However, the response to recent droughts by Texas and California does not provide much confidence in facing future drought conditions. Despite conservation measures by Texas and California farms and cities, increased ground water pumping served as the primary solution to deal with drought conditions—a very shortsighted strategy.[7]

Many water problems have been created or significantly exacerbated by the law applicable in the region or locality. For example, the Colorado 'river is in trouble, and water laws are one significant cause'.[8] Legal rights and state water allocations give away more water than the river can provide. Meanwhile, as the river flow declines, policymakers are trying to wring more supply out of the Colorado. Yet, as of 2010, the total US water use dropped to approximately 355 billion gallons per day,[9] representing the first drop in water use since 1985.[10] The declines in water use came primarily from improvements in technology—a key to solving water problems. For example, irrigation water use declined as more farms are shifting to water-efficient irrigation systems, and thermoelectric-power water reductions resulted from shifts to cooling systems and generation technologies with lower water requirements.[11] Because agriculture and energy production account for the greatest water use, technology improvements, often encouraged with tax incentives, are extremely important.[12]

a. Energy Production

As a critical part of US society, energy production depends on significant amounts of water that is either irreplaceable or extremely costly to replace.[13] Fuel production, hydropower generation, and thermoelectric power plant cooling consume huge amounts of water. For example, in 2010, 45% of national water withdrawals went to thermoelectric cooling.[14] In addition, 'degraded water is often a waste byproduct that creates management and disposal challenges'.[15] Often policymakers prioritize other national problems—such as inexpensive energy, national security concerns associated with foreign energy dependence, climate change mitigation and adaption, public health issues and a robust economy—over water issues in determining their stance on energy policy.[16]

While prioritization of national problems requires an understanding and ranking of extremely complex problems, water management must be at the top of the list of US national priorities. The energy–water nexus is explained and evaluated in this section. Energy is necessary to deliver water in the many ways it is used, and water is a necessary input to energy production. As policymakers acknowledge the extreme water vulnerability of US water supplies, the impact of energy production's water use must be reduced. This vulnerability is exemplified by increased water demands, temperature increases attributable to global warming and drought conditions exacerbated by climate change. In the summer of 2011, Texas's very high temperatures increased electricity demand, and a continuing drought resulted in reduced water flows. The water needed to cool electric generators became compromised.[17] The state deemed consumer conservation critical as peak demand electricity purchases reached the market cap ($3000 per megawatt hour).[18] The state avoided disaster *only* because weather conditions abated.[19] In the aftermath of the 2011 disaster, Texas electricity plants instituted a number of safety measures.[20] However, more can be done to reduce vulnerability to water disruptions in the production of electricity. For example, expanding the nation's electricity portfolio to 20% wind by 2030 would reduce water consumption by 1.2 billion gallons daily.[21] Reliable water is essential for US electricity security.

Water is also a key input and output of fossil fuel production. The Congressional Research Service (CRS) identifies several key factors that impact water needed for fuel production: '(1) which fuel is being produced in the region, (2) the local and regional significance of its water use, and (3) regional conditions for management of wastewaters'.[22] The amount of water necessary for fuel production depends on the type of fuel. At the low end is conventional natural gas needing 1 gallon of water per MMBtu, and at the high end are irrigated biofuels needing 100–1000 gallons of water per MMBtu. An estimated 4.6 billion gallons per day of fresh water is used for fuel production.[23] However, the water needed to produce fuels using different techniques is poorly documented.[24] The water required to produce oil from conventional wells represents the largest water use by the US oil and gas sector.[25] Although water needed for conventional drilling is expected to increase, the latest increase in demand—for water used in hydraulic fracturing—raises the biggest questions.[26] In the early 2000s, as the industry's water use began climbing, the US Geological Survey (USGS) estimated that, for fracked wells, gas wells needed 4.1 million gallons of water per well and oil wells needed 2 million gallons of water per well.[27] While such water needs are staggering, the USGS notes that these figures are incomplete. First, the data only includes information provided by the industry. Second, the USGS survey stopped in 2010, early on in the drilling boom.[28] The USGS continues to update its information; however, that the average water use per well will increase substantially is a virtual certainty.[29]

In addition to water needed as an input for fuel production, water is also the biggest byproduct of fuel production, called 'produced water'. In the United States, an estimated 2.3 billion gallons per day are produced from onshore oil and gas wells.[30] The average ratio of produced water to oil is 7.6 to 1. This ratio is predicted to increase to an average 12:1 by 2025 as a result of aging, less productive wells.[31] In addition, because of the growth of fracking (25,000 wells drilled per year),[32] policymakers and the public are disturbed by increasing wastewater and problems associated with its disposal.[33] 'Hydraulic fracturing . . . uses large amounts of water to crack open rocks and help coax oil and gas from underground wells . . . After the gas and oil have been extracted, the chemical-laced water is typically pumped back underground.'[34] As fracking operations attract more attention, scientific research to improve disposal and reuse is on the rise. 'Water impacts are a central issue addressed in new rules for fracking on US public land. The Bureau of Land Management tightened requirements for well construction and for the storage of wastewater.'[35] In a 2015 comprehensive review of fracking, the US Environmental Protection Agency (EPA) sought to provide state and local governments with information on fracking's impact in their locality, and provide guidance for regulation.[36] As part of the study's goals, the EPA worked 'to identify how streams, aquifers, and wells might be vulnerable to fracking—either through contamination from chemicals, wastewater spills or natural gas intrusion, or through the draining of wells or groundwater'.[37] While acknowledging specific instances of pollution and depleted ground water, drinking wells, and streams, the EPA stated that fracking to date has not caused widespread harm to US drinking water.[38] *However*, the EPA also concluded that hydraulic fracking poses many threats to water.[39] The EPA study identified the following:

possible contamination from well failures; badly managed wastewater; and chemical spills. In a bizarre twist, scientists have linked disposal of fracking wastewater to earthquakes.[40] Industrial wastewater disposal makes certain areas more prone to seismic activity, linking US earthquakes near wastewater injection sites to quakes in Japan and Chile.[41] Three areas in the United States had increased seismic activity in the days following devastating earthquakes on the other side of the globe. Texas, Colorado and Oklahoma experienced 'triggered quakes' following earthquakes across the world. One thing the affected areas had in common was wastewater injections for a sustained period. For example, 16 hours after a huge quake in South America, Prague, Oklahoma suffered a 4.1 magnitude earthquake. Bolstering this research, a separate study suggests that pumping water into and out of an underground reservoir to produce geothermal power can also induce earthquakes.[42] So in addition to water use and water waste on a huge scale, removing underground water and injecting water underground pose additional environmental problems.

b. Agriculture

Agricultural water uses in the United States, particularly in the western states, account for significant amounts of water waste. Perverse state and federal incentives, along with inefficient farming practices, result in wasted water, polluted water, dry river beds, destroyed ecosystems and water shortages with serious consequences to the US water supply. As discussed in Part II, state law encourages water waste and nonsensical farming practices. Because of the 'use it or lose it' water laws in the western United States, water owners divert water from rivers and streams whether they need it or not.[43] This practice compounds water problems in many ways. As water is diverted upstream, downstream flows are reduced or eliminated, causing water shortages downstream and ecosystem loss in the waterway. Even if upstream owners do not need their full allotment of water, they risk having their allotment reduced if they fail to take all of their allotted share. Moreover, states have allocated more water than exists in many rivers and streams, guaranteeing downstream water shortages. These problems are compounded because each state governs its own water resources, and the laws from state to state are not standardized.[44] Because water rights are so valuable, states operate with regard for their state only—not the needs of the waterway or neighboring states.[45]

Another side effect of 'use it or lose it' is production of crops that *need* lots of water. For example, water-thirsty crops like cotton are grown in Arizona which, but for 'use it or lose it', could not be grown in this arid state. Federal agricultural incentives significantly contribute to this problem. For example, although Arizona is one of the driest states in the United States,[46] its cotton production ranks 10th in the United States.[47] Billions of gallons of water must be pumped onto cotton fields each year. Cotton needs lots of water to grow—six times more than lettuce and 60% more than wheat.[48] Absurd? The federal government offers farmers so many financial incentives to continue these practices that they can't afford to change.[49] According to one Arizona farmer, 'Some years all of what you made came from the government . . . Your bank would finance your farming operation . . . because they knew the support was guaranteed. They wouldn't finance wheat, or alfalfa. Cotton was always dependable, it would always work.'[50] Over the last two decades, the federal government has paid Arizona farmers over $1.1 billion to grow cotton. Although other crops receive federal subsidies, cotton subsidies outstrip other crop subsidies by 9 times.[51]

As the world's biggest cotton exporter, seventeen of the US's southern states produce about 8 billion pounds of cotton every year.[52] Moreover, while California and Arizona produce more than twice the cotton per acre than cotton powerhouses like Texas and Georgia, they also irrigate their fields two to four times more per acre.[53] Often, this water comes from hundreds of miles away.[54] Yet western farmers are not ignorant. They understand that such water use is unsustainable, but state property law and enormous federal subsidies make it very difficult for cotton farmers to change their practices.[55] Sadly, Arizona officials predict that the state will run out of water within a few decades. These perverse subsidies must be eliminated.

c. Public Supply

While domestic use (households) accounts for the lowest use of available water, households are also enormously wasteful in their water use. Public suppliers deliver water to users for domestic, industrial, commercial and other purposes. About 57% of total public supply withdrawals go to domestic uses. These include indoor and outdoor residential uses, such as drinking water, sanitation and landscape watering.[56] As with the other sectors of the economy, domestic use has declined. Although the US population continues to increase, total public supply use has declined by 5%.[57] However, declines in water use must continue and on a significantly greater scale because, despite this slight decline, Americans use, on average, 150 gallons of water per day per person.[58] Such usage is an abomination on the world stage, even when compared with countries of similar economic status. For example, the English use only 40 gallons of water per day per person. One of the most bizarre aspects of water in the United States is that virtually no one pays for it! The water bills that US customers pay are based on a cost-of-service model. Water rates are set so that customers pay for the extraction, storage, delivery and treatment of water, but not the water itself—the water is free.[59] Free water does not engender any sense of scarcity or the need for frugality. Consumers need to know the *real* cost of water—the cost of obtaining additional supplies of water. Also, free water fails to provide the necessary funds to maintain water supply and disposal systems.[60] As with the other sectors of the water-using economy, the public supply seriously needs reform.

While this section of the article has described some of the major water issues in the three most water-thirsty sectors of the US economy, this next section describes how the US legal system contributes to these problems. Both state and federal laws that have perverse effects on US water usage will be explored.

II. WATER LAW IN THE UNITED STATES: HOW THE LAWS UNDERMINE ENVIRONMENTAL PROTECTION

a. State Law

Property law in the United States (including water rights) is governed by the laws of each separate state. As with many areas of domestic law, water law developed over time and subject to the exigencies of the era. Historically, water scarcity involved only limited localities. As a result, localities, perhaps with state help, resolved these issues. Depending upon where water problems occurred, the manner of resolution could vary significantly. Moreover, because no state property regime considered adverse environmental effects of water management, 'agricultural interests, industry, municipalities and other water managers have manipulated and degraded our freshwater resources in a relentless fashion'.[61]

US water law depends on geography. In general, one approach to water rights developed in the eastern states, while quite a different approach developed in the western states. The laws that governed during the expansion of the United States from east to west remain largely intact, creating a legal regime resistant to national oversight or coordination. The doctrine of riparian rights grew in the eastern United States where water is plentiful. Developed around the turn of the 19th century, the riparian rights system replaced a natural flow rule that impeded the burgeoning industrial expansion.[62] Riparian owners have the right to reasonable use of their water as long as such use does not impede the reasonable use by downstream users.[63] Water owners must exercise their own judgement in determining the amount and manner in which the water will be used.[64] The reasonable use approach, however, suffers from a lack of specificity regarding the amount of water use constituting 'reasonable use'.[65] As east coast populations grew along with per capita water use, the riparian rights doctrine failed to accommodate 'too little' water. Thus many riparian rights states have enacted regulatory formulations to determine water allocations. For example, about half of these jurisdictions have developed a riparian rights exception that allows the grant of permits for large-scale water withdrawals.[66] State variations of water rights continue to plague any comprehensive water ownership regime.

Unlike the eastern United States, as the US population spread west, water ownership developed based on water scarcity. Settlers detached water rights from riparian ownership because ranches and farms were often located far from streams. As settlers grabbed land, so too did they grab the rights to adjacent and underlying water. Thus, water ownership in the west is determined under the 'prior appropriation' doctrine. During the gold rush in the late 1800s, gold miners diverted upstream water panning for gold in contravention of water rights of downstream users.[67] Protecting landowners, courts held that upstream users had to save water for 'first in time' owners downstream.[68] The doctrine considers those settlers who are 'first in time' to be 'first in right'.[69] Beneficial use and seniority—not need, utility or reasonableness—determined an owner's right to fixed quantities of water. 'Since most property was located far from streams and there was little rain, officials then gave settlers formal rights to take water out of rivers and move it across dry land where it could be used to mine minerals or turn rocky fields into farms'.[70] In times of water shortages, those with senior rights received their quantities of water in full before junior rights.[71]

Consider the Colorado River as a prime example of the problems created by the prior appropriation doctrine. In the early 1900s, the seven states depending upon Colorado River water began to compete for its water. Eventually, the US Secretary of Commerce divided Colorado River water among these seven states. Regrettably, the water allocated exceeded the actual water in the river. For example, in 2015, the amount of Colorado River water allocated, 16.5 million acre-feet, exceeds the actual river flow of 12.4 million acre-feet.[72] Complicating matters, each state (enforcing its laws) asserts authority to address water issues. Buying and selling of water rights is also part of the law. The result is that the prior appropriation doctrine treats water as a commodity. Thus, despite the negative effects of Western water law, development of water markets (perhaps, increasing water allocation efficiency) is available under such a water regime,[73] suggesting that market instruments, such as tax mechanisms, can be used to change the effects of existing law.

The prior appropriation doctrine also undermines environmental stewardship because leaving unneeded, but appropriated, water for other users or uses hurts the owner of the water rights.[74] A water owner who fails to 'use' their water allotment risks loss of this right.[75] Colorado even keeps a log of property owners who have failed to exercise their water rights. If a water owner fails to exercise the full extent of their rights for 10 years, the state can consider confiscation of any unused water.[76] Thus, despite inefficiency, people will divert as much water as possible.[77]

Today, western states recognize the destructiveness of the prior appropriation doctrine. To protect the public interest, western states will deny water permits that might compromise water recreation or the ecology.[78] States are also recognizing the importance of protecting instream water flows by requiring minimum stream flows. However, because instream rights typically stand behind more senior rights, minimum stream flow requirements take a back seat during low-flow periods.[79] Moreover, markets for water rights have been slow to develop. Although government purchases of water rights have resulted in transfers to instream flows, even these transfers must give way to junior water owners if the transfer would negatively affect those rights.[80] Not surprisingly, states are fiercely protective of their existing water allocations. Moreover, the federal government has repeatedly pledged not to interfere.[81] In sum, although states recognize the need to protect water, current property right systems fall short. Without some major (and coordinated) legal changes, both eastern and western states' ability to protect water remains limited.

b. Federal Law

Federal regulation of most water issues is difficult because the US legal property regime regarding water resides primarily at the state level. In addition to federal agricultural subsidies discussed in Part I,[82] three federal doctrines and several federal statutes constrain state implementation of their water laws. The federal common law doctrine of equitable apportionment permits federal courts to adjudicate issues that concern the division of interstate water resources as between states.[83] In applying equitable apportionment, a federal court must balance the equities presented by the case at hand. The court need not use a formulary approach or consider the laws of the affected states.[84] The federal public trust fund doctrine prevents states from selling or leasing public land underneath navigable waters. The doctrine preserves the public's right to such uses as commerce and fishing in navigable waters. The doctrine of federal reserved rights protects Indian reservations and federal lands set aside for a specific purpose. The doctrine is supposed to ensure that these lands will have enough water to satisfy their purpose.[85]

Federal statutes impacting water appropriation focus on water use and value issues, and thus, only indirectly affect withdrawal and consumption problems. The Clean Water Act (CWA) regulates point source discharges of pollutants in US waters.[86] The CWA uses uniform technology-based effluent limitations to limit discharges. States may impose stricter ambient-based water quality standards, and the federal government encourages states to design programs that reduce non-point source pollution. Important to this discussion, the CWA grants states the power to certify any federally permitted activity that might impair water quality or the aquatic ecosystem. This power includes the authority to review, approve, veto, or condition such federally permitted activity.[87] Requiring minimum stream flows is certainly within the realm of states' control. Thus, the scope of federal power in water issues is limited.

Federal statutes that protect wildlife and ecosystems may also impact water issues otherwise governed by state law. The Endangered Species Act requires federal agencies to guarantee that any action funded, permitted, or carried out under an agency's authority will not jeopardize the continued existence of any endangered or threatened species.[88] The Act also makes it illegal for any private or state action to significantly modify any habitat in a way that results in death or injury to any protected species. The EPA enforcement of this provision has resulted in the recovery and management of a number of waterways. Moreover, enforcement has resulted in the release of water from federally operated dams.[89] Construction of hydroelectric facilities, governed by the Federal Power Act, requires the regulatory agency to consider fish and wildlife and other aspects of environmental quality to be an equal part of project authorization. In addition, any construction license issued must include conditions requiring protection or enhancement of fish and wildlife affected by the project.[90] Under the CWA, the US Army Corps of Engineers (ACE) regulates other water-based projects in US waters. The ACE issues permits for activities involving dredged or fill material. Pursuant to EPA guidelines, the ACE must deny permits for any project resulting in degradation of the aquatic system.[91] The EPA also has the authority to reject ACE-issued permits that 'result in "an unacceptable adverse effect" on wildlife, fisheries, recreation, or municipal water supplies'.[92]

Resulting from a multitude of legal approaches, US water law is highly fragmented. Both state water law and federal law impacting state law fail to comprehensively address US water problems—problems that are increasing—threatening the water future for the United States. While a complete water law overhaul is needed, this article discusses alternative approaches to environmentally friendly water laws designed to fill the gaps that exist under the current regulatory mess.

III. FEDERAL INTERVENTION ADDRESSING WATER ISSUES

This article analyzes how the federal government might take a more prominent and comprehensive role in addressing US water issues. The magnitude of water problems in the United States is unprecedented and growing. Greater federal participation in dealing with water problems is crucial. Water issues predominate every state, and state conflicts over water are increasing. Prior research advocates the use of market instruments to achieve higher value water use. Trading schemes and tax incentives have frequently been used to influence environmentally friendly behavior.

a. Water Issues Amenable to Federal Intervention

Water problems include damaging water flows; water use increases from various sectors of the economy; damaging water disposal—polluted water, seismic issues; distorted and wasteful agricultural use of water; water waste by consumers and industry; and climate change issues. All of these water problems are amenable to federal intervention. Because water problems span from east to west, the US government must take a leadership role in developing a comprehensive and coordinated approach to coping with water problems.

1. Water allocation issues

Water allocation presents a significant challenge. A federally run water trading market would encounter significant legal and geographic obstacles. For example, reallocation of water from lower-value to higher-value uses by allowing willing buyers and sellers to engage in a transfer might make economic sense, but would require physically moving water from one location to another. Moving water may be feasible for short distances and small amounts, but geography becomes an obstacle at some point. However, a national trading system could operate in such a way that geography is taken out of the equation by using a national water bank. Those with excess water could deposit the water into a national bank which would facilitate locating and arranging water sales to buyers.

US water law expert, Robert Glennon, describes water trades in the western United States as 'vibrant'.[93] Between 1987 and 2005, western states traded more than twice the annual flow of the Colorado River (10 trillion gallons). Transfers between farmers and cities comprised the bulk of the water trades. Glennon extols the market's ability to minimize waste and maximize water allocation.[94] Capitalizing on such trades would have enormous economic impacts in addition to enormous water savings.

Finally, the federal government must alter its agricultural policies. Foremost, federal farm subsidies paid to farmers for growing cotton, and the subsidies they receive for growing water-hungry crops like alfalfa must be abolished.[95] For some farmers, the financial incentives provided by the Farm Bill are so great that many farmers cannot afford to choose less water-intensive crops.[96] Unfortunately, eliminating these subsidies may not be so easy. In some years, a farmer's entire income comes from government subsidies.[97] Obviously, the perverse behavior created by federal dollars clearly disrupts attempts to solve US water problems.

2. Water scarcity and pollution

Many approaches to solving water problems are amenable to federal intervention, especially through incentive programs. Water conservation programs often include financial incentives that have proved effective. In New Mexico, both Santa Fe and Albuquerque have dramatically reduced water use through conservation.[98] Since 1995, Santa Fe has reduced water use by 42%, and Albuquerque has achieved a 36% per capita decline in water use.

In Albuquerque, incentives constituted a big part of the conservation efforts. The city gave rebates to a substantial number of citizens that installed water saving devices, including high-efficiency toilets, high-efficiency washing machines, hot water recirculating systems and a wide array of outdoor water rebates. In conjunction with the incentive scheme, Albuquerque instituted several fines and penalties. The city also increased its water rates. Like Albuquerque, Santa Fe also implemented a wide array of rebates.[99] Santa Fe's citizens can qualify for rebates for buying high-efficiency clothes washers, low-flow toilets for both residential and commercial customers and waterless or no flush urinals. Commercial, industrial and institutional customers are eligible for rebates by installing new equipment and processes that conserve water at existing facilities. The city has also increased the cost of water to its customers.[100] Financial incentives and penalties, along with other water-reduction measures, have resulted in two of the most successful water reduction programs in the country.

Many other water problems are amenable to incentive solutions. For example, the reuse of reclaimed water requires investment in infrastructure to clean dirty water.[101] Desalination is an option for increasing our water supply. However, desalination is very costly and creates significant fallout with regard to ocean ecosystems.[102] Incentives can promote the development of new agricultural conservation technology. Likewise, the development of electricity efficiency improvements is also responsive to incentive programs. Clearly, federal measures in addressing water issues can be effective. However, effectiveness depends on choice of policy instrument and the targeting of these tools.

b.   Market Instruments: Using Tax Incentives and/or Tax Penalties

Water issues in the United States are complicated, enormous and growing. No single solution is possible. States must overhaul antiquated water laws. The federal government must also eliminate perverse agricultural subsidies. However, even more important, federal policymakers must assert bold leadership in solving both domestic and global water challenges. Delay is not an option. This section discusses various types of market instruments and the characteristics incorporated in these market instruments that target specific government objectives.

Before choosing subsidies or tax incentives to address an issue, understanding the types of problems tax incentives can address is critical. Likewise, crafting the tax incentive so that it actually accomplishes the desired result is also imperative. Tax incentives can be effective to overcome a number of market situations that can hinder government goals. The reasons tax incentives can be effective are basically the same as they were 100 years ago when Congress enacted tax incentives to stimulate the petroleum industry: (a) to overcome the high initial start-up costs; (b) to minimize the high risk associated with new industries; and (c) to send a message of support for this new technology.[103] In general, federal incentives to stimulate industry have been defended on two grounds: (a) to promote a new technology during the early stages of its development; and (b) to pay the difference between the value of an activity to the private sector and its value to the public sector.[104]

For example, individuals and businesses underinvest in energy-saving technologies because the private returns from those investments are lower than the total benefits to society.[105] Social benefits include reduced air pollution and greenhouse gases in the atmosphere, and reduced dependence on oil imports. When potential investors only consider the private benefits in making decisions, they may underinvest in technologies that are worthwhile from the point of view of society as a whole, but not profitable to the individual making the investment. Tax incentives are an appropriate tool for addressing the failure of market prices to achieve the desirable level of investment in energy-saving technologies because they can increase the private return from the investment by reducing its cost. This increase in the private return induces additional investment in energy-saving technologies.[106]

Tax incentives may also help to overcome market barriers that hinder investment in energy-saving technologies, such as lack of information on the energy and environmental benefits of certain products and the uncertainty regarding the return to the investment.[107] Tax incentives improve buyers' awareness of highly energy-efficient products and improve the return on investments in those products. They encourage buyers to be early purchasers of advanced new products and, in turn, encourage firms to innovate and supply them. By helping to assure future demand for highly energy-efficient products, the incentives reduce the supplier's risk that demand for innovative new products will fail to materialize. The prospect of additional demand may also stimulate competition from new suppliers and create pressure to improve product quality and upgrade technology. Thus, the incentives facilitate a mutually reinforcing process whereby buyers are encouraged to purchase highly energy-efficient products and suppliers are encouraged to innovate to produce them. Of course, measures designed to encourage water conservation are good incentive candidates.

Economic activities generate several types of environmental pressures on the environment (here, water).[108] For example, input demands, pollution/waste flows and spatial intrusions in natural areas can all stress the natural environment.[109] To ensure sustainable use of environmental resources and the maintenance of stricter levels of environmental quality, one environmental policy strategy is 'influencing the decision making process at the micro level (influencing consumers, producers and investors)'.[110] This approach leads to the use of economic incentives or market stimuli. If the environmentally more appropriate behavior is made more rewarding for the target (consumer, producer, investor), then attitudes and behaviors will shift in favor of the more socially desirable behavior or alternatives. Environmental concerns are internalized by altering the agent's context rather than the agent's value structure or preferences.[111] Economic instruments influence decisions such that cost-effective, environmentally friendly alternatives are chosen.[112] Because environmental degradation stems from decision making and policies instituted, government intervention is needed to ensure the incorporation of environmental externalities.[113] Selected instruments must satisfy not only effectiveness and efficiency, but also societal and political acceptance.[114]

For example, policymakers can enact incentives designed to reduce energy consumption and greenhouse gas emissions by encouraging the deployment of highly efficient energy technologies that use renewable energy sources. Proposed incentives should also be designed to minimize windfalls for investments that would have been made even absent the incentives and to facilitate tax administration. If taxpayers claim a credit, the credit rewards the purchase of items that produce energy savings and reductions in greenhouse gas emissions. The design of the tax incentives incorporates the following considerations:

(1) *Superior energy efficiency compared to conventional equipment.* The eligible items should meet higher standards for energy efficiency than conventional equipment or use renewable energy sources. This helps to ensure that tax benefits promote energy efficiency and reduce greenhouse gas emissions.

(2) *High threshold for eligibility.* The eligible items should presently account for a small share of the market. This minimizes windfalls for purchases that would have been made with or without the credit.

(3) *High up-front costs compared to conventional equipment.* The targeted technologies have significantly higher purchase prices than conventional equipment and, at current market prices, are not universally cost effective. These high upfront costs are another reason relatively few would be purchased without the credit.

(4) *Commercially available.* The items should be commercially available or near commercialization. This ensures that the incentives encourage the deployment of new technologies that private markets have already developed.

(5) *Ease of administration.* The items must be able to be defined precisely enough so that the IRS can administer the incentives. This helps to ensure that tax benefits are claimed only for items for which they are intended.[115]

Considering the above criteria, tax incentives are a cost-effective way to encourage US consumers and industry to invest in technologies designed to cut energy waste, including water waste. To create stability and inspire further innovation, Congress should also eliminate the practice of enacting expiring incentives. Moreover, policymakers must improve existing incentives to ensure that they are performance-based, technology-neutral incentives with maximum impact but minimum cost.[116]

The improved resource allocation through subsidy reform depends on several factors: price sensitivity of the subsidized activity; the form of the subsidy; the conditions attached to the subsidy; and how the subsidy interacts with other policies.[117] Water pricing is politically controversial, but often vital in generating sufficient revenues to maintain water systems and extend water services, particularly to the poor. Charging for water can encourage more efficient use of water. The use of targeted subsidies can encourage efficient water use and avoid adverse effects on disadvantaged populations.[118] Yet water resource management is inherently political because of the numerous competing water claims by both the rich and the poor.[119] Water infrastructure is not supported by water users. If policy-makers undertake water pricing reform then several policy objectives must be included. These include: improving the efficiency of using and allocating water and encouraging water conservation; cost recovery to cover infrastructure and recurring costs and ease the burden on public budgets; and increasing coverage and access to water services.[120]

Tax incentives have been politically popular because once enacted they do not require an annual appropriation and also because they reduce taxes for voters.[121] Experience with past tax incentives demonstrates effective ways to apply limited funds. Federal energy incentives should target only technologies or processes that provide a societal good in the energy sector, such as reducing energy use and saving money or encouraging new energy sources. A number of 2005 tax incentives have succeeded in influencing permanent transformation of the energy market.[122] Experience with recent energy efficiency tax incentives indicates that future energy tax incentives should: (a) target energy-saving equipment and practices with substantial energy savings; and (b) target only technologies or processes that provide a societal good in the energy sector. Examples include reducing energy use; encouraging new energy sources that have long-term potential; targeting efficiency levels and new energy sources that have a small market share; paying substantial incentives to motivate significant sales; and enacting incentives for a significant time period so that market players will invest. After this initial period, incentives should be phased out or restricted as indicated by market indices.[123] In a recent ACEEE (American Council for an Energy-Efficient Economy) working paper, tax incentives targeted towards energy efficiency produced highly cost-effective results. Moreover, these energy-efficiency tax incentives leverage substantial private investments because the tax incentives cover only a portion of the cost of the measure. This same study concludes that targeted incentives for energy efficiency creates jobs.[124]

One study concludes that cost-effective energy efficiency can result in significant cost savings.[125] However, a number of market barriers preclude such investment. For example, demand-side barriers include lack of awareness, uninformed decision makers, panic purchases, third-party decision-makers and financial procedures that overemphasize initial costs and de-emphasize operating costs.[126] Likewise, supply-side barriers include limited stocking of efficient products, efficiency bundled into premium products only and a shortage of skilled contractors.[127]

Experience with tax incentives shows that, when incentives are substantial enough to make a difference and have targeted measures with a very small market share, the tax incentives can help to develop a market that can be sustained after the tax incentives end.[128] These tax incentives will help our economy as investments in energy efficiency help to create jobs, including direct jobs in the field of energy efficiency technology and induced jobs created as consumers and businesses re-spend their energy bill savings.[129]

Tax incentives improve buyers' awareness of highly energy efficient products and improve the return on investments in those products.[130] Tax investments encourage buyers to be early purchasers of advanced new products and, in turn, encourage product innovation to meet demand. By helping to assure future demand for highly energy efficient products, the incentives reduce the supplier's risk that demand for innovative new products will fail to materialize. The prospect of additional demand may also stimulate competition from new suppliers and create pressure to improve product quality and upgrade technology. Thus, the incentives facilitate a mutually reinforcing process whereby buyers are encouraged to purchase highly energy-efficient products and suppliers are encouraged to innovate to produce them.

This section illustrates the success of tax incentives in encouraging environmental outcomes. Certainly, water concerns caution that the US efforts are insufficient and suggest public ignorance of the severity of water issues. State tax law variations can allow us to identify the effect of tax incentives on energy conservation investment. Using a data set on individuals followed over a three-year period, we find that the conservation incentive programs offered by state governments, in addition to federal programs, have a statistically significant effect on investment once controlled for individual (fixed) effects. This result contributes to the existing empirical literature by shedding new light on the question of whether consumers irrationally ignore tax incentives for home improvements. Based on our preferred estimate of the tax price coefficient, a 10 percentage point change in the tax price for energy investment would lead to a 24% increase in the probability of energy conservation investment. Whether the government should be involved in the business of providing tax incentives for conservation investments is another matter and cannot be resolved in this paper. For one, any subsidy to conservation investment is earned by households already planning to make conservation investments with or without the credit. For these households, the credit is a windfall. Moreover, one must ask whether energy consumption does, in fact, fall after investment (assuming reduced energy consumption is the policy goal) and how the public interest benefits from promoting energy conservation. However, as the policy debate unfolds, an important piece of information will be whether tax incentives can increase the probability at the margins of making conservation investments. The evidence reported here suggests that they can.[131]

IV.   FINAL THOUGHTS

The United States must face the water crisis at hand. The water crisis is multi-faceted, impacting every sector of the US economy. The current legal regime governing water issues is outdated and even perverse. Local and/or regional remedies need supplementation. Policymakers must consider alternative options and solutions—such as market instruments (tax incentives). This article discusses water problems affecting the biggest US water sectors. US water law is discussed and integrated into the water issues previously reviewed. Policymakers and water experts have identified a number of options for addressing water issues. Market instruments, such as water trading markets, and tax incentives must be a part of these solutions. Yet, as always, opponents to change will always try to discredit new alternatives. However, naysayers will not bend the will of those soldiers dedicated to water law reform.

NOTES

1. Theodore Roosevelt, *The New Nationalism*, at 52 (1910) (Theodore Roosevelt's speech before the Colorado Live Stock Association, Denver, Colorado, August 29, 1910. This sentence is one of the quotations inscribed on a first floor corridor in the US Capitol).
2. Brian Clark Howard, *2015 to Be Hottest Year on Record*, NATIONAL GEOGRAPHIC, December 20, 2015, http://news.nationalgeographic.com/2015/11/151124-2015-hottest-year-record-global-warming.
3. Howard, *supra* note 2, at 2.
4. Nicole T. Carter, ENERGY–WATER NEXUS: THE ENERGY SECTOR'S WATER USE, at 9 (Cong. Res. Ser. Aug, 30, 2013).
5. Sandra Postel, *Climate Change Poses Existential Water Risks, Water Currents*, NATIONAL GEOGRAPHIC, December 21, 2015, http://voices.nationalgeographic.com/2015/02/17/climate-change-poses-existential-water-risks.
6. Postel, *supra* note 5, at 1. The study was conducted by NASA, Cornell and Columbia University.
7. Postel, *supra* note 5, at 1.
8. Abrahm Lustgarten, *Use It or Lose It: Across the West, Exercising one's Right to Waste Water*, at 2, June 9, 2015, https://projects.propublica.org/killing-the-colorado/story/wasting-water-out-west-use.
9. Nancy L. Barber, *United States Geological Survey, Summary of Estimated Water Use in the United States in 2010*, http://pubs.usgs.gov/fs/2014/3109.
10. United States Geological Survey, *Trends in Water Use in the United States, 1950 to 2010*, http://water.usgs.gov/edu/wateruse-trends.html.
11. USGS, Water Use in 2010, at 2. In 2010, thermoelectric power, irrigation, and public supply accounted for 90% of total water use. USGS, *Summary of Estimated Water Use in the United States in 2010*, Department of the Interior (November 2014), http://water.usgs.gov/watuse/wutrends.html. *See also* Carter, *supra* note 4, at 1.
12. USGS, Water Use in 2010, at 2.
13. Nicole T. Carter, ENERGY–WATER NEXUS: THE ENERGY SECTOR'S WATER USE, at Summary (Congressional Research Service, August 30, 2013).
14. USGS, Water Use in 2010, at 2; Carter, *supra* note 4, at Summary.

15. Carter, *supra* note 4, at Summary.
16. Carter, *supra* note 4, at Summary.
17. Carter, *supra* note 4, at 7.
18. Carter, *supra* note 4, at 7.
19. Carter, *supra* note 4, at 8. Other plants were near curtailment when the weather provided relief.
20. Carter, *supra* note 4, at 8. Power plant operators built pipelines accessing additional water sources, sought out and purchased new water rights, and built additional capacity for groundwater pumping. Moreover, as of 2013, all new facilities had to provide proof of their water rights before inclusion in grid planning. *See* Carter, *supra* note 4, at 8 (footnote 26).
21. Carter, *supra* note 4, at 2. Citing DOE, *20% Wind Energy by 2030: Increasing Wind Energy's Contribution to U.S. Electricity Supply*, July 2008, http://www1.eere.energy.gov/witn/pdfs/41869.pdf. The water saved by increasing wind energy amounts to 41% in the Midwest/Great Plains, 29% in the West, 16% in the Southeast, and 14% in the Northeast. *Id.*
22. Carter, *supra* note 4, at 3.
23. Carter, *supra* note 4, at 5.
24. Carter, *supra* note 4, at 4.
25. Carter, *supra* note 4, at 5.
26. Christina Nunez, *Energy Snapshot: Water Use for Fracking Has Skyrocketed, USGS Data Show*, NATIONAL GEOGRAPHIC, March 25, 2015, http://news.nationalgeographic.com/energy/2015/03/150325-water-use-for-fracking-over-time.html.
27. Nunez, *supra* note 26, at 2.
28. Nunez, *supra* note 26, at 2.
29. *Id.* Scott Anderson, a senior policy analyst at the Environmental Defense Fund, stated that 'Once the statistics are available, I'm sure they will show that the average amount of water used for fracturing horizontal wells has continued to grow since 2010.' *Id.*
30. Carter, *supra* note 4, at 5.
31. Carter, *supra* note 4, at 6.
32. Craig Welch, *Fracking Pollutes Some Water, But Harm is Not Widespread, EPA Says*, NATIONAL GEOGRAPHIC, at 7, June 4, 2015, http://news.national geographic.com/2015/06/150604-fracking-EPA-water-wells-oil-gas-hydrology-poison-toxic-drinking.html.
33. Carter, *supra* note 4, at 6. Problems include seismic impacts and quality of water disposal. *Id.*
34. Ker Than, *Fracking Wastewater Disposal Linked to Remotely Triggered Quakes*, NATIONAL GEOGRAPHIC, at 7, July 12, 2013, http://news.nationalgeographic.com/news/energy/2013/07/130711-fracking-wastewater-injection-earthquakes.html.
35. Nunez, *supra* note 26, at 2.
36. Welch, *supra* note 32, at 6.
37. Welch, *supra* note 32, at 7.
38. Welch, *supra* note 32, at 7.
39. Craig Welch, *Fracking Pollutes Some Water, But Harm is Not Widespread, EPA Says*, National Geographic, June 4, 2015, http://news.national geographic.com/2015/06/150604-fracking-EPA-water-wells-oil-gas-hydrology-poison-toxic-drinking.html.
40. Than, *supra* note 34, at 5.
41. Than, *supra* note 34, at 6.
42. Than, *supra* note 34, at 9.
43. Lustgarten, *supra* note 8, at 2.
44. Lustgarten, *supra* note 8, at 3.
45. Lustgarten, *supra* note 8, at 4. *See also* Abrahm Lustgarten and Naveena Sadasivam, *How Federal Dollars are Financing the Water Crisis in the West*, PROPUBLICA, at 1, 9 (May 27, 2015), http://projects.propublica.org/killing-the-colorado/story/

arizona-cotton-drought-crisis. *Id.* at 9. This article describes how Arizona built an expensive canal to be able to claim all its allotted water from the Colorado River. The state was concerned that if it did not take all of its allotted water from the Colorado River each year they risked losing any unclaimed allotment.

46.   Lustgarten, *Federal Dollars, supra* note 45, at 4.
47.   Lustgarten, *Federal Dollars, supra* note 45, at 4. Despite Arizona's decreases in the number of acres irrigated, in 2013, farmers planted over 161,000 acres of cotton—the second biggest crop planted in the state. *Id.* at 3. USDA, National Agricultural Statistics Service, *Crop Production; U.S. Cotton Production*, Stuff About States.com.
48.   Lustgarten, *Federal Dollars, supra* note 45, at 1.
49.   *Id.*
50.   *Id.*
51.   *See* Lustgarten, *Federal Dollars, supra* note 45, at 4. Cotton also gets more support than other crops in California, with cotton farmers receiving more than $3.3 billion over the last 20 years. *Id.*
52.   Lustgarten, *Federal Dollars, supra* note 45, at 5.
53.   *Id.*
54.   *Id.* at 8.
55.   *Id.* at 5. For example, cotton growers are protected from price drops through subsidies and crop losses with federally subsidized insurance. *Id.* at 8.
56.   USGS, Water Use in 2010. Another 44.5 million people get water from self-supplied sources such as wells.
57.   *Id.*
58.   Doug Pushard, *The Tale of Two Cities—Billions Conserved* (www.harvesth2o.com, visited September 23, 2015).
59.   Robert Glennon, *Diamonds in Disguise: Using Price Signals and Market Forces to Address the Water Crisis, in* Last Call at the Oasis: The Global Water Crisis and Where We go From Here, at 158 (ed. Karl Weber, May 12, 2012).
60.   Glennon, *Diamonds in Disguise, supra* note 59, at 159.
61.   William L. Andreen, *Water Law and the Search for Sustainability: A Comparative Analysis, in* Water Resources Planning and Management, Ch. 8, at 155 (eds R. Quentin Grafton and Karen Hussey, Cambridge University Press, 2011).
62.   Andreen, *supra* note 61, at 156. The natural flow rule permitted each riparian land-owner to use a stream in its natural condition without artificial interference.
63.   *Id.*
64.   *Id.*
65.   Andreen, *supra* note 61, at 157.
66.   Andreen, *supra* note 61, at 156.
67.   Abrahm Lustgarten, *Use It or Lose It: Across the West, Exercising One's Right to Waste Water*, Propublica, at 5 (September 23, 2015) http://projects.propublica.org/killing-the-colorado/story/wasting-water-out-west-use-it-or-lose-it.
68.   Lustgarten, *supra* note 67, at 5.
69.   Andreen, *supra* note 61, at 157.
70.   Lustgarten, *supra* note 67, at 5.
71.   Andreen, *supra* note 61, at 157. *See also* Lustgarten, *supra* note 67, at 5.
72.   Lustgarten, *supra* note 67, at 6.
73.   Andreen, *supra* note 61, at 157.
74.   Sandra Postel, *Groundbreaking State Law Tested in Colorado Headwaters Stream*, Water Forum, National Geographic, December 2, 2015 (http:/voices.nationalgeographic.com/2015/09/21/groundbreaking-state-law-tested-in-colorado-headwaters-stream).
75.   Lustgarten, *supra* note 67, at 8.
76.   Lustgarten, *supra* note 67, at 8.
77.   Andreen, *supra* note 61, at 158. *See also* Postel, *Groundbreaking State Law, supra* note 74, at 1. One recent Colorado law strikes at this antiquated system in a small but groundbreaking way. Water rights owners now have flexibility to leave part of their

allocated water in the waterway during critical low flows. Willow Creek, at the head-waters of the Colorado River, is a test case for application and analysis of the new law. One rancher with rights to divert water from Willow Creek developed a plan, working with the Colorado Water Trust, to leave water in the creek for up to five years during a 10 year period. Leaving water in the creek will not jeopardize his water rights. Under the plan, the rancher leaves some of his allocable water in the stream during danger-ously low flows. Even a small amount of water left in the stream during critical times is enough to enhance water quality, and support fish and other aquatic species. While small, the law mitigates the incentive for water owners to claim their entire water allot-ment in times when it is needed by the water source. *Id. See also*, Lustgarten, *supra* note 67, at 9. Kansas has also passed legislation protecting the total allotment of farmers who choose to use less in any given year. *Id.*

78. Andreen, *supra* note 61, at 158.
79. *Id.* at 158.
80. *Id.*
81. Lustgarten, *supra* note 67, at 9.
82. *See* Part I, B.
83. Andreen, *supra* note 61, at 158. The doctrine will apply if no interstate compact or congressional action supersedes.
84. *Id.* at 158.
85. *Id.* at 158. These reserved water rights must be determined in a state court proceeding. Thus, the federal government tends to be disadvantaged in these cases.
86. Andreen *supra* note 61, at 159. *See* 33 USC §§ 301, 402.
87. *Id.* States' authority extends to non-federally operated hydroelectric facilities, nuclear power plants, US Army Corps of Engineers projects, and CWA discharge permits issued by the EPA.
88. *Id.* at 159. *See* 16 USC §1536(a)(2).
89. *Id.*
90. Andreen, *supra* note 61, at 159. *See* 16 USC §803(j)(1).
91. Andreen, *supra* note 61, at 160. *See* 40 Code of Federal Regulation (CFR) §230.10(c).
92. *Id. See also* 33 USC § 1344(c).
93. Glennon, *Diamonds in Disguise*, *supra* note 59, at 166.
94. *Id.*
95. Lustgarten, *Federal Dollars*, *supra* note 45.
96. *Id.*
97. Lustgarten, *Federal Dollars*, *supra* note 45.
98. Doug Pushard, *The Tale of Two Cities—Billions Conserved*, http://harvesth2o.com/tale_of_two_cities.shtml (visited September 23, 2015).
99. *Id.*
100. *Id.*
101. Robert Glennon, *Water Scarcity, Marketing, and Privatization* 83 Texas L. Rev. 1873, 1881 (2005).
102. *Id.*
103. Mona L. Hymel, *Americans and their Wheels*, Critical Issues in Environmental Taxation, at 22 (2006).
104. Bruce W. Cone and Alex G. Fassbender, *An Analysis of Federal Incentives used to Stimulate Energy Production*, at Executive Summary 7 (1978).
105. Department of Treasury, *Analysis of the Administration's Proposed Tax Incentives for Energy Efficiency and the Environment*, at 1 (June 28, 1999) [hereinafter DOT, *Analysis*].
106. *Id.*
107. *Id.*
108. OECD, Managing the Environment: The Role of Economic Instruments (1994).
109. *Id.* at 14.
110. *Id.*

111.   *Id.* at 15.
112.   *Id.* at 17.
113.   *Id.* at 47.
114.   *Id.* at 48. Economic incentives operate best in combination with other instruments, such as direct regulation. DOT, *Analysis, supra* note 105, at 2.
115.   OECD, *supra* note 108, at 48.
116.   NRDC Issue Brief, *Federal Energy Efficiency Tax Incentives: Driving innovation and investment in our buildings and appliances to save money and energy* (December 2013).
117.   The World Bank, *Environmental Fiscal Reform, What Should Be Done and How to Achieve It*, at 34 (May 2005).
118.   *Id.* at 101.
119.   *Id.*
120.   *Id.* at 104.
121.   Steven Nadel, *Energy Efficiency of Tax Incentives*, at iii (ACEEE Working Paper, July 2012).
122.   Nadel, *supra* note 121, at iii.
123.   Nadel, *supra* note 121, at iv.
124.   Nadel, *supra* note 121, at v.
125.   Nadel, *supra* note 121, at 8.
126.   *Id.*
127.   Nadel, *supra* note 121, at 9.
128.   Nadel, *supra* note 121, at 14.
129.   *Id.* at 15.
130.   DOT, *Analysis, supra* note 105, at Intro.
131.   Kevin A. Hassett, Gilbert E. Metcalf, *Energy Tax Credits and Energy Conservation Investment: Evidence from Panel Data*, 57 J. OF PUB. ECONOMICS 201–217, 216 (1995).

5. The impact of hydraulic fracturing on fresh water resources in the United States

Hans Sprohge, Bill Butcher, Mary Margaret Callison and Larry Kreiser

INTRODUCTION

Hydraulic fracturing in the United States is rewarded for polluting the atmosphere and destroying fresh water with federal tax breaks that equate to billions of dollars in subsidies. Hydraulic fracturing, also known as fracking, is a well drilling method that extracts natural gas from very far below the surface of the Earth. Natural gas is composed of many hydrocarbons that are inimical to the atmosphere. Proponents of fracking argue that natural gas is a plentiful bridge fuel that allows society to continue to rely on fossil fuels while reducing greenhouse gas emissions compared with other fossil fuels until such time as economically viable green energy sources are developed. Empirical studies show that, although the combustion of natural gas emits less carbon dioxide (CO_2) into the atmosphere than other fossil fuels, over a 20-year period or so the impact on the atmosphere may be worse than that from using other fossil fuels. The process of hydraulic fracturing depletes the supply of fresh water and pollutes both underground aquifers and above-ground sources of water. The Internal Revenue Code provides many generous tax breaks to the natural gas industry despite the environmental damage caused by fracking. Two of the biggest tax breaks are deductions for intangible drilling costs and a depletion allowance.

CHEMICAL COMPOSITION OF NATURAL GAS

Natural gas is a hydrocarbon. Hydrocarbons are made up of the elements hydrogen and carbon, plus impurities. Natural gas consists of hydrocarbons that are gaseous at ordinary temperatures (20°C) and

Table 5.1   Typical composition of natural gas

Methane	CH_4	70–90%
Ethane	C_2H_6	
Propane	C_3H_8	0–20%
Butane	C_4H_{10}	
Carbon dioxide	CO_2	0–8%
Oxygen	O_2	0–0.2%
Nitrogen	N_2	0–5%
Hydrogen sulfide	H_2S	0–5%
Rare gases	A, He, Ne, Xe	Trace

Sources: naturalgas.org; http://www.naturalgas.org/overview/background.asp.

pressures. The principal constituents of natural gas are methane, ethane, propane and butane. Methane accounts for 70–90% of the total volume produced. Dry natural gas is gas containing more than 95% methane (Table 5.1).[1] Wet natural gas is gas containing less than 95% methane and more than 5% ethane, propane and butane. Wet natural gas usually produces hydrocarbon liquids during production. Natural gases also can contain small and variable quantities of nonhydrocarbons such as carbon dioxide, carbon monoxide, sulfur dioxide, hydrogen sulfide, nitrogen, hydrogen, oxygen, helium, and argon.[2] These impurities must be removed from the natural gas stream prior to sale. Sour natural gas is gas with high levels of hydrogen sulfide, which is highly undesirable owing to corrosion.[3] It is called 'sour' because of the sour smell of sulfur. In the absence of sulfurous compounds, natural gas is colorless and odorless.[4] The smell associated with the gas coming from a stovetop is due to an odorization process that adds mercaptan compounds to the end-use gas.[5] Adding an odorant before gas is sold to the public aids in detection of gas leaks.

Liquefied natural gas is the liquid product produced by cooling methane to −161.5°C.[6] Methane may also be converted to liquid fuels through gas-to-liquids processes. Liquefied petroleum gas refers to propane and butane that is stored, transported, and marketed in pressurized containers.[7]

AIR POLLUTION

Natural gas is promoted as a clean-burning fuel because it produces less carbon dioxide (CO_2) when burned than oil or coal. On a burned British thermal unit basis, natural gas emits 29% less CO_2 than oil and 44% less than coal.[8] With respect to sulfur dioxide, natural gas is 1122 times cleaner than oil and 2591 times cleaner than coal.[9] However, regardless of whether greenhouse gasses are emitted into the atmosphere a little bit at a time or all at once, the end result is the same.

A 2011 study by the International Energy Agency reports that a large global shift to natural gas would still put CO_2 emissions on a trajectory resulting in a global average temperature increase of more than 3.5°C in the long term.[10] Although burning natural gas releases less CO_2 than burning coal, natural gas is not an environmentally friendly alternative to coal. Natural gas is composed primarily of methane, which according to the Intergovernmental Panel on Climate Change is 86 times worse over 20 years than CO_2.[11] The environmental benefits of natural gas are vitiated when it leaks into the atmosphere before it is burned. Leaks may occur when a well is drilled, fracked, compressed into pipelines, transported by pipeline, and after the well is plugged or abandoned.[12] Independent studies by the National Oceanic and Atmospheric Administration,[13] Purdue University,[14] and Cornell University[15] show that the greenhouse gas footprint of natural gas will be significantly greater than that of coal over the next several decades.

In 2011, the US House of Representatives Committee on Energy and Commerce Minority Staff released a report on hydraulic fracturing.[16] In a mere four year period, between 2005 and 2009, 14 oil and gas service companies used more than 595 hydraulic fracturing products containing 24 different hazardous air pollutants. The 14 companies were as follows:

> Basic Energy Services
> BJ Services
> Calfrac Well Services
> Complete Production Services
> Frac Tech Services
> Halliburton
> Key Energy Services
> RPC
> Sanjel Corporation
> Schlumberger
> Superior Well Services
> Trican Well Service
> Universal Well Services
> Weatherford.

Hydrogen fluoride is a hazardous air pollutant. It is a highly corrosive and systemic poison that causes severe and sometimes delayed health effects because of deep tissue penetration. Absorption of substantial amounts of hydrogen fluoride by any route may be fatal.[17] One of the hydraulic fracturing companies used 67,222 gallons of two products containing hydrogen fluoride in 2008 and 2009.[18]

Lead is a hazardous air pollutant that is a heavy metal that is particularly harmful to children's neurological development. It also can cause health problems in adults, including reproductive problems, high blood pressure, and nerve disorders.[19] One of the hydraulic fracturing companies used 780 gallons of a product containing lead in this five-year period.[20]

Methanol is the hazardous air pollutant that appeared most often in hydraulic fracturing products. Other hazardous air pollutants used in hydraulic fracturing fluids included formaldehyde, hydrogen chloride, and ethylene glycol.

THE PROCESS OF HYDRAULIC FRACTURING

Natural gas resources are classified as conventional or unconventional on the basis of whether the gas remains trapped in the sedimentary rock in which it was formed or rises towards the surface. Natural gas tends to rise towards the surface through pore spaces in the rock because of its low density compared with the surrounding rock.[21] Conventional natural gas is gas that has to migrate into a highly porous and permeable rock until it reaches a layer of impermeable rock where it becomes trapped before it can reach the surface and escape into the atmosphere.[22] Unconventional gas is gas that has been created in rocks without the permeability necessary to allow migration.[23] These include:

- tight sands gas—formed in sandstone or carbonate with low permeability that prevents the gas from flowing naturally;
- coalbed methane—formed in coal deposits and adsorbed by coal particles;
- shale gas—formed in fine-grained shale rock with low permeability in which gas has been adsorbed by clay particles or is held within minute pores and microfractures.

Unconventional gas formations are 'continuous', deposited over large areas rather than in discrete traps.[24]

Conventional natural gas is easier to extract than unconventional gas. It can be extracted by a well drilled vertically until the impermeable rock preventing the gas from rising is breached. Once breached, the gas flows from the higher pressure underground to the lower pressure wellhead.[25] Extracting unconventional gas requires directional drilling and hydraulic fracturing.

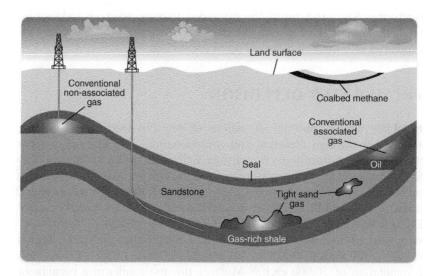

Figure 5.1   Illustration of vertical and horizontal drilling

Horizontal drilling is used to reach the horizontal dimensions of uncon-ventional gas reservoirs. A well is drilled vertically to a subsurface location just above the unconventional gas reservoir.[26] At that point the well bore is deviated from the vertical plane around a curve to intersect the reservoir at a near-horizontal inclination and continues horizontally for up to a mile (Figure 5.1).[27]

After the drill is pulled out, hydraulic fracturing (also known as fracking) creates fractures that extend from the well bore into rock forma-tions.[28] These fractures allow the gas to travel from the rock pores, where it is trapped, to the production well. Fractures are created by pumping millions of gallons of water at extremely high pressure, accompanied by sand and chemicals into the rock or coal formation.[29] Water does not compress under pressure the way air does. Water or a water-based liquid pumped into a well at sufficient pressure will force open gaps in the rock through which gas can more easily flow. The water-based liquid pressure is as high as 10,000–15,000 psi (pounds per square inch).[30] At 15,000 psi, the pressure is 1000 times sea level air pressure or the equivalent of 7.5 tons pressing on each square inch. Merely opening cracks is not enough. They need to remain open. A proppant—granular materials, commonly sand—is used to keep the cracks open. The proppant is injected in a slurry that seeps throughout the network of fissures created by the hydraulic fracturing. The sand enters the expanded fissures, where it lodges and holds them open. Unconventional gas bubbles through the newly created capillaries into the well bore and up to the surface.

FRESH WATER DEPLETION

Fracking removes millions of gallons of precious freshwater from the water cycle through depletion and contamination. The amount of fresh water used for hydraulically fracturing a well varies owing to differences in formation geology, well construction, and the type of hydraulic fracturing process used.[31] The water used is likely to come from surface water (rivers, lakes, ponds) and groundwater aquifers. In 2011, the US Environmental Protection Agency estimated that 70–140 billion gallons of fresh water were used to fracture 35,000 wells in the United States each year. This is roughly equivalent to the annual water consumption of 40–80 cities with a population of 50,000 each.[32] Most of this use results in a permanent loss of water resources within a region. Fracture treatments in coalbed methane wells use from 50,000 to 350,000 gallons of water per well, while deeper horizontal shale wells can use anywhere from 3 to 12 million gallons of water when it is first fractured.[33] Similar huge amounts of water are needed each time a well is refractured to maintain well pressure and gas production. Wells may be refractured several times over the life of each well.

Depleting nearby streams and rivers may decrease downstream flows, making them more susceptible to changes in temperature: increases in the summer and decreases in the winter.[34] Higher temperatures could harm aquatic life. Many fish and invertebrates need specific temperatures for reproduction and proper development.[35] Furthermore, decreased flows could damage or destroy vegetation living in or located on the banks of rivers and streams. Depleting water from shallow aquifers could lower water levels in the nearby streams and springs to which they are connected, which in turn could damage or remove riparian vegetation and aquatic life. In Pennsylvania, water has been withdrawn for fracking to the extent of streams being sucked dry. Two streams in southwestern Pennsylvania— Sugarcamp Run and Cross Creek—were drained by water withdrawals for fracking, triggering fish kills.[36] Depleting water from deeper aquifers could have longer-term effects on connected streams and springs because replenishing deeper aquifers with precipitation generally takes longer.

In the United States, more than half of the wells drilled, 55%, were in drought-stricken areas.[37] Nearly half (47%) were in regions under high or extremely high water stress.[38] Extremely high water stress means that more than 80% of a region's available surface and groundwater is already allocated for municipal, agricultural or industrial use.[39] High stress means that 40–80% of the water is already allocated. More than a third (36%) of all US wells were in areas experiencing groundwater depletion. Fracking can create or exacerbate existing water problems for other uses and could constrain future natural gas production in some areas. For example, at an auction of unallocated water in Colorado by the Northern Water Conservancy District during the spring of 2012, natural gas companies successfully bid for water that had previously been largely claimed by farmers.[40] Farmers raised concerns about the impacts on agriculture in the region. 'How do we continue to sustain agriculture when there's just more and more demand on our water resources in this state?' said Bill Midcap, director of the Rocky Mountain Farmers Union, which represents 22,000 producers in Colorado, Wyoming and New Mexico.[41] In August 2011, 13 previously approved water withdrawal permits in Pennsylvania's Susquehanna River Basin were temporarily suspended owing to low stream levels; 11 of these permits were for natural gas projects.[42] Although parts of Pennsylvania were abnormally dry, the basin was not, suggesting that natural gas operations were creating conflict with other uses under normal conditions. As the number of fracking wells increases, conflicts between natural gas companies and other users are very likely to intensify.

UNDERGROUND WATER CONTAMINATION

Fracking has contaminated underground aquifers and surface water across the United States with methane and chemicals. In 1980, the US Environmental Protection Agency identified six major pathways of contamination, or ways in which fluids injected into a gas well could escape the well and enter underground sources of drinking water.[43] Figure 5.2 shows four of the six different pathways.

One way in which contaminants can reach underground sources of drinking water is by leaking through a hole in the casing.[44] Well casing supports the well bore to prevent collapse of the hole and consequent loss of the well, serves as a means for injecting fluids into the underground formation in which they will be stored, and supports other components of the well. If a well casing is defective, fluids may leak through a hole or other fault in the well's casing, or a steel pipe that is placed into the wellbore.

For example, in 2007, a well that had been drilled almost 4000 feet into a tight sand formation in Bainbridge, Ohio was not properly sealed with cement, allowing gas from a shale layer above the target tight sand formation to travel through the annulus into an underground source of drinking

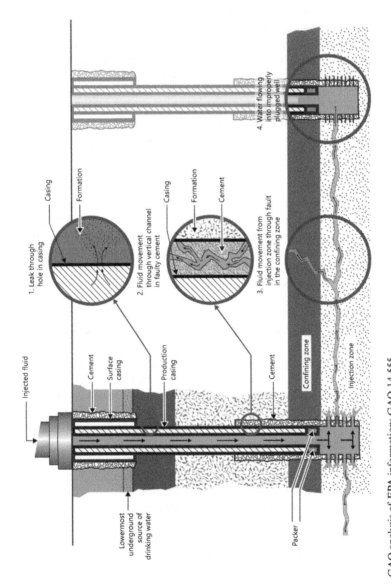

Source: GAO analysis of EPA information; GAO-14-555.

Figure 5.2   Contamination pathways

water where it caused an explosion that severely damaged one home and forced the evacuation of 19 others.[45] The buildup of methane resulted in an explosion in a resident's basement. The risk of contamination from improper casing and cementing is not limited to the development of shale formations. Casing and cementing practices also apply to conventional gas development. However, wells that are hydraulically fractured are commonly exposed to higher pressures than wells that are not hydraulically fractured. Furthermore, hydraulically fractured wells are exposed to high pressures over a longer period of time as fracturing is conducted in multiple stages, and wells may be refractured multiple times to extend the economic life of the well when production declines significantly or falls below the estimated reservoir potential.

Data from Pennsylvania's Department of Environmental Protection also confirm these initial leakage rates, with a 6% structural integrity failure rate observed for shale gas wells drilled in 2010, 7.1% observed for wells drilled in 2011 and 8.9% observed for wells drilled in 2012.[46] The failure rate of casings and of other parts of the well structure only grows with age. Schlumberger, one of the world's largest companies specializing in fracking, published an article in its magazine in 2003 showing that 50% of wells leak after 15 years and a whopping 60% leak after 30 years.[47] The industry has no solution for the problem of well casing leakage.

A second way by which contaminants can reach underground sources of drinking water is by contaminants migrating upward through vertical channels in faulty cement.[48] This can occur when friction and resistance are created in the formation into which fluid is being injected and the fluid takes the path of least resistance back through the casing and the wellbore.

A third way by which contaminants can reach underground sources of drinking water is by contaminants migrating from an injection zone, or the underground formation into which it is injected, through faults in the confining zone around it.[49] Fluids injected into a formation under pressure will normally travel laterally through the formation, away from the well. Typically, the formation is separated from overlying formations that contain drinking water by a confining layer, or a layer of relatively impermeable rock. If there are permeable or fractured areas in the confining layer that separates the injection zone from an overlying underground source of drinking water, the fluids can migrate out of the receiving formation and into the protected region.

Even in the absence of naturally occurring fractured areas in the confining layer, pressure from injection wells may cause underground rock layers to crack.[50] For example, toxic chemicals pumped underground at two injection wells in the 1980s that were supposedly secure for at least 10,000 years, migrated into a well within 80 feet of the surface over the course of two decades.[51] Investigators believe that excessive pressure within the injection well caused the rock to fracture.[52]

A fourth way by which contaminants can reach underground sources of drinking water is by migration through improperly abandoned and improperly completed wells.[53] This will occur if fluids injected into a formation move laterally through the formation and encounter a well that has been abandoned and not properly plugged or an operating well that has not been properly completed (i.e. weaknesses are present). Fluids injected under pressure will take the path of least resistance and flow upward within the well until entering an overlying underground source of drinking water or overflowing onto the land surface. Because of the large number of wells drilled in the past and because of lax regulatory scrutiny of well operation and abandonment, contamination by this route can be a significant risk to public health. There are approximately 17,000 improperly abandoned or improperly completed wells that could cause this problem. The location or condition of many old wells is not known.

A fifth way by which contaminants can reach underground sources of drinking water is by migration from one part of a formation to another that is not meant to be used for wastewater storage.[54] Usually, the injection zone of a particular well is segregated from underground sources of drinking water by impermeable materials. In some cases, fluids may be injected into an unprotected portion of an aquifer which in another area is designated for drinking water purposes. In this event, there may be no impermeable layer or other barrier to prevent migration of fluids into underground drinking water.

Lastly, contaminants can reach underground sources of drinking water by direct wastewater fluid injection into a drinking water source. The last pathway of contamination of groundwater is potentially the most worrisome. The injection of fluids into or above underground sources of drinking water can present the most immediate risk to public health because it can directly degrade groundwater, especially if the injected fluids do not benefit from any natural attenuation from contact with soil, as they might during movement through an aquifer or separating stratum.

SURFACE WATER CONTAMINATION

Surface water contamination results from above-ground leaks, spills of waste water, and erosion. Leaks and spills occur as a result of tank ruptures, blowouts, equipment or waste pit failures, overfills, vandalism, accidents, ground fires, or operational errors.[55] Tanks storing toxic chemicals or hoses and pipes used to convey wastes to the tanks could leak. Waste pits are of particular concern because improper liners can tear and wastewater can overflow from heavy rainfall or during the spring melt season. In 2010 and 2011, wastewater overflowed in North Dakota during the spring melt season because operators did not move fluids from the impoundments to a proper disposal site before the spring thaw. In New Mexico, substances from oil and gas pits have contaminated groundwater at least 421 times.[56] Additionally, in New Mexico, state records show 743 instances of all types of oil and gas operations polluting groundwater—the source of drinking water for 90% of the state's residents.[57] In Colorado, approximately 340 of the leaks or spills reported by drilling operators engaged in all types of oil and gas drilling over a five-year period polluted groundwater.[58] In Pennsylvania, state regulators identified 161 instances in which drinking water wells were impacted by drilling operations between 2008 and the fall of 2012.[59]

Natural gas development can contribute to erosion that carries sediments and pollutants into surface waters. Natural gas development requires under-taking a number of earth-disturbing activities, such as clearing, grading, and excavating land to create a pad to support the drilling equipment.[60] Access roads to transport equipment and other materials to the site may be constructed. Surfaces are exposed to precipitation and runoff. Without erosion controls to contain or divert sediment away from surface water, precipitation and runoff could carry sediment and other harmful pollut-ants into nearby rivers, lakes, and streams. Sediment clouds water, decreases photosynthetic activity, reduces the viability of aquatic plants and animals, and ultimately destroys organisms and their habitat.[61] Sediment runoff rates from construction sites are generally 10–20 times greater than from agricultural lands and 1000–2000 times greater than from forest lands. Examples of erosion controls are vegetative cover, rocks, and hay bales to filter storm water, or terracing slopes to divert and slow runoff.

INTANGIBLE DRILLING COSTS

The costs of a new oil well can be divided into two broad categories: intan-gible and tangible. Intangible drilling costs (IDCs) are all expenditures made in connection with drilling and preparing wells for the production of natural gas.[62] IDCs include expenditures for wages, fuel, repairs, hauling, supplies, etc., that are used:

- in the drilling, shooting and cleaning of wells;
- in the clearing of ground, draining, road making, surveying, and geological works as are necessary in preparation for the drilling of wells; and

- in the construction of such derricks, tanks, pipelines, and other physical structures as are necessary for the drilling of wells and the preparation of wells for the production of oil and gas.

IDCs also include the cost of any drilling or development work performed by contractors under any form of contract including a turnkey contract. IDCs do not include items that are part of the acquisition price of an interest in the property or expenses for items that have a salvage value. IDCs include the cost of installing salvageable items required to complete the well. The well is completed when the casing has been installed.

A taxpayer is allowed to make a binding one-time election to immediately write off IDCs.[63] The deduction may be taken even for prepayments provided drilling of the well commences within 90 days after the close of the tax year.[64] The IDC expenditures are deductible even when they result in a dry hole. Integrated oil companies that have elected to expense IDCs are required to capitalize 30% of the IDCs on productive wells and amortize them over a 60-month period.[65] The deductibility of IDCs applies only to those IDCs associated with American properties. For this purpose, the United States includes certain wells drilled offshore.

IDCs usually represent 70–85% of the cost of a well and may be deducted 100% against taxable income in the first year. For example, taxpayers investing $100,000 in a well that had 80% of its costs in IDCs can deduct $80,000 from taxable income for that year. For taxpayers in the top 39.6% federal tax bracket, that deduction would save $31,680 in federal income taxes for that tax year.[66]

TANGIBLE DRILLING COSTS

Tangible drilling costs (TDCs) are expenditures for property that has a salvage value regardless of whether or not the property is actually salvaged after it is installed. TDCs include the cost of: (a) equipping wells and structures that are constructed on the property, such as derricks, tubing, tanks, pumping units, flow lines, valves and other fittings, separators and compressors, and (b) wages, fuel, repairs, hauling supplies, etc., incurred in connection with installing equipment and structures. TDCs include the cost of casing, even though such casing is cemented in the well to such an extent that it has no salvage value.[67]

Continuing with the example above, the remaining $20,000 (20% of the cost of the well) would be TDCs. These costs are capitalized and depreciated over a seven-year period, utilizing the Modified Accelerated Cost Recovery system or MACRS.[68] Under MACRS, following the half year convention, $1429 may be deducted the first year ($20,000 × 14.29% × ½). At a 39.6% tax rate the net tax saving is $565. The total first year tax saving on a $100,000 investment in a natural gas well from IDC and TDC deductions is $32,245:

Initial investment		$100,000
First year deductions		
Intangible drilling costs	$80,000	
Tangible drilling costs	1,429	(81,429)
Tax rate		× 39.6%
First year tax savings		$ 32,245

The tax saving from IDC and TDC reduces the true cost of the investment from $100,000 to $67,755:

Initial investment	$100,000
First year tax savings	(32,245)
True cost of the investment	$ 73,895

DEPLETION

Depletion is the using up of a natural gas by drilling. Depletion allowance, like depreciation, is a form of cost recovery for capital investments. Cost recovery under percentage depletion is based on the income rather than depreciation of capitalized costs. Percentage depletion allows a tax deduction equal to 15% of the gross revenue from a gas-producing property.[69] This deduction is limited to 100% of the taxable income from the property and 65% of the taxpayer's taxable income for the year.[70] This deduction is generally only available to independent producers and royalty owners (taxpayers who are not retailers or refiners) from so much of the taxpayer's average daily production of natural gas as does not exceed the taxpayer's average daily production of natural gas.[71] This means that the deduction continues throughout the life of a gas well, even after the taxpayer's capitalized costs have long since been fully amortized and deducted!

According to a 2011 report by the US Energy Information Administration, intangible drilling costs and percentage depletion deductions are two of the most valuable subsidies for the oil and gas industry. The Energy Information Administration estimated that for 2010 the IDC subsidy amounted to $400 million and the percentage depletion allowance subsidy amounted to $980 million, for a total of about $1.38 billion. A study by a venture capital firm specializing in energy investments estimates that, from 1918 to 2009, oil and gas firms have received $447 billion in subsidies, measured in 2010 dollars.

Numerous other federal tax provisions also favor gas production. These include, among many others, depreciation of natural gas pipelines over 15 years and natural gas gathering lines over seven years; an allowance for 'tax-exempt bond-financed prepayments' for natural gas; a 'passive loss exception for working interests in oil and natural gas properties'; and limited time periods for amortization of 'geological and geophysical' expenses (seven years for large, integrated companies and two years for independents) that allow for a higher annual deduction than might otherwise apply.

'PERVERSE' SUBSIDIES

The tax benefits conferred on the fracking industry fall into the category of perverse subsidies. Perverse subsidies are those which do harm to both the environment and the economy. The federal tax subsidies for fracking encourage that environmentally harmful drilling process, constitute a significant cost to the federal budget, and distort markets by imposing downward pressure on gas prices and discourage investment in renewable energy sources.

Subsidies develop a sense of entitlement and dependence among their beneficiaries. Their removal can cause industrial and labor market upheaval, at least in the short term, and can be electorally unpopular. However, there are precedents for their successful removal. New Zealand, for example, eliminated most of its longstanding agricultural subsidies in the mid-1980s bringing budget relief and leading to less damaging land use, without resulting in the rural calamity some commentators predicted.[72] In recent years the US government has proposed removing tax credits for IDCs, which would result in substantial budget savings.[73] Naturally, this has met with strong opposition from the gas industry and has yet to be implemented.

CONCLUSION

Fracking is not the environmentally safe source of energy the natural gas industry claims it is. The claim that natural gas is a bridge fuel is pure fantasy. In a few decades, greenhouse gas emissions from the production and burning of natural gas will be worse than those from other fossil fuels. The use of natural gas will not stop in a few decades. The full extent of the impact of fracking on ground and surface water is almost impossible to determine. Incredibly, hydraulic fracturing is exempted from the Safe Drinking Water Act. Equally incredible is the recent defeat of Senator Kirsten Gillibrand's (D., NY) proposed legislation to close this loophole for fracking in the Safe Drinking Water Act.[74] It is almost impossible to find data on gas spills in most states. No data exists about abandoned gas wells that are still spewing methane. No action is taken by any governmental authority to even look at the problem of abandoned wells. Federal regulators are unlikely to step up enforcement of potential water contamination cases linked to natural gas drilling.[75]

Industry assurances that groundwater is protected from chemicals because fracking is separated by thousands of feet of rock from the aquifers high above and that steel casings and cement liners prevent any gas or chemicals from escaping into the aquifer are meaningless. The industry cannot even construct wells that are leak proof today, let alone predict what will happen to so-called protective rock layers and steel casing and cement. Groundwater contamination could be permanent because it occurs slowly and can go undetected; cleanup may be impossible. What if someday in the future the country needs to draw drinking water from a mile-deep aquifer?

In the United States, the Internal Revenue Code should be changed to eliminate all tax preference items for the natural gas industry, particularly the IDC deduction and the percentage depletion deduction. In a form of double dividend, at least a portion of the resulting billions in increased tax revenue for the government could be put to use in funding research or providing other support for environmentally friendly sources of energy. The natural gas industry should not be rewarded for polluting the atmosphere and destroying fresh water with federal tax subsidies.

NOTES

1. Vivek Chandra, *What is Natural Gas?* (visited August 22, 2011) <http://www.natgas.info/html/whatisnaturalgas.html>.
2. Arkansas Geological Survey, *Gas* (visited August 23, 2011) <http://www.geology.ar.gov/fossil_fuels/gas.htm>.
3. American Chemical Society, *Natural Gas* (visited on July 22, 2011) <http://www.ems.psu.edu/~pisupati/ACSOutreach/Natural_Gas.html>.
4. American Chemical Society, *Natural Gas* (visited on July 22, 2011) <http://www.ems.psu.edu/~pisupati/ACSOutreach/Natural_Gas.html>.
5. American Chemical Society, *Natural Gas* (visited on July 22, 2011) <http://www.ems.psu.edu/~pisupati/ACSOutreach/Natural_Gas.html>.

6. Vivek Chandra, *What is Natural Gas?* (visited August 22, 2011) <http://www.natgas. info/html/whatisnaturalgas.html>.
7. Vivek Chandra, *What is Natural Gas?* (visited August 22, 2011) <http://www.natgas. info/html/whatisnaturalgas.html>.
8. OtegoNY.com, *Un-Natural Gas* (visited September 5, 2015) <http://otegony.com/ un-natural-gas>.
9. OtegoNY.com, *Un-Natural Gas* (visited September 5, 2015) <http://otegony.com/ un-natural-gas>.
10. International Energy Agency, World energy outlook 2011 special report: Are we entering a golden age of gas? (visited on September 4, 2015) <http://www.worldenergyoutlook.org/media/weowebsite/2011/WEO2011_GoldenAgeofGasReport.pdf>.
11. Earthworks, *Fracking, Methane and Climate* (visited September 3, 2015) <https://www. earthworksaction.org/issues/detail/fracking_methane_and_climate>.
12. Earthworks, *Fracking, Methane and Climate* (visited September 3, 2015) <https://www. earthworksaction.org/issues/detail/fracking_methane_and_climate>.
13. Nature.com, *Methane Leaks Erode Green Credentials of Natural Gas* (visited September 3, 2015) <http://www.nature.com/news/methane-leaks-erode-green-credentials-of-natural-gas-1.12123>.
14. Proceedings of the National Academy of Sciences, *Toward a Better Understanding and Quantification of Methane Emissions from Shale Gas Development* (visited September 3, 2015) <http://www.pnas.org/site/aboutpnas/index.xhtml>.
15. Howarth-Marino Lab Group, *Greenhouse Gas Footprint of Shale Gas Obtained by High-Volume, Slick-Water Hydraulic Fracturing* (visited September 4, 2015) <http://www.eeb. cornell.edu/howarth/web/Marcellus.html>.
16. United States House of Representatives Committee on Energy and Commerce Minority Staff, *Chemicals Used in Hydraulic Fracturing* (visited July 18, 2015) <http://democrats.energycommerce.house.gov/sites/default/files/documents/Hydraulic-Fracturing-Chemicals-2011-4-18.pdf>.
17. US Department of Health and Human Services, Agency for Toxic Substances and Disease Registry, *Medical Management Guidelines for Hydrogen Fluoride* (visited September 8, 2015) <http://www.atsdr.cdc.gov/MMG/MMG.asp?id=1142&tid=250>.
18. United States House of Representatives Committee on Energy and Commerce Minority Staff, *Chemicals Used in Hydraulic Fracturing* (visited July 18, 2015) <http://democrats.energycommerce.house.gov/sites/default/files/documents/Hydraulic-Fracturing-Chemicals-2011-4-18.pdf>.
19. US Environmental Protection Agency, *Learn about Lead* (visited September 8, 2015) <http://www2.epa.gov/lead/learn-about-lead#effects>.
20. United States House of Representatives Committee on Energy and Commerce Minority Staff, *Chemicals Used in Hydraulic Fracturing* (visited July 18, 2015) <http://democrats.energycommerce.house.gov/sites/default/files/documents/Hydraulic-Fracturing-Chemicals-2011-4-18.pdf>.
21. Union of Concerned Scientists, *How Natural Gas is Formed* (visited August 1, 2015) <http://www.ucsusa.org/clean_energy/technology_and_impacts/energy_technologies/ how-natural-gas-works.html>.
22. Union of Concerned Scientists, *How Natural Gas is Formed* (visited August 1, 2015) <http://www.ucsusa.org/clean_energy/technology_and_impacts/energy_technologies/ how-natural-gas-works.html>.
23. enerdynamics, *The Rise of Unconventional Gas* (visited July 11, 2015) <http://www. enerdynamics.com/documents/Insider91807_000.pdf>.
24. Vello A. Kuuskraa, *The Unconventional Gas Resource Base* (visited July 11, 2015) <http://www.adv-res.com/pdf/ARI%20OGJ%202%20Unconventional%20Gas%20 Resource%20Base%207_24_07.pdf>.
25. Bob Shively, *The Natural Gas Fracking Debate: What Is Fracking and Why Does It Matter? Part I* (visited September 3, 2015) <http://marketing.enerdynamics.com/ Energy-Insider/2011/Q3NaturalGas.htm>.

26. Lynn Helms, *Horizontal Drilling* (visited August 22, 2015) <https://www.dmr.nd.gov/ndgs/documents/newsletter/2008Winter/pdfs/Horizontal.pdf>.
27. Ellis Boal, *Green Fracking* (visited July 20, 2015) <http://www.ausableanglers.org/files/Riverwatch61-web-1(2).pdf>.
28. Earthworks, *Hydraulic Fracturing 101* (visited July 22, 2015) <http://www.earthworks-action.org/FracingDetails.cfm>.
29. Ellis Boal, *Green Fracking* (visited July 20, 2015) <http://dontfrackmichigan.org/green-Fracking.shtml>.
30. Marcellus-Shale.us, *FRACKING* (visited September 1, 2015) <http://www.marcellus-shale.us/fracking.htm>.
31. Union of Concerned Scientists, *Environmental Impacts of Natural Gas* (visited September 1, 2015) <http://www.ucsusa.org/clean_energy/our-energy-choices/coal-and-other-fossil-fuels/environmental-impacts-of-natural-gas.html#.VeZCFGfJDs0>.
32. Union of Concerned Scientists, *Environmental Impacts of Natural Gas* (visited September 1, 2015) <http://www.ucsusa.org/clean_energy/our-energy-choices/coal-and-other-fossil-fuels/environmental-impacts-of-natural-gas.html#.VeZCFGfJDs0>.
33. Union of Concerned Scientists, *Environmental Impacts of Natural Gas* (visited September 1, 2015) <http://www.ucsusa.org/clean_energy/our-energy-choices/coal-and-other-fossil-fuels/environmental-impacts-of-natural-gas.html#.VeZCFGfJDs0>.
34. Government Accountability Office, *Shale Oil and Gas Development* (visited September 15, 2015) <http://www.gao.gov/assets/650/647791.pdf>.
35. Government Accountability Office, *Shale Oil and Gas Development* (visited September 15, 2015) <http://www.gao.gov/assets/650/647791.pdf>.
36. One Green Planet, *No Fraccident: How Animals Are Hurt By Fracking* (visited September 22, 2015) <http://www.onegreenplanet.org/animalsandnature/no-fraccident-how-animals-are-hurt-by-fracking/>.
37. Ceres, *Hydraulic Fracturing & Water Stress* (visited September 2015) <http://www.ceres.org/issues/water/shale-energy/shale-and-water-maps/hydraulic-fracturing-water-stress-water-demand-by-the-numbers>.
38. Ceres, *Hydraulic Fracturing & Water Stress* (visited September 2015) <http://www.ceres.org/issues/water/shale-energy/shale-and-water-maps/hydraulic-fracturing-water-stress-water-demand-by-the-numbers>.
39. USA TODAY, Report: Fracking raising water supply worries (visited September 2, 2015) <http://www.usatoday.com/story/money/business/2014/02/05/ceres-report-fracking-water-supplies/5230583/>.
40. Bruce Finley, 'Colorado Farms Planning for Dry Spell Losing Auction Bids for Water to Fracking Projects,' *The Denver Post*, April 1 <http://www.denverpost.com/environment/ci_20299962/colorado-farms-planning-dryspell-losing-auction-bids>.
41. Bruce Finley, 'Colorado Farms Planning for Dry Spell Losing Auction Bids for Water to Fracking Projects,' *The Denver Post*, April 1 <http://www.denverpost.com/environment/ci_20299962/colorado-farms-planning-dryspell-losing-auction-bids>.
42. Susquehanna River Basin Commission, *13 Water Withdrawals Remain on Hold to Protect Streams in the Susquehanna Basin* (visited September 24, 2015) <http://www.srbc.net/whatsnew/Newsletters/article_58.asp>.
43. Environmental Protection Agency, Office of Drinking Water, *Statement of Basis and Purpose: Underground Injection Control Regulations* (visited September 24, 2015) <http://www.epa.gov/safewater/uic/pdfs/rept_uic_statemt_basis_purpose_uic_1979.pdf>.
44. Environmental Protection Agency, Office of Drinking Water, *Statement of Basis and Purpose: Underground Injection Control Regulations* (visited September 24, 2015) <http://www.epa.gov/safewater/uic/pdfs/rept_uic_statemt_basis_purpose_uic_1979.pdf>.
45. Ohio Department of Natural Resources, *Report on the Investigation of the Natural Gas Invasion of Aquifers in Bainbridge Township of Geauga County, Ohio* (visited September 25, 2015) <http://oilandgas.ohiodnr.gov/portals/oilgas/pdf/bainbridge/report.pdf>.

46. Concerned Health Professionals of NY, *Compendium of Scientific, Medical, And Media Findings Demonstrating Risks and Harms of Fracking (Unconventional Gas and Oil Extraction)* (visited September 25, 2015) <http://concernedhealthny.org/wp-content/uploads/2014/07/CHPNY-Fracking-Compendium.pdf>.
47. Concerned Health Professionals of NY, *Compendium of Scientific, Medical, And Media Findings Demonstrating Risks and Harms of Fracking (Unconventional Gas and Oil Extraction)* (visited September 25, 2015) <http://concernedhealthny.org/wp-content/uploads/2014/07/CHPNY-Fracking-Compendium.pdf>.
48. Environmental Protection Agency, Office of Drinking Water, *Statement of Basis and Purpose: Underground Injection Control Regulations* (visited September 24, 2015) <http://www.epa.gov/safewater/uic/pdfs/rept_uic_statemt_basis_purpose_uic_1979.pdf>.
49. Environmental Protection Agency, Office of Drinking Water, *Statement of Basis and Purpose: Underground Injection Control Regulations* (visited September 24, 2015) <http://www.epa.gov/safewater/uic/pdfs/rept_uic_statemt_basis_purpose_uic_1979.pdf>.
50. Environment America, *Fracking by the Numbers* (visited September 25, 2015) <http://www.environmentamerica.org/sites/environment/files/reports/EA_FrackingNumbers_scrn.pdf>.
51. ProPublica, *Whiff of Phenol Spells Trouble* (visited September 25, 2015) <http://www.propublica.org/article/whiff-of-phenol-spells-trouble>.
52. ProPublica, *Whiff of Phenol Spells Trouble* (visited September 25, 2015) <http://www.propublica.org/article/whiff-of-phenol-spells-trouble>.
53. Environmental Protection Agency, Office of Drinking Water, *Statement of Basis and Purpose: Underground Injection Control Regulations* (visited September 24, 2015) <http://www.epa.gov/safewater/uic/pdfs/rept_uic_statemt_basis_purpose_uic_1979.pdf>.
54. Environmental Protection Agency, Office of Drinking Water, *Statement of Basis and Purpose: Underground Injection Control Regulations* (visited September 24, 2015) <http://www.epa.gov/safewater/uic/pdfs/rept_uic_statemt_basis_purpose_uic_1979.pdf>.
55. Government Accountability Office, *Shale Oil and Gas Development* (visited September 15, 2015) <http://www.gao.gov/assets/650/647791.pdf>.
56. Joanna Prukop, 'Setting the Record Straight on Pit Rule,' *Farmington Daily Times*, September 17, 2008. Available at <http://www.daily-times.com/columns/ci_10482677>.
57. New Mexico Oil Conservation Division, Environmental Bureau, *Generalized Record of Ground Water Impact Sites* (visited September 24, 2015) <http://www.emnrd.state.nm.us/OCD/documents/rptGeneralizedGWImpact.pdf>.
58. Bruce Finley, 'Drilling Spills Reaching Colorado Groundwater; State Mulls Test Rules,' *The Denver Post*, December 9, 2012. Available at <http://www.denverpost.com/ci_22154751/drilling-spills-reaching-colorado-groundwater-state-mulls-test>.
59. Laura Legere, 'Sunday Times Review of DEP Drilling Records Reveals Water Damage, Murky Testing Methods,' *The Times-Tribune (Scranton, Pa.)*, May 19, 2013. Available at <http://thetimes-tribune.com/news/sunday-times-review-of-dep-drilling-records-reveals-water-damage-murky-testing-methods-1.1491547>.
60. Government Accountability Office, *Shale Oil and Gas Development* (visited September 15, 2015) <http://www.gao.gov/assets/650/647791.pdf>.
61. Government Accountability Office, *Storm Water Pollution* (visited September 15, 2015) <http://www.gao.gov/assets/250/245272.pdf>.
62. Treas. Reg. § 1.612-4(a).
63. I. R. C. § 263(c) and Treas. Reg. 1.612–4.
64. I. R. C. § 461(i)(2)(A).
65. I. R. C. §§ 291(b)(1)(B), 291(b)(2).

66. Investopedia, Oil, *A Big Investment with Big Tax Breaks* (visited October 3, 2015) <http://www.investopedia.com/>.
67. Rev. Rul. 70-44, 1970-2CB132.
68. I. R. C. § 168(b) and (c).
69. I. R. C. § 613(b)(2).
70. I. R. C. §§ 613(a), 613A(c)(1).
71. I. R. C. § 613A(c)(1)(B).
72. Henning Steinfeld et al., *Livestock's Long Shadow: Environmental Issues and Options*, Food and Agriculture Organization of the United Nations, Rome 2006, p. 232 (visited February 11, 2016) <ftp://ftp.fao.org/docrep/fao/010/a0701e/a0701e00.pdf>, <https://books.google.com.au/books?id=1B9LQQkm_qMC&pg=PA232&lpg=PA232 &dq=nz+removal+agricultural+subsidies+1980s&source=bl&ots=LNZ-cY9LtN& sig=BFx3pyb39-X6JaJjiddWGr3s8Yg&hl=en&sa=X&ved=0ahUKEwjh0IfD7u7KAh VLlJQKHUHxCQ8Q6AEISjAG#v=onepage&q=nz%20removal%20agricultural%20 subsidies%201980s&f=false>.
73. Withdrawal of the IDC credit alone was calculated to save $3.49bn in 2013: Jim Snyder and Wingfield, B. *Obama Budget Would Cut $40 Billion in Fossil-Fuel Credits*, February 14, 2012 (visited February 10, 2016) <http://www.bloomberg.com/news/ articles/2012-02-13/obama-proposes-cutting-40-billion-in-u-s-fossil-fuel-credits>.
74. Kirsten Gillibrand, *As Keystone Debate Continues, Gillibrand Introduces Amendments To Protect Clean Water, Hold Oil & Gas Companies Accountable* (visited October 9, 2015) <http://www.gillibrand.senate.gov/newsroom/press/release/as-keystone-debate-continues-gillibrand-introduces-amendments-to-protect-clean-water-hold-oil-and-gas-companies-accountable>.
75. Huffington Post, *EPA Unlikely To Pursue Fracking Contamination Cases Anytime Soon, Analysts Say* (visited October 10, 2015) <http://www.huffingtonpost.com/2014/01/06/ epa-fracking-contamination_n_4544961.html>.

6. Policy instruments to support water conservation and support the ecosystem: A California example

Rahmat Tavallali and Paul Lee

1. INTRODUCTION

The drought in the southwestern part of the United States is now in its fourth year. Many cities are running out of water.[1] Ranchers are struggling to feed livestock and farmers are having difficulty raising crops. The entire area has also become extremely vulnerable to wild fires.

Following three dry years, many irrigation districts have exhausted surface water reserves and groundwater has been drawn-down in many parts of the Central Valley of California. The current drought is more severe than in the past in part because of the growth in the state's population. Today, California has 16 million more people than during the severe 1976–1977 drought and nearly 10 million more than during the long 1987–1992 drought.[2] It is estimated that the current situation could deteriorate further and the socio-economic impacts of an extended drought could be much more severe.[3] As a result of the drought, in the last four years, California has lost 8 trillion gallons of its water reserves. Over time, warming temperatures, changing rain and snowfall patterns are expected to have severe negative effects on California's ability to manage water supplies and other natural resources.

California is not alone in experiencing the growing impacts of global warming and climate change. There is evidence that climate change is influencing hydrologic events all over the world including heat waves, droughts and decreasing water supply. It is important for California and the rest of the world to adopt a comprehensive strategy to deal with this growing impact of climate change.

This chapter makes a quantitative analysis of the use of tax incentives to curb climate change versus the current policies of regulations, fines and penalties.

2. THE MAJOR CAUSE OF DROUGHT IN CALIFORNIA

Most scientists agree there is overwhelming evidence that climate change is a major cause of the current drought in California. Carbon dioxide (CO_2) is an important compound for plant and animal life, as part of the carbon cycle, and as a greenhouse gas (GHG). CO_2 is the primary GHG emitted in California, accounting for 84% of total GHG emissions in 2013.

2.1 Sources of Carbon Dioxide in California for 2013

Transportation is the single largest source of CO_2 in California, which primarily comprises on-road travel. Electricity production, industrial and residential sources also contribute to CO_2 emissions. Figure 6.1 shows the sources of carbon dioxide in California for 2013 by different sector.

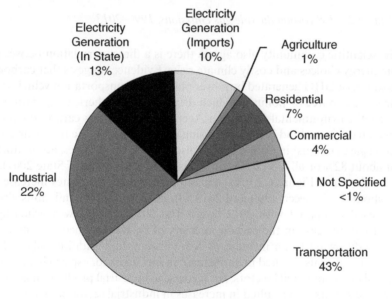

2013 Total CO_2 Emissions: 386.6 MMTCO2e

Source: California Environmental Protection Agency, Air Resource Board California Greenhouse Gas Emission Inventory, 2015 edn, June 30, 2015, http://www.arb.ca.gov/cc/inventory/background/co2.htm.

Figure 6.1 Sources of carbon dioxide in California for 2013

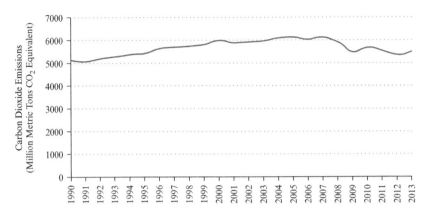

Note: All emission estimates from the *Inventory of US Greenhouse Gas Emissions and Sinks: 1990–2013.*

Source: US Department of State, Sources of Greenhouse Gas Emissions, EPA, http://epa. gov/climatechange/ghgemissions/sources.html.

Figure 6.2   US carbon dioxide gas emissions, 1990–2013

The scientific community also agrees there is a direct correlation between our energy choices and costly climate risks. Evidence suggests that carbon dioxide as a GHG generated by power plants and transportation vehicles is the largest source of pollution which drives up atmospheric temperatures. The US Environmental Protection Agency (EPA) claims carbon dioxide generated by mankind is the largest single contributor to the rise of greenhouse gases not just in California but also in the United States, accounting for about 82% of all US GHG emissions (US Department of State 2007).

As shown in Figure 6.2, CO_2 emissions in the United States increased by about 7% between 1990 and 2013.[4] In 2013, US GHG emissions also increased compared with 2012 levels. The 2013 increase was primarily due to an increase in the carbon intensity of fuels consumed to generate electricity owing to an increase in coal consumption. Additionally, cold winter conditions resulted in an increase in fuel demand, especially in residential and commercial sectors. An increase in industrial production across multiple sectors also resulted in increases in industrial sector emissions.[5]

Since the combustion of fossil fuels is the largest source of GHG emissions, changes in emissions from fossil fuel combustion have historically been the dominant factor affecting total US emission trends. Changes in CO_2 emissions from fossil fuel combustion are influenced by many long- and short-term factors, including population growth, economic growth, changing energy prices, new technologies, changing behavior, and seasonal temperatures.

2.2 The Source of California's Precipitation

Most of California's precipitation comes from storms moving across the Pacific Ocean. The path followed by the storms is determined by the position of an atmospheric high-pressure belt that normally shifts southward during the winter months, allowing low pressure zones to move into the state. On average, 75% of California's annual precipitation occurs from November through March, with 50% occurring from December through February.[6] In an average year, about 30% of California's urban and agricultural water supplies come from groundwater.[7] In the last four years, reliance on groundwater has increased owing to reduced availability of surface water.[8]

3. ECONOMIC IMPACT OF THE WATER SHORTAGE

California has experienced four consecutive years of below-average rain and snow and is currently facing severe drought conditions in all 58 counties. The extended drought is expected to be worse for California's agricultural economy this year because of reduced water availability.[9]

Table 6.1 estimates that farmers will have 2.5 million acre-feet less surface water than they would in a normal water year, about a 33% loss of average water supply. The impacts are concentrated mostly in the San Joaquin Valley and are not evenly distributed. Individual farmers will face severe losses.

Table 6.1   Estimated drought impacts to California agriculture, 2015

Drought impact	Loss quantity
Water supply	
Surface water reduction	8.7 million acre-feet
Groundwater pumping increase	6.2 million acre-feet
Net water shortage	2.5 million acre-feet
Statewide costs	
Crop revenue loss	$856 million
Additional groundwater pumping cost	$595 million
Total statewide economic cost	$2.7 billion

Source: Howitt, R. E., Medellín-Azuara, J., MacEwan, D., Lund, J. R. and Sumner, D. A. (2015) 'Preliminary Analysis: 2015 Drought Economic Impact Study', UC Davis Center for Watershed Sciences.

While farmers are having difficulty in watering their crops and environmentalists are working to protect the ecosystem, the Governor of California has ordered statewide water restrictions.

On April 1, 2015, the Governor issued an Executive Order that, in part, directs the State Water Board to impose restrictions on water suppliers to achieve a statewide 25% reduction in potable urban water usage through February 28, 2016; it requires commercial, industrial, and institutional users to implement water efficiency measures; it prohibits irrigation with potable water of ornamental turf in public street medians; and it prohibits irrigation with potable water outside newly constructed homes and buildings that is not delivered by drip or micro-spray systems.[10]

The damage to ecosystems and the economic loss of climate change have affected California's infrastructure while the governor has outlined bold steps directing the first ever statewide mandatory water reductions, increased enforcement of water use standards and investment in new water energy technologies. To accelerate the deployment of innovative water and energy saving technologies and reduce GHG emissions, California's Energy Commission, jointly with the Department of Water Resources and the State Water Resources Control Board, will implement a Water Energy Technology Program to provide funding for innovative technologies that meet the following criteria:

- display significant water savings, energy savings, and GHG emission reductions;
- demonstrate actual operation beyond the research and development stage;
- document readiness for rapid, large-scale deployment.[11]

Despite mandatory water restriction policies, it is not clear that these measures will decrease water consumption enough to avoid serious water shortages. In addition, the California drought has shifted the sources of electricity with adverse economic and environmental consequences. The Pacific Institute has just completed and released a report that evaluates how diminished river flows have resulted in lost hydroelectricity, more expensive electricity from the combustion of natural gas, and increased production of GHG emissions.[12] During 2011–2014, burning more natural gas to compensate for limited hydropower led to an 8% increase in emissions of carbon dioxide and other pollutions from California power plants.[13]

3.1 California Emergency Drought Responses

Following the lowest snowpack ever recorded, in April 2015, the governor of California signed an Executive Order B-29-15[14] directing the first ever statewide mandatory water reductions.[15] As a result, the state's emergency drought response is strategically guided by accelerating the following key actions in the California Water Action Plan:

- $1.9 billion for drought relief and water infrastructure;
- reduced potable urban water use by 25% statewide;
- a requirement for agricultural water users to report more water use information, increasing the state's ability to enforce against illegal diversions, waste and unreasonable use of water;
- $28 million Cap-and-Trade funds for the Department of Water Resources and Energy Grant Program to reduce energy demand and GHG emissions through local projects that also support water use efficiency and conservation;[16]
- $75 million ($40 million Cap-and-Trade funds and $35 million Proposition 1 funds) for agricultural water efficiency programs, which will enable the Department of Food and Agriculture and DWR to provide incentives to agricultural operations to invest in water irrigation technologies that reduce water and energy use and GHG emissions;
- $37.1 million General Funds to assist drought impacted communities and enforce water use restrictions (Executive Order B-29-15, State of California).

A major purpose of the economic incentives provided by Executive Order B-29-15 is to influence water management and to promote water management practices that meet federal, state, regional, and local policy goals. These incentives include financial assistance, water pricing, and water marketing policies. Also, fines can be used to discourage undesirable water user behavior.

4. THE INFLUENCE OF CLIMATE CHANGE ON THE CALIFORNIA DROUGHT

The California drought currently is by some metrics the worst in state history. Combined with unusually warm temperatures and stagnant air conditions, the lack of precipitation has triggered a dangerous increase in wildfires and incidents of air pollution across the state. A Stanford

University report estimated that the water shortage would result in direct and indirect agricultural losses of at least \$2.2 billion to the state.[17]

While attention has been focused on alleviating the current crisis situation, the question of whether or not climate change can be linked to the severity, duration, or frequency of drought in California has been discussed. New research from Stanford earth scientists Noah Diffenbaugh, Daniel Swain, and Danielle Touma seeks to provide insights into the drought–climate linkage questions by examining the influence of temperature in contributing to the severity and/or likelihood of drought, an issue that until recently has received less attention than the causes of precipitation deficits.[18]

Scientists agree that there is growing evidence to support the influence of human behavior on climate change, including the fingerprints of higher temperatures and changes in the atmospheric circulation patterns. Professor Noah Diffenbaugh also claims that the extreme atmospheric conditions associated with California's drought are far more likely to occur under today's global warming conditions than in the climate that existed before humans emitted large amounts of greenhouse gases. By using a novel combination of computer simulations and statistical techniques, he shows that a persistent region of high atmospheric pressure hovering over the Pacific Ocean that diverted storms away from California is more likely to form in the presence of modern GHG concentrations.[19]

Under current conditions, scientists believe that California will see more drought while the west could suffer more wildfires, and the east coast could be battered by heavy rains and storm surges, such as were experienced in 2015.

5.   CALIFORNIA CAP-AND-TRADE AND INNOVATION

In order to fight climate change, California has launched a Cap-and-Trade Program (Global Warming Solution Act of 2006 or AB32), which is second in size only to the European Union's Emissions Trading System on the amount of emissions covered. This Act (AB32) requires that the California Air Resources Board (ARB) determine the statewide 1990 GHG emissions level and approve a statewide GHG emissions limit equal to the 1990 level, to be achieved by 2020. The program will reduce GHG emissions by more than 16% between 2013 and 2020.[20] Under the Cap-and-Trade system, California will implement energy efficiency mandates by imposing several tax incentive formulas assuming that these incentives will motivate manufacturers and consumers to reduce energy consumption, cut pollution and reduce the damages caused by each additional ton of carbon dioxide emitted into the atmosphere. The California Cap-and-Trade Program is designed to achieve cost-effective emissions reductions across the capped sectors. The Program sets maximum, statewide GHG emissions for all covered sectors each year (the 'cap'), and allows covered entities to sell off allowances.[21] An allowance is a tradable permit that allows the emission of 1 metric ton of CO_2e. The California carbon price is driven by allowance trading. By 2020, the Cap-and-Trade Program in California is expected to drive approximately 22% of targeted GHG reductions still needed in capped sectors after reductions from AB32's complementary policies.[22]

Under the California Cap-and-Trade system, companies must hold enough emissions allowances to cover their emissions, and are free to buy and sell allowances on the open market. Ultimately, the California program offers opportunities for the most cost-effective emissions reductions. However, many challenging issues must be addressed. Once the program matures, a well-designed Cap-and-Trade market will achieve emission reduction goals in a cost-effective manner and drive GHG innovation.

The fallacy of efficiency mandates, however, is that the cost of energy efficiency standards will surpass the savings and tax incentives. In 2009, President Obama made a commitment to reduce US GHG emissions in the range of 17% below 2005 levels by 2020 and efficiency standards for appliances and federal buildings will reduce carbon pollution by at least 3 billion metric tons cumulatively by 2030.[23] Under this plan, an overall national cap on carbon emissions would be established by the government which would limit heat-trapping pollution from factories, refineries and power plants. Those that are able to reduce pollution at a low cost could sell their extra allowances to companies facing higher costs. The Cap-and-Trade system would also require all pollution credits to be auctioned. The revenues generated from these auctions would be reinvested into promoting a clean energy economy and in energy efficiency improvements.

6.   THE SOCIAL COST OF CLIMATE CHANGE

In spite of California's economic incentives policy for reducing water use, it is not clear that these policies alone can solve the state's water shortage. A long-term solution is needed to reduce pollution which has generated the climate change that has intensified droughts in California. One issue which is being discussed is the controversial cost of climate change, which economists call 'the social cost of carbon' or SCC.[24] The $SC\text{-}CO_2$ is meant

Table 6.2   Social cost of CO_2, 2015–2050 (in 2007 dollars per metric ton CO_2)

Year	Discount rate and statistic			
	5% Average	3% Average	2.5% Average	3% 95th percentile
2015	$11	$36	$56	$105
2020	$12	$42	$62	$123
2025	$14	$46	$68	$138
2030	$16	$50	$73	$152
2035	$18	$55	$78	$168
2040	$21	$60	$84	$183
2045	$23	$64	$89	$197
2050	$26	$69	$95	$212

Note: The SC-CO_2 values are dollar-year and emissions-year specific and have been rounded to two significant digits.

Source: Technical Support Document (PDF, 21 pp, 1 MB): Technical Update of the Social Cost of Carbon for Regulatory Impact Analysis under Executive Order 12866 (May 2013, Revised July 2015). Available at http://www3.epa.gov/climatechange/EPAactivities/economics/scc.html (accessed February 9, 2016).

to be a comprehensive estimate of climate change damages and includes changes in net agricultural productivity, human health, property damages from increased flood risk, and changes in energy system costs, such as reduced costs for heating and increased costs for air conditioning. In other words, the SCC is a measurement of the price that society must pay for the damages caused by each additional ton of carbon dioxide added to the atmosphere. The SCC is also an estimate of the monetized damages associated with an incremental increase in carbon emissions in a given year. It is intended to include changes in net agricultural productivity, human health, property damages from increased flood risk, and the value of ecosystem services owing to climate change. The value of SCC is calculated based on discount rates of 2.5, 3 and 5%.[25]

Table 6.2 shows the SCC values in five year increments from 2015 to 2050. Values for 2015, 2020, 2040 and 2050 are calculated by first combining all outputs (10,000 estimates per model run) from all scenarios and models for a given discount rate.

In January 2016, NASA announced that 2015 was the hottest year on record and many computer models project a warmer temperature in 2016. As the world gets hotter, it is anticipated that the social cost of carbon dioxide will increase.

At the present time, most environmentalists believe that, in order to achieve any progress with climate change and reduce carbon dioxide emissions, the US government should consider 'the social cost of carbon' as a basis for any energy tax proposals in the United States. Economists say it makes sense to tax carbon at a level that reflects its social cost.

7. CONCLUSION

For the last four years, California has been feeling a shift in weather patterns that suggests that there is a link to climate change that will influence future environmental and economic conditions. Scientists see parallel lines of evidence of the influence of human-induced climate changes causing higher temperatures and changes in atmospheric circulation patterns. It is time for all nations to establish standards through comprehensive cost-effective plans to tackle climate change and reduce damages to the environment caused by global warming. The obvious long-term solution is to reduce the human pollution that has caused the climate change that has intensified droughts in California.

Most environmentalists believe that to achieve any progress in dealing with climate change, all states should consider 'the social cost of carbon' as a basis for any energy tax proposals in the United States. Economists say it makes sense to tax carbon at a level that reflects its social cost.

NOTES

1. There is no single definition of 'drought'. Drought, most simply defined, is the mismatch between the amounts of water nature provides and the amounts of water that humans and the environment demand, see Glieck, P. (2014) 'The Growing Influence of Climate Change on the California Drought', The California Drought, Pacific Institute, December 2014. Available at http://www.californiadrought.org.
2. *Ibid.*
3. *Ibid.*
4. According to the Fourth Climate Action Report to the UN, CO_2 emissions in the United States are projected to grow by about 1.5% between 2005 and 2020, see the US Department of State (2007). *Fourth Climate Action Report to the UN Framework Convention on Climate Change: Projected Greenhouse Gas Emissions*. US Department of State, Washington, DC. Available at http://www.state.gov/e/oes/rts/rpts/car4/90324.htm. To learn about projected GHG emissions to 2020, visit the US Climate Action Report 2014. Available at: http://www.state.gov/documents/organization/219038.pdf.
5. US Department of State, Sources of Greenhouse Gas Emissions, EPA, http://epa.gov/climatechange/ghgemissions/sources.html.
6. Drought and Precipitation, Drought Background (2015) Department of Water Sources, July 2015. Available at http://www.water.ca.gov/waterconditions/backgound.cfm.
7. Drought and Precipitation, Drought Background (2015) Department of Water Sources, July 2015. Available at http://www.water.ca.gov/waterconditions/backgound.cfm.
8. Two of the state's largest water systems—the state Water Project and federal Center

Valley Project—move water through the Sacramento–San Joaquin River Delta to more than 25 million people in the San Francisco Bay Area, Central Valley and Southern California and to more than 2.5 million acres of farmland, see Department of Water Resources, 'California State Water Projects' (2014). Available at http://saveourwater.com/environmental problems (accessed July 27, 2015).

9. Howitt, R., MacEwan, D., Medellin Azuara, J., Lund, J. and Sumner, D. (2015) 'Preliminary Analysis: 2015 Drought Economic Impact Study', May. Available at http://www.npr.org/sections/thesalt/2015/06/03.

10. See Proposed Text of Emergency Regulation, Article 22.5. Drought Emergency Water Conservation (2015). Available at http://www.waterboards.ca.gov/waterrights/water_issues/programs/drought/docs/emergency.

11. California Energy Commission (2015) 'Investing in Innovative Water and Energy Saving Technologies', July. Available at http://www.energy.ca.gov/wet.

12. According to the Pacific Institute, between October 2011 and October 2014, California's ratepayers spent $1.4 billion more on electricity than in average years because of the drought-induced shift from hydropower to natural gas, see Gleick, P. (2015) 'The Impacts of California's Drought on Hydroelectricity Production', March 2015. Available at http://californiadrought.org/the-impacts-of-californias-drought-on-hydroelectricity-production.

13. A longer view reveals an even more startling economic impact: factoring in the dry years the total additional energy cost to the state's electricity users during the recent drought was $2.4 billion; see: Gleick *ibid.*

14. For more information, see Executive Order B-29-15, State of California. Available at http://gov.ca.gov/docs/4.1.15_Executive_Order.pdf.

15. In late April 2015 the Governor issued a continued proclamation of drought emergency to enable regulatory streamlining that will allow several urgent actions to be expedited, including voluntary water transfers, emergency drinking water projects, crucial habitat protection measures, and the purchase of essential equipment for fire suppression and drought response, see Executive Order B-29-15.

16. In July 2015, the Department of Water Resources' Water-Energy Grant Program awarded $28 million in grants to 25 projects using proceeds from the state's Cap-and-Trade Program for saving water (an estimated 270,000 acre-feet of water) and energy to combat climate change by reducing GHG emissions, see 'Funding Grants to Save Water and Energy' (2015). Available at http://www.water.ca.gov/waterconditions/.

17. Causes of California Drought Linked to Climate Change (2014) Stanford Report, September 2014. Available at http://news.stanford.edu/FINAL.pdf.

18. Diffenbaugh, N. (2015) 'California Drought and Climate Linked—But Rain Isn't the Only Factor' (2015). Available at https://woods.stanford.edu/sites/default/files/files/PNAS-Diffenbaugh-Drought-Climate-Brief-03032015-FINAL.pdf.

19. This study was led by Woods Senior Fellow Noah Diffenbaugh (Associate Professor, Environmental Earth System Science) in collaboration with coauthors Daniel Swain and Danielle Touma (graduate students in the Department of Environmental Earth System Science), is conducted by a group of scientists from Stanford University and is supported in part by a National Science Foundation CAREER Award and by a grant from the National Institutes of Health; see 'California Drought and Climate Change Linked—but Rain Isn't the Only Factor' (2015) Stanford Woods Institute for the Environment. Available at https://woods.stanford.edu/sites/default/files/files/PNAS-Diffenbaugh-Drought-Climate-Brief-03032015-FINAL.pdf.

20. Prior to California's program, GHG Cap-and-Trade programs were operating in the European Union, Australia, and New Zealand.

21. California is a leader in reducing GHG emissions in all sectors of the state's economy. Investments in water saving appliances and devices reduce energy use, thereby reducing GHG emissions. The transportation and treatment of water and wastewater, and the energy used to heat water, accounts for nearly 20% of the total electricity and 30% of non-power plant related natural gas consumed in California. Saving water allows California to achieve multiple environmental benefits.

22. California Carbon Dashboard (2015) A project of Climate Policy Initiative. Available at http://calcarbondash.org/.
23. The President's Climate Action Plan (2013). Available at https://www.whitehouse.gov/ sites/default/files/image/president27sclimateactionplan.pdf.
24. In 2009, an interagency workgroup composed of members from six federal agencies and various White House offices was convened to develop estimates of the 'social cost of carbon' for regulatory impact analysis. This process represents a step forward in increasing transparency and consistency in benefit–cost analyses of federal regulatory actions and can serve as a model for future revisions of the social cost of carbon estimates to keep pace with the evolving state of the science, see 'Technical Support Document: Technical Update of the Social Cost of Carbon for Regulatory Impact Analysis. Under Executive Order 12866' Interagency Working Group on Social Cost of Carbon, United States Government, May 2013. Available at http://www.whitehouse.gov/sites/ default/files/omb/inforeg/for-agencies/Social-Cost-of-Carbon-for-RIA.pdf.access.
25. The most recent estimate for the cost of a ton of carbon emissions—referred to as the social cost of carbon—is $37. That number was calculated in 2013 by 12 federal agencies using three models that incorporate both our physical understanding of climate change and the cost of climate impacts around the globe, see 'Technical Support Document, Technical Update of the Social Cost of Carbon for Regulatory Impact Analysis. Under Executive Order 12866' Interagency Working Group on Social Cost of Carbon, United States Government.

PART III

Shifting the tax burden to effect environmentally responsible outcomes

7. From fossil fuels to renewable energy: Subsidy reform and energy transition in African and Indian Ocean island states

Kai Schlegelmilch, Jacqueline Cottrell and François Fortier

1. INTRODUCTION

Energy is key to prosperity and the discovery and use of fossil fuels in the past few centuries has generated tremendous wealth. Yet, this energy paradigm has now become a liability that threatens the very sustainability of all it enabled. Coal, petroleum and gas not only induce climate instability through emissions of greenhouse gases, but also entail numerous other economic, social and environmental externalities, adding up to a dangerously negative balance sheet.

This chapter, a summary of a recent report,[1] analyses the impacts of fossil fuel energy in the multiple dimensions of sustainability, modelling the relationships, externalities and opportunities that a transition to a new energy paradigm can offer, based on energy conservation, efficiency and low-carbon renewable sources. It first explores the 'sustainability doughnut' as an integrative model, which facilitates the overlaying of policy choices, including energy-related ones, with the economic, social and environmental sustainability impacts they have. This provides a cogent framework for the comparison of the fossil fuel and renewable energy paradigms, highlighting their costs and opportunities.

Based on this modelling and rationale, the bulk of the chapter then turns to analysing fossil fuel subsidy reforms and renewable energy (RE) transitions in the context of island states, with particular reference to Small Island Developing States (SIDS) in the Indian Ocean and Atlantic African coast.[2] With policy-relevance as key objective, the chapter makes a series of general recommendations for these island states, underlining the most important policy areas of fossil fuel to renewable energy (FFRE) transition.[3] While island states were the focus of the original report, these recommendations have broader policy relevance for countries wishing to pursue a fossil fuel subsidy reform and renewable energy transition.

2. ISLAND STATES IN FOCUS

The majority of island territories referred to in this chapter are SIDS, although some are not considered as such by international practice, notably for not being small in either size or population. For this reason, the broader term 'island states' is used here. Nevertheless, as a general rule, the country cases reviewed in the report share many of the characteristics and vulnerabilities common to SIDS, namely small population and few natural resources, prone to disasters, dependent on foreign trade and costly imports, and limited economies of scales in industry, infrastructure and public administration.

Excessive dependence on international trade in island states includes energy dependence on fossil fuel imports, making those countries extremely vulnerable to changes in global energy prices. At the same time, many island states have considerable potential for renewable energy generation, in terms of solar, wind, hydro, ocean, biomass and geothermal power. Thus, many island states are in the position to bring together the related aims of reducing wasteful spending on fossil fuels—in relation to fossil fuel subsidies (FFS) and/or high spending on fossil fuel imports—and increasing the rate of renewable energy technology deployment.

This approach would have several benefits. A gradual shift away from fossil fuels and towards renewable energy could enable island states to achieve energy independence in the medium term, freeing up foreign exchange needlessly wasted on energy imports and government revenues spent or foregone owing to fossil fuel subsidies, reducing both budget deficits and balance of payments deficits. In fiscal and economic terms, RE transition makes sense, particularly in the context of island states.

FFS reforms and RE transitions also have a number of climate, environmental and social benefits: reduced greenhouse gas emissions; improved local air quality with reduced SO_2, NO_x and particulate matter emissions; improved respiratory health; and net job creation from the RE sector. Subsidy reform can also free up revenues for spending, for example, on education and health activities previously crowded out as a result of high levels of government expenditures to keep the price of fossil fuels low.

Thus, a gradual and carefully planned energy transition offers island states—and others—the chance to reap the benefits of a win–win solution to several of their most pressing economic and fiscal problems.

The report has been produced on the basis of background research on island states and information kindly provided by participants of the United Nations Office for Sustainable Development workshop on fossil fuel subsidy reform and energy transition held in Mauritius on 12–16 May 2014. The authors would like to thank all participants for their contributions and comments.

3. GENERAL RECOMMENDATIONS FOR FFRE TRANSITIONS IN ISLAND STATES

On the basis of workshop inputs and research, including the baseline study completed for the information of participants prior to the Mauritius FFRE event of May 2014, the remainder of this chapter makes a series of recommendations for FFRE policies specifically relevant to the needs of island states.[4] However, many of the conclusions drawn here are also more widely applicable to developing, transition and emerging economies. Not all recommendations will be relevant to all countries, thus readers are invited to pick up on those elements most relevant to the specific circumstances of their country, taking into account, for example, existing RE strategies and policies as well as the national developmental and political economic context.

3.1 Increasing Fiscal Space by Means of EFR

The World Bank defines environmental fiscal reform as 'a range of taxation or pricing instruments that can raise revenue, while simultaneously furthering environmental goals. This is achieved by providing economic incentives to correct market failure in the management of natural resources and the control of pollution'.[5] The European Environment Agency also emphasises the importance of subsidy reform: 'Environmental Fiscal Reform (EFR) . . . focuses not just on shifting taxes and tax burdens, but also on reforming economically motivated subsidies, some of which are harmful to the environment and may have outlived their rationale'.[6]

Environmental fiscal reform can be used to raise revenues by means of environmental taxation, or reduce government spending by means of reform of harmful subsidies. Thus, implementing EFR can increase fiscal space and free up government revenues for investment in FFRE transition.

In the majority of the island states participating in the workshop, and in the majority of SIDS as a whole, tax revenues are worth less than 20% of GDP, while in OECD countries, tax revenues are as a general rule worth 30–40% of GDP, sometimes more. This means that SIDS and island state governments have limited budgetary room to provide resources for a desired purpose, such as fostering energy transition. Budgetary room can be increased in a number of ways. Diversification of revenue sources is one possibility. EFR is another—increasing environmental taxation and reforming fossil fuel subsidies—and has the added advantage that it can give government revenues a much-needed boost and change relative pricing in the energy sector at the same time, thus incentivising more environmentally friendly behaviour.

Increasing taxes or consumer prices is politically controversial and as a general rule does not go unchallenged. For this reason, policy-makers should be very explicit about the purpose of EFR measures and ensure that revenue expenditures are transparent. Revenues should generally be used for the highest national priority, as this is most likely to ensure sustained and broad political support for such reforms, particularly in critical times. The list below summarises recommended environmentally related taxes applicable to island states:

- taxes on energy consumption (fossil fuels and electricity), apart from taxes on RE;
- taxes on road transport fuels, domestic flights, domestic shipping, cooking fuels and fossil fuels used for electricity generation;[7]
- taxes on the import of cars, differentiated according to CO_2 emissions in g/km, fuel efficiency, engine size or import price (in this order of preference);
- annual circulation taxes on road vehicles, using a similar differentiation;
- water charges to ensure cost coverage and incentivise efficient water consumption;
- removal of levies on import of RE products and components;
- tourism taxes for the use of infrastructure (e.g. fixed fee per night) or introduction of an 'ecosystem contribution' for tourists (on arrival or departure);
- air ticket tax on all departing flights, differentiated according to flight distance and taxing first and business class higher than economy class; inclusion of freight transport.

Clearly, these measures cannot all be implemented at the same time—and not all measures will be feasible in all countries. Generally, all of these changes should be announced well in advance, giving stakeholders time to plan ahead, and should subsequently be implemented gradually in small steps. Policy-makers should prepare an appropriate communication strategy to ensure a broad and shared understanding of the rationale of the measures, to make the benefits of the measures clear, to facilitate changes in behaviour by communicating how economic actors can respond to changing prices and to inform which sectors and stakeholders are the beneficiaries of increased spending.

3.2 Subsidy Reporting and Subsidy Reform

Island countries are highly dependent on imports and spend a great deal of limited foreign exchange on fossil fuels. For this reason, they are extremely vulnerable to fluctuations in global fuel prices. This problem is compounded in those countries that subsidise fossil fuels, as an increase in global prices can result in a substantial—and unexpected—increase in government spending. Because prices of petroleum products in island countries are amongst the highest in the world, these fluctuations can have a particularly severe impact on small fossil fuel-dependent economies.[8] Perhaps in part as a result of this, awareness of the problem of energy dependence seems in general to be higher in island states than in many other countries. In some cases, this awareness might help foster an enabling environment for subsidy reforms and feed into government strategies to garner support and ensure that a reform is sustained in the long term.

Fossil fuel subsidies are not necessarily transparent or easy to identify or quantify. Often, the fiscal or environmental impacts of a particular measure have not been quantified at all. For this reason, regular subsidy reporting can be a useful tool. Subsidy reports should analyse all expenditures and subsidies and all reduced tax rates to evaluate whether they have, or could potentially have, negative impacts on the environment. Publishing such an analysis on a regular basis can help raise awareness of wasteful spending and the negative impacts of fossil fuel subsidies, and create a political consensus in favour of reform.

In Germany, for example, biannual reporting on general subsidies has taken place since the late 1960s, and was recently supplemented by regular reporting from the Federal Environmental Agency on environmentally harmful subsidies.[9]

If tax revenues are earmarked or ring-fenced, these links should be carefully analysed against environmental and sustainability criteria, as such links often reveal environmentally harmful subsidies, for example excise duties on road transport fuels that must be spent on road infrastructure.

Renewable energy transition can create an enabling framework for FFS reform, as in the case of El Hierro. El Hierro, the smallest of the Canary Islands was 100% dependent on fossil fuels in the 1990s, before it set itself the target of being the first 100% RE-powered island in the world. From 2012–2013, 12 MW of wind and 11 MW of pumped hydro power generation for energy storage were installed, alongside solar PV, to replace the 13 MW generators powered by heavily subsidised diesel. Already in the first year of operation, 70–80% of total electricity came from RE sources and the system uses diesel generators as a back-up only in times when there is no wind or hydro power available. In this case, the transition to RE generated massive savings owing to reduced expenditures on fossil fuel subsidies – which amounted to US$2.4 million in 2013 – as a result of reduced fuel use. It is estimated that revenues from the sale of RE will generate a further US$5.4 million each year.[10]

Thus, as the case of El Hierro shows, single large solar PV or wind farm facilities can account for a large proportion of total electricity consumed in smaller island states, and substantially reduce fossil fuel imports and subsidy expenditures.

Nonetheless, fossil fuel subsidy reforms are politically contentious processes and governments should prepare the ground well in advance. A roadmap for reform should develop a strategy for how, when and over what timescale to reduce subsidies. It is also essential that governments develop flanking measures to protect the vulnerable from the impact of rising prices.[11]

3.3   Protecting the Vulnerable

As a general rule, EFR will result in increased energy prices. Green taxes or subsidy reforms must be accompanied by flanking measures to ensure that vulnerable groups are protected from the impact of such price increases. This is important even in cases where many people are off-grid and rely mainly on fuel wood for their energy needs, because higher energy prices will have a knock-on effect on the prices of other commodities, including staple foods.

The following compensation measures could be considered:

- vouchers or green cheques, which can be distributed by local government or post offices;
- cash transfers, e.g. in Iran, compensation payments were paid into accounts set up for almost 80% of the population;
- provision of alternatives, e.g. LPG or solar stoves to replace kerosene;
- lifeline tariffs, i.e. zero or lower rates for first units of consumption, targeting the poorest households.

Compensation measures should minimise market distortions. The impact of rising energy prices should be visible and tangible to incentivise more energy-efficient behaviour, while compensation should ensure that the poor are not adversely affected. Programmes should also be temporary, targeted and tailored to minimise costs and prevent subsidy dependence.

3.4 Develop a Detailed Country-specific FFRE Strategy with Binding RE Targets

A clear, overarching FFRE strategy is essential as a basis for the development of effective, relevant, feasible and complementary RE policies. A country-specific strategy should start with an in-depth analysis of current fiscal policies, looking at all expenditures, subsidies and tax policies, particularly reduced tax rates and exemptions, to identify any negative environmental impacts and options to increase revenues. Planners should also undertake an in-depth analysis of the political economy of FFRE transition, identifying key political obstacles to transition and subsidy reforms, understanding key stakeholders and consider possible solutions.

The setting of renewable energy objectives should be guided by SMART binding targets: Specific, Measurable, Achievable, Relevant and Time-bound. The process should include as much of the following as possible:

- RE resource mapping and feasibility studies, clarifying what potentials exist and where;
- explicit R&D investment planning;
- exploration and exploitation of the potential of a range of RE sources;
- improvement and strengthening of the existing infrastructures (grids, transformer stations, meters), including RE sources as backup (e.g. hydro [pump] power, biogas);
- mobilisation of public and private capital for the energy sector, for example by providing low-interest loans for investors and/or high-interest funds for bond owners—in some cases, funds can help to finance such investments;
- improved availability of energy services;
- improved on- and off-grid energy access;
- investment in demonstration plants/projects.

3.5 Develop a Communication and Awareness-raising Strategy that Explains and Makes FFRE Attractive to as Many Stakeholders as Possible

RE transition is a gradual and incremental process. Policy-makers should look to easy, low-cost solutions to initiate a shift towards RE and reduced energy dependence—e.g. promotion of energy efficiency, or pilot projects to prove viability and foster acceptance of RE transition. Once it has been demonstrated that RE technologies are feasible, acceptance of RE policies and willingness to invest will increase, making the next steps easier.

The ultimate objective of RE policy formulation should be to develop a series of collaborative recommendations and strategies for FFRE transition that have been developed with a wide range of stakeholders and meet with broad acceptance within the country. Creating a sense of ownership can boost support and help ensure that energy transition policies are a success.

4.   DEVELOPMENT OF SOUND TRANSITION POLICY PACKAGES

4.1   Multi-faceted Environmental Problems

The complex nature of environmental problems is such that a single policy is not sufficient to effectively address all aspects of the problem. Instead, several policy instruments are required, each addressing one facet of the problem. One example might be a raft of measures to tackle several market failures, which may require better information flows, clearer property rights and internalisation of external costs. In this way, policy instruments can mutually underpin and complement one another.[12]

As a result, implementation of a complementary – but not overlapping – policy package is necessary to realise energy transition, for example, using taxation to create a level playing field in energy markets and regulation to create stable conditions for RE deployment by guaranteeing prices and grid access to investors.

4.2   Creating a Level Playing Field in Energy Markets

Environmental fiscal reform, as described in detail above, is the best means of guaranteeing full-cost pricing within energy markets and reducing distortions from non-internalised costs of fossil fuel combustion.[13] Fossil fuel combustion has a range of environmental and social costs – impacts on air and water quality, ecosystems, climate change and human health. Subsidy reforms and environmental taxes can internalise these costs in the price of fuels, avoiding them being borne by those who suffer most from the consequences of pollution. Correcting these market distortions improves conditions for RE and enables it to compete in energy markets, as it is not burdened by high pollution externalities. Alongside EFR – particularly when technologies are just starting out in the market – other policy measures can support RE technology deployment by fostering a stable investment climate, guaranteeing return on investment and reducing the cost of importing RE technologies.

4.3 Taxes and Other Instruments to Enhance Energy Efficiency

A natural complement to renewable energy transition is energy efficiency, which curbs demand and reduces the investment required in RE generation. Energy efficiency gives policy-makers the option to use savings on the deployment of renewables, for which upfront capital costs can be relatively high. Once RE generation facilities are operational, costs are often much lower than with fossil fuel-based plants (sometimes close to zero), as for wind, hydro and solar facilities. This means that the targeted deployment of RE combined with improved energy efficiency can significantly reduce the long-term costs of energy service.[14]

Energy efficiency can be incentivised by environmental fiscal reform, with both fossil fuel subsidy reform and increased energy taxation as a means of encouraging efficient behaviour through higher energy prices. Other measures to encourage behavioural change or facilitate technology transfer may include:

- differentiated import duties;
- efficiency standards;
- green procurement;
- incentives to make larger energy-saving purchases (low-cost loans, grants, etc.);
- feebate schemes—to eliminate or reverse price spread between more and less efficient appliances, in favour of energy efficiency;
- clear, compulsory energy efficiency labelling.

4.4 Instruments to Reduce Risk and Foster a Stable Investment Environment

Creating a stable low-risk investment climate for RE is essential to facilitate transition. There is evidence that commitment, stability, reliability and predictability can increase the confidence of market actors and reduce regulatory risk, which can have the knock-on effect of reducing the levelised cost of renewable electricity by 10–30%.[15] The policy instruments below are supportive of this aim:

- stable and enforceable contracts for electricity purchases (preferred grid access for RE);

- clear long-term policy and objectives;
- institutional support—including technical and training assistance;
- supportive infrastructure;
- streamlined permitting and grid connection procedures;
- credit or loan guarantees, insurance mechanisms to reduce cost of financing.

As with all sources of power generation, RE requires significant up-front investments, although facilities are much cheaper to run, with free RE resources, than fossil-fuelled power plants. Nevertheless, private investors are often deterred from island states, owing to their small energy markets and the resulting lack of economies of scale. Thus, not surprisingly, the bulk of energy foreign direct investment flows to island states thus far have been directed at a very few high- or upper-middle-income island states.[16]

Failure to access up-front finance for RE projects can act as a significant barrier to technology deployment. Thus, it is essential that governments foster an attractive and stable investment climate to appeal to private investors. Reducing risk, as discussed above, is an integral part of this process. However, creating an attractive investment climate for RE also requires a multi-aspect approach to FFRE transition policy. The International Renewable Energy Agency (IRENA) has developed a framework for attracting investments to islands, focussed on four priority areas: making attracting investment a political priority; creating a market framework for investment; introducing technical and integrated resource planning; and capacity building.[17]

The case of Cabo Verde highlights the benefits of a government commitment to renewable energy. In the country, a commitment has been made to cover 50% of total electricity supply from RE sources by 2020 and an effective and supportive structure has been introduced for market investment in RE, with power purchasing agreements for independent power producers of 15–20 years duration.[18] Cabo Verde has also tested innovative approaches to financing. The 2010 European Investment Bank and African Development Bank-funded project to design, build and operate onshore wind farms on four islands in the Cabo Verde archipelago exemplifies how innovative financing can provide for FFRE transition. The project is a public–private partnership held between the Cabo Verde government, a government-owned utility company, Electra and InfraCo, a publicly financed, privately managed company.[19]

On the other hand, in spite of the success of such innovative approaches, in Carbo Verde limited technical development and lack of capacity continue to act as a constraint on the island state for private investment and it will have to step up the pace of RE deployment if the 2020 target is to be reached—exemplifying the importance of all four elements of the IRENA framework to attract private investment to island states.

4.5 Exploring Regional Cooperation to Fund RE Transition

Renewable energy finance has boomed in the last decade, with $244 billion invested globally in 2012, of which $112 billion has been invested in non-OECD countries.[20] A key question for policy-makers in island states is how to exploit these opportunities.

It is difficult for island states to access international climate finance for a number of reasons. International donors tend to focus on larger emerging economies and often seem unaware of the special difficulties faced by island states, and of opportunities available to them. As a result, foreign development assistance to island states remains under-funded.[21] Furthermore, a major criterion for accessing climate finance is per capita income, rather than structural needs and vulnerabilities, which often puts island countries at a clear disadvantage.[22]

On the other hand, some barriers stem from within island states themselves. Scarce human resources may result in lack of institutional capacity to navigate the complex funding access criteria and application procedures. Some island states also lack in-country coordination systems necessary to monitor and enforce climate funds, or to report to donors in compliance with international fiduciary requirements.[23] Finally, lack of fiscal space and high levels of debt may also act as a barrier. The development of institutional capacity by the governments concerned, with assistance and facilitation by donors and international financial organisations, is a key enabling priority. One means of addressing this might be for island states to explore ways of cooperating and jointly applying for climate finance, enhancing their visibility with donors and making the most of their scarce human resources. This could reduce transaction costs and create opportunities to access higher levels of climate finance.

One possible strategy to attract renewable energy investment to island states would be to aggregate RE projects and develop new models of ownership. This could attract investors seeking larger-scale opportunities and enable island states to access more attractive terms and conditions for investments and, in so-doing, reap the benefits of economies of scale. An example of this has been documented in the US state of Massachusetts, which recently aggregated all municipal property to attract a large investor, identifying 10 MW of opportunities in solar PV and offering to develop the project at rates considerably below ongoing utility ones.[24]

At the same time, the 'traditional donor-based "North–South" partnership model' has been criticised, for example, by the Seychelles roving

Ambassador for Climate Change and SIDS, Roland Jumeau, for not living-up to the expectations of island states. Jumeau proposed instead exploring sustainability and energy transition financing from non-traditional sources, including the private sector, philanthropic trusts and foundations.[25] At the same time, there is also considerable potential for renewable energy in island states to be partly citizen or community owned and to generate substantial additional economic impacts for local communities.

Island states will also benefit from new coordinated and regional approaches to partnership and cooperation, including improved mechanisms for research, technology transfer and new approaches to financing FFRE transitions. Sharing innovative developments and research findings, as well as collaborating on research and pilot projects, could help all island states to advance their FFRE agendas and to develop RE-generation technologies appropriate to their specific contexts. The German Ministry for the Environment has carried out a feasibility study in Cabo Verde to design a wind electricity plant that would power sea water desalination whenever the wind blows and electricity is generated, thus using this fluctuating resource in a way that does not require grid integration—which can be a challenge, notably in island states. This is just one example of the development of island-appropriate technologies, from which all islands could potentially benefit.[26]

Island states could also consider regionally coordinating tax policies targeting the tourism industry. For example, air ticket taxes introduced unilaterally might be considered politically sensitive, particularly given the high dependency on tourism in many island states. However, an alliance between African and Indian Ocean island states, along with other countries in a similar situation, could be formed to coordinate air ticket taxation policies and implementation.

The Maldives have introduced a $6 per bed tax on tourism in November 2015, with revenues being used to fund waste management on the islands. If other island states were to follow suit, tax competition between countries would be reduced and any leakage of tourism in response to the tax would be minimised.[27]

5.   CONCLUSIONS

There is increasing focus and innovation in island states on RE, and for energy transitions along the 2030 Agenda for Sustainable Development adopted by the UN General Assembly in September 2015 (and previously referred to as the Post-2015 Agenda[28]). Many island states have drafted or adopted national and regional energy policies and strategies. They seek to improve energy efficiency and make use of their renewable solar, wind, ocean, geothermal, hydropower and biomass potential, notably to minimise future dependence on imported fossil fuels.[29] To ensure the success of FFRE transitions, however, key measures need to be followed up and implemented with determination, and as soon as possible.

Given that most island states have market economies, prices are crucial for investment and consumption decisions. Influencing prices via taxes and subsidies provides strong leverage for governments to change behaviour and reduce fossil fuel consumption. Moral appeals, information campaigns and awareness-raising may be important too, but are often not as effective as price signals, a key factor in household and business decision-making. Bearing these factors in mind, the challenge for island states today has shifted to how these countries can benefit from the falling price of renewable energy, as soon and as much as possible.

As always, context is vital and generalisations are only helpful to a limited extent. While the challenges faced by island states are often similar, best responses vary, and policy approaches need to be carefully tailored to the specific socio-economic and environmental conditions within each country. All island states need to identify sectors, actions and priorities in order to achieve their FFRE transition effectively and efficiently. Nonetheless, it is possible to make some general recommendations for island states on how to best undertake such transition.

5.1 Policy Mainstreaming and FFRE Transition Roadmaps

One clear and useful generalisation is that governments should mainstream FFRE transitions within all national policy planning processes, becoming part and parcel of national decision-making. In supporting this integration, planning authorities need to conduct RE resource mapping and feasibility studies, exploration of policy options and accurate modelling and cost–benefit analysis of FFRE transition impacts.

Beyond this macroeconomic review, a political economy analysis must also be undertaken, mapping the stakeholders of the energy landscape with their interests, strategies, resources, relations and discourses. Together, such comprehensive groundwork will enable a FFRE transition strategy based on realistic and sustainable assumptions, aimed at relevant objectives and guided by a clear time-bound roadmap of SMART indicators. It will also ensure that the politics of transition is well understood and planned for, nurturing a collaborative and participatory policy process that increases the chance of success and minimises disruption.

Further to such groundwork, the role of policy-makers in demonstrating the value of an RE transition is crucial. 'Low-hanging fruits' solutions should be identified, such as simple energy efficiency measures and high-return RE pilot projects that will reduce fossil fuel dependence, improve fiscal and trade balances, and quickly demonstrate the viability of the RE transition. Acceptance of RE policies and willingness to invest will increase, making subsequent steps easier.

5.2   Addressing FFRE Concerns

The need for a reliable base-load electrical supply has raised doubts about the feasibility of high levels of RE in the energy mix, particularly in small and unconnected island markets. As argued in the report, however, intermittence can be overcome through enhanced energy efficiency that reduces base-load demand, along with new grid management and storage technologies that buffer both various power sources and peak demand.

Another area of concern has been the recent falling prices of fossil fuels, perceived as a threat to RE value and viability. Falling prices can favour FFRE transitions in several ways, however. For one, low fuel prices create a political opportunity to reform subsidies, even eliminating them altogether, without public resistance—as recently seen in several countries, notably Indonesia, Malaysia and Mexico. Low prices also create opportunities for policy-makers to internalise fossil fuel externalities by introducing new taxes and keep prices stable—similarly, with little public resistance. Such measures increase national fiscal space, while levelling playing fields in energy markets, and incentivising investment in efficiency and RE. Finally, currently low fossil fuel prices result from overproduction and sluggish demand. This is not expected to last much beyond 2016 and possibly signals an era of widely unstable and unpredictable prices. This, in itself, is good news for investments in FFRE transitions, which offer structurally declining RE prices and predictable stability.

Overcoming other barriers—such as access to grants and climate finance from donors, and technology transfer—requires innovative approaches and greater regional coordination. There is great potential for island states to learn from each other's experiences, such as from the public–private funding model applied in Cabo Verde, and to tailor these approaches to their own particular country context.

5.3   Fiscal Space and EFR

To create an economic climate which fosters FFRE transitions, island states also need to adjust energy pricing in a way appropriate to their national context by means of EFR. Increased domestic revenue mobilisation (through environmental taxation and subsidy reform) can thus promote the FFRE agenda by increasing fiscal space and delivering much-needed revenues to meet critical spending needs.

Island states should also consider regionally coordinating and harmonising fiscal policies that leverage the tourism and aviation sectors. This could include a standardised levy per overnight stay, conservation fees or an infrastructure service charge paid on entry or exit. If taken unilaterally, such measures may encounter political resistance among industry stakeholders. Coordination among major destinations, for example of the Indian Ocean basin, will at least partly address concerns, and avoid a race to the bottom in the tax treatment of the two sectors.

Along those reforms, regular reviews of the fiscal system should be institutionalised to monitor and report on government revenues and expenditures. Impact assessments can then inform adjustments, particularly in protecting the vulnerable. Consistent communication strategies on the rationale and benefits of reforms will also help gain further acceptance.

5.4 Mobilising Investment

Creating a stable investment climate is essential to facilitate a FFRE transition. Policy measures should take the multi-faceted nature of energy markets into consideration and provide for:

- making mobilisation of private investment a political priority;
- creating a level playing field in energy markets through FFS reform and green taxation, including varied customs and duties on fossil fuel and RE technologies and components;
- introducing technical and integrated resource planning;
- supporting capacity development with institution building (e.g. nurturing relevant trade associations) and training of human resources (e.g. specialised RE skills);
- ensuring a good return on investment by means of feed-in tariffs and appropriate power purchasing agreements;
- facilitating access to RE solutions by fostering technology transfer and removing import duties on RE technologies and components;
- considering aggregating FFRE projects to develop new models of ownership between islands, taking advantage of economies of scale in the RE sector and reducing the cost of RE transition in each individual island state;
- reducing investment risk by making contracts clear and transparent, providing infrastructure and loan guarantees to instil investor confidence.

5.5 Working Together

Finally, island states should maximise the benefits of new coordinated and regional approaches to partnership and cooperation, including improved mechanisms for research, technology transfer and new approaches to financing FFRE transitions. Sharing innovative developments and research findings, as well as collaborating on research and pilot projects, could help all island states to advance their FFRE agendas and to develop island-appropriate technologies for RE generation.

NOTES

1.   The paper is broadly based on the following report: Cottrell, Jacqueline, François Fortier and Kai Schlegelmilch, 'Fossil Fuel to Renewable Energy: Comparator Study of Subsidy Reforms and Energy Transitions in African and Indian Ocean Island States', United Nations Office for Sustainable Development, Incheon, Republic of Korea, January 2015, available at http://www.unosd.org/content/documents/958FFRE%20 Islands%20Comparator%20Study%202015-02-02.pdf (accessed 4 December 2015). The report was researched and written by Jacqueline Cottrell and Kai Schlegelmilch. The introductory chapter on energy transitions and the United Nations Office for Sustainable Development fossil fuel to renewable energy policy support workshops was written by François Fortier, who also edited the report.
2.   The islands considered are Cabo Verde, Comoros, Madagascar, Mauritius, São Tomé and Príncipe, Seychelles, Sri Lanka and Zanzibar.
3.   The report also contains a series of country-specific recommendations for the island states that participated in a capacity-building workshop organised in Mauritius, in May 2014, by United Nations Office for Sustainable Development and the *Maurice Ile Durable* Commission. More details are available at http://www.unosd.org/index.php?pa ge=view&type=13&nr=22&menu=229 (accessed 1 July 2014).
4.   For a generic review of RE transition in island contexts, see also IRENA, 2013, Pacific Lighthouses. Renewable Energy Roadmapping for Islands, available at http://www. irena.org/DocumentDownloads/Publications/Pacific-Lighthouse-Roadmapping.pdf (accessed 10 May 2014). Although the focus is on the Pacific region, many of the conclusions apply more widely.
5.   World Bank, 2005, Environmental Fiscal Reform: What Should be Done and How to Achieve it?, p. 1.
6.   European Environment Agency, Market-based instruments for environmental policy in Europe, Report No. 8/2005, p. 84.
7.   An electricity tax incentivises energy efficiency, while input taxes on fossil fuels for electricity generation incentivise renewables (as they create a level playing field in energy markets) and efficient electricity-generation technologies.
8.   UNEP, UNDESA and FAO, 2012, SIDS-FOCUSED Green Economy: An Analysis of Challenges and Opportunities, available at http://www.unep.org/pdf/Green_Economy_ in_SIDS.pdf (accessed 22 April 2014).
9.   http://www.umweltbundesamt.de/publikationen/environmentally-harmful-subsidies-in-germany (accessed 12 June 2014).
10. IEA-RETD, 2012, Renewable Energies for Remote Areas and Islands, available at http://iea-retd.org/wp-content/uploads/2012/06/IEA-RETD-REMOTE.pdf   (accessed 5 May 2014), pp. 164–168.
11. The GSI Guidebook to Fossil Fuel Subsidy Reform for Policy-makers in South East

Asia provides a useful introduction to developing reform frameworks, available at http://www.iisd.org/gsi/sites/default/files/ffs_guidebook.pdf (accessed 21 August 2014).

12. Organisation for Economic Co-operation and Development, 2007, Instrument Mixes for Environmental Policy, OECD, Paris.
13. Above n. 10.
14. Above n. 12.
15. de Jaeger, D. and Rathmann, M., 2008, Policy Instrument Design to Reduce Financing Costs in Renewable Energy Technology Projects, study commissioned by IEA-RETD.
16. UNDESA, 2013, Financing for Sustainable Development in Small Island Developing States, available at http://sustainabledevelopment.un.org/content/documents/1153FFSD_SIDS_final.pdf (accessed 23 April 2014).
17. IRENA, 2014, Renewable Islands: Settings for Success, available at http://www.irena.org/DocumentDownloads/Publications/GREIN_Settings_for_Success.pdf (accessed 18 August 2014).
18. Above n. 17.
19. For details see e.g. http://eleqtra.com/projects/cabeolica-wind/ (accessed 5 May 2014).
20. UNEP, 2013, Global Trends in Renewable Energy Investment 2013, Frankfurt School-UNEP Centre/Bloomberg New Energy Finance.
21. Caribbean Development Bank, 2013, Financing Low Carbon Climate Resilient Development in the Caribbean, presentation at the 2013 High-Level Caribbean Forum, Nassau, Bahamas, by Selwin Hart, Climate Finance Advisor Office of the Vice-President, 20 September, available at http://www.imf.org/external/np/seminars/eng/2013/caribbean/pdf/selwin-hart.pdf (accessed 5 May 2014).
22. Above n. 13.
23. Above n. 21.
24. Above n. 13.
25. http://www.un.org/en/development/desa/newsletter/desanews/feature/2014/05/index.html (accessed 5 May 2014).
26. German Federal Ministry for the Environment, Nature Conservation and Nuclear Safety: Windbetriebene und regulierbare Meerwasserentsalzung auf Kap Verde [Wind-powered Seawater Desalinisation on Cabo Verde], MARIVENTO, unpublished feasibility study, Berlin, August 2011.
27. http://www.ttgasia.com/article.php?article_id=24482 (accessed 28 January 2015).
28. AIMS SIDS, 2013, http://sids-l.iisd.org/news/aims-states-outline-post-2015-priorities-for-sids/, https://sustainabledevelopment.un.org/index.php?menu=1300.
29. Above n. 7.

8. Using environmental taxation to improve outcomes for e-waste in Australia[1]

Wayne Gumley

1. INTRODUCTION

This chapter considers the role of environmental taxation as a regulatory response for dealing with the escalating cost of managing the disposal and recycling of end-of-life electrical and electronic products ('e-waste') in Australia. The e-waste problem presents a very clear example of a market failure requiring some form of government intervention. On the one hand the producers and distributors of electronic communication and entertainment products are amongst the most successful corporations in the global market place, providing consumers with an ever increasing range of exciting new gadgets, ranging from smart phones to photo-voltaic panels.[2] Meanwhile, the quantity of e-waste has grown rapidly and less than 16% is currently recovered for re-use, recycling or safe disposal.[3] In earlier times State and Territory governments commonly relied upon landfills to deal with most industrial, construction and household waste streams. The rapid growth in e-waste and a shift to recognising the economic value in waste streams has caused governments to re-think the traditional landfill approach. The Australian Federal Government recognised the need for a national approach, when it introduced a 'product stewardship' scheme for computers and televisions in 2011. The National Television and Computer Recycling Scheme (NTCRS) requires manufacturers and importers of televisions, computers and ancillary products to be responsible for collecting and recycling a prescribed proportion of those products when they are discarded by consumers at 'end-of-life'.

This chapter will first outline some quantitative aspects of the e-waste problem and then describe the regulatory measures that have been used to address this problem with particular focus upon the NTCRS. Observations from that analysis will then be used to suggest how environmental taxation strategies can be applied to overcome weaknesses in the current arrangements.

2. THE NATURE AND EXTENT OF THE PROBLEM

Human society is now profoundly committed to information technology with our lifestyles increasingly centred on electronic entertainment and communication devices. The rapid transition into the information age has provided numerous commercial and social advantages, but has also created new waste management challenges. A recent report by the United Nations University estimated that the total amount e-waste generated worldwide in 2014 was 41.8 million metric tonnes (Mt), and this was forecast to increase to 50 Mt by 2018.[4] That study also found that Australians produced about 20 kg of e-waste per capita in that year, placing Australia amongst the top tier of e-waste producers.[5] An earlier Australian report found that 106,000 tonnes (17 million units) of televisions, computers and peripheral equipment became e-waste in Australia in 2007–2008, with 84% going into landfill, 10% recycled and 6% exported.[6] The total volume of e-waste is expected to grow to 181,000 tonnes (44 million units) by 2027/2028.[7]

This rapid growth in e-waste poses not only a logistic problem for waste management agencies, but also a potentially serious public health hazard owing to the increasing range of metals and other toxic components that may leach out of e-waste within a landfill.[8] Another important aspect of this problem is the growing realisation that e-waste is not merely a community hazard, but also a potential resource that can create new economic opportunities.[9] Thus the recovery of valuable materials from e-waste is becoming an important part of the larger international commodity chain for metals. It has been estimated that about 12 Mt of metals were consumed in Australia during 2012–2013 (520 kg per person). Of that total, about 5 Mt accumulated as 'in-use' stocks of buildings and products, leaving about 7 million tonnes in the waste stream (300 kg per person). About 5 Mt was collected and recycled (and/or exported), 1 Mt became obsolete or degraded and 1 Mt was disposed of to landfill. The potential value of metals lost to landfill was estimated to be over $6 billion.[10] E-waste such as mobile phones and computer circuit boards contains a wide range of high-value metals (including copper, gold and silver), often at much higher concentrations than in virgin ore bodies.[11] It has been calculated that the market value of metals and other materials embedded in e-waste is on the order of $300–400 per tonne, but recovery may cost about $970 per tonne.[12] This cost barrier is reflected in a recent United Nations Development Programme report, which found that only around one-third of the 60 metals it studied had a recycling rate of 25% or more.[13]

There is also a strong resource security argument for better recovery of metals from waste streams, as the supply of many metals that are 'critical' for industrial development may become much more limited in future,[14] and our quantitative knowledge of this important economic constraint has been described as 'rudimentary' and 'totally inadequate'.[15] A related problem is that most of the high grade natural mineral deposits have been exhausted long ago, and thus mineral extraction processes must work with much lower ore grades which produce far greater waste and environmental degradation, whilst using much higher inputs of other vital resources such as energy and water.[16]

3. TRADITIONAL WASTE MANAGEMENT REGULATION IN AUSTRALIA

Historically, household and consumer waste management in Australia has been regulated by local and State and Territory agencies. The traditional model adopted a linear 'take–make–waste' approach that directed most solid waste into landfills, on the assumption that it had no economic value. The cost of this system was generally covered by property 'rates' paid by households to local government. More recently, a range of factors, including population growth and increasing volumes of waste per capita, have greatly increased the cost and external effects of managing landfill sites. Landfill levies have been introduced in most (but not all) States and Territories to discourage excessive dumping of solid waste. The levies have limited the volume of solid waste going to landfills, but have probably also contributed to illegal dumping and transhipment to unregulated sites in regional areas or non-levy jurisdictions. One clear benefit of landfill levies is that substantial revenue is raised, which can offset waste management costs and facilitate other environmental management programmes.[17] However, the landfill levy approach has minimal impact upon the dumping of smaller lightweight electronic products that are can be easily included in household waste collections (eg. used batteries). Bulkier forms of e-waste, such as computers and televisions create different problems (eg. lead content of glass screens), and as a consequence some State governments are now considering a ban on all e-waste in landfills.[18]

Most local governments have encouraged separation of the readily recyclable waste streams to assist recycling opportunities, including e-waste, paper, metals, glass, plastics and organic waste. These strategies have frequently been promoted through cooperation with non-governmental organisations and the charity sector.[19] Unfortunately, the scope for recycling is often limited by competition with industries using virgin raw materials at lower cost (eg. recycled metals compete with the traditional mining sector and cheap imports, recycled paper competes with subsidised forestry operations in native forests, recycled plastics compete with new plastic produced as a by-product of petro-chemical industry). Another market barrier is the effect of globalisation and free-trade policies that have facili-tated re-location of manufacturing and production facilities to developing countries with much lower input costs and less direct regulation of their operations. Countries like Australia are now major importers of most con-sumer goods, particularly the increasingly complex new lines of electronic goods. Thus the production processes, product design and material inputs of most new electronic products now occur at locations far away from the countries where they are consumed and discarded.

4. FEDERAL GOVERNMENT INTERVENTION IN WASTE REGULATION

Historically, the Australian Federal Government has been reluctant to intervene in waste management, despite judicial affirmations of its legisla-tive power across a wide spectrum of environmental issues.[20] However the global dimensions of the e-waste problem has prompted a range of Federal Government actions. Before the e-waste problem emerged, the 1989 *Basel Convention on the Control of Transboundary Movements of Hazardous Wastes and their Disposal* committed Australia to reduce the production of hazardous waste and to restrict its transboundary movements.[21] A few years later in 1992, the Federal Government released a National Waste Minimisation and Recycling Strategy.[22] By 2005, it was apparent that a stronger focus upon sustainability and conservation was required, and the Productivity Commission was instructed to review policy options, with a greater focus upon pricing and extended producer responsibility.[23] The Productivity Commission took a relatively narrow view in recommending that only local impacts should be addressed by pricing strategies, whereas 'upstream' issues such as resource conservation and climate change should be removed from this policy area altogether.[24] The Commission also argued that many existing measures such as the waste hierarchy, collec-tion targets and waste minimisation objectives should be replaced. The Government rejected most of the Commission's recommendations on the grounds that they were too theoretical, and a Senate Inquiry was instigated to provide a more workable approach.[25] The Senate Committee also found many defects with the current State and Territory arrangements on waste management and attributed many of the problems to the lack of a coordi-nating national policy.[26] A new National Waste Policy was developed and released in 2009, aiming 'to set a clear direction for Australia over the next 10 years, toward producing less waste for disposal, and managing waste *as a resource*' (emphasis added).[27] The cost issue was addressed by a guiding principle that 'participants in the product supply and consumption chain, rather than the general community, bear responsibility for the costs of resource recovery and waste management'. A longer-term objective was that, by 2020 'Governments, industry and the community have embraced product stewardship and extended producer responsibility approaches . . . leading to improvements in the design, longevity and disassembly of products, a reduction in hazardous content, less waste, and more thoughtful consumer choices'.[28]

One of the first Australian Government schemes to apply these principles was the *National Packaging Covenant*, introduced in 1999, which provided a voluntary framework for collaborative management of packaging waste across all levels of the supply chain.[29] This collaborative approach was more recently elevated into a broader legislative scheme under the *Product Stewardship Act* 2011 (Cth), which requires certain manufacturers and relevant parties to take responsibility for the environmental impacts of certain classes of products designated under the Act. In particular, any 'liable party' in relation to a designated class of products must become a member of an 'approved co-regulatory arrangement' (and thus subject to certain statutory obligations), or else be liable for civil penalties under s 18 of the Act.

Televisions and computers were the first products designated under the new Act,[30] following a Decision Regulatory Impact Statement that considered a range of regulatory options and ultimately recommended a co-regulatory scheme backed by Commonwealth legislative penalties. The NTCRS provides that television and computer suppliers are to be jointly responsible for collection of their products when discarded by consumers (including historic and orphan products).[31] Liable parties are defined as importers and manufacturers of televisions, computers, printers and peripherals, of over 5000 units of televisions, computers or printers, or over 15,000 units of peripherals per annum. Regulation 3.01(1) specifies the required outcomes of the co-regulatory arrangement, as:

(a) reasonable access to collection services in metropolitan, inner regional, outer regional and remote areas must be provided free of charge to households or small business;
(b) certain recycling targets for each product in the class must be met (as determined under Regulation 3.04); and
(c) from 1 July 2014 a material recovery target must be met (as determined under Regulation 3.06).

The NTCRS commenced operating from 1 July 2012 and the results of the first two years are summarised in Table 8.1. The table also shows the

Table 8.1   NTCRS targets and results for the first two years[32]

Year	Total waste arising (tonnes)	NTCRS collection target (tonnes)	Actual NTCRS collections (tonnes)
2012–2013	137,756	41,327 (30%)	40,813 (30%)
2013–2014	131,607	43,430 (33%)	52,736 (40%)
2014–2015	121,869	42,654 (35%)	Not yet reported

scheme target for the third year (2014–2015) but at the time of writing the results for that year have not been reported.

The early progress of the NTCRS has been investigated as part of a collaboration project between several Australian universities and Yale University funded by the Commonwealth Scientific and Industrial Research Organisation, called *Wealth from Waste*.[33] The following comments are partly based upon interviews with various NTCRS participants and other stakeholders conducted by the Monash team during the early stages of that project. It is clear that the legislated scheme targets have been met in the first two years of operation, including a significant 'over-achievement' by exceeding the collection target in 2014. Furthermore, the volume collected in the first year was nearly double the level occurring before the scheme commenced, estimated at 21,200 tonnes in 2009–2010. Despite those successes, it should be noted that up to 60% of disused televisions and computers are currently not being recovered under the scheme, leaving a substantial cost to be borne by governments and the broader community.

In the first year of the NTCRS five 'co-regulators' were engaged by the liable parties to satisfy the NTCRS requirements.[34] Each co-regulator was contracted to provide collection services for a particular group of liable parties, and thus they took no responsibility for handling any surplus e-waste from other sources. Interviews with several scheme participants indicated that in 2014 significantly more e-waste units were drawn into collection centres than was expected (particularly for televisions), which imposed a significant cost burden upon some co-regulators. This problem arose partly because the scheme set its original targets using a simplistic formula based on import records and a fixed assumption about product discard patterns. Whilst the collection targets for future years have now been adjusted upwards following an Operational Review of the NTCRS in 2015,[35] the reliance upon rigid weight-based targets may continue to present problems for co-regulators, as collection patterns are subject to many unpredictable factors. For instance, changes in broader economic conditions, technology innovations, product designs, product lifespans and consumer behaviour can all influence discard and re-use patterns. The combination of computers and televisions under the same target also creates some distortion as there are clear differences in technology trends and discard patterns. For example, a one-off change in television technology occurred when the Australian network shifted from analogue to digital systems over 2010–2013, which greatly accelerated disposal of many bulky analogue units. In computing there is a continuing trend away from large desktop computers to lighter and smaller laptop and tablet style units, with less weight and different material composition.[36] Even if the targets were better formulated, a more fundamental problem with the current NTCRS approach is its failure to encourage liable parties to deliver outcomes beyond the prescribed targets.

The material recovery target specified under Regulation 3.06 is set at '90% of television or computer products based on weight',[37] and the most recent annual reports by co-regulators indicate full compliance with this target. This target is currently a matter of some uncertainty as reporting requirements were not yet finalised at the time of writing. However resale values of the various materials extracted from e-waste are dependent upon global commodity markets and thus highly variable. One area of concern is that the recycling task is commonly carried out by a wide range of sub-contractors, and much of the recovered material is then exported for re-processing overseas, where little further scrutiny is possible.[38] A new joint Australian and New Zealand Standard (AS/NZS 5377:2013) has been established to set minimum requirements for the safe and environmentally sound handling of e-waste within Australia.[39] However, when e-waste or recovered materials is exported to poorly regulated 'dumping ground' countries, best practice cannot be guaranteed. Nevertheless, under the Basel Convention, Australia must ensure, *inter alia*, that any exported waste 'will be managed in an environmentally sound manner at the place of its destination'.[40] There is clearly a need for better monitoring of e-waste that is exported, including quantitative information on the degree, location and type of processing and recovery.

One clear achievement of the NTCRS is diversion of a substantial amount of e-waste from Australian landfills. However, the proportion of televisions and computers being diverted at present is only around 40% (increasing to 50% in 2015–2016) and the long-term target is 80% by 2026–2027. Thus the scheme deliberately apportions responsibility for e-waste between the liable parties and the broader community— particularly state and local government waste management agencies and various not-for-profit organisations engaged in this sector. The role of the not-for-profit organisations is important—in particular they have played an important role in brokering the re-use of discarded second-hand goods (including electronic goods) through second-hand stores and welfare programmes. This activity provides a highly desirable outcome from both an environmental and social equity viewpoint, by prioritising re-use over recycling, whilst also providing important work and community engagement opportunities for volunteers and disadvantaged citizens. Interviews with scheme participants suggest that the NTCRS has appropriated much of the e-waste previously directed to the not-for-profit sector, and thereby increased the flow of used electronics that are dismantled and/or exported rather than re-used as second-hand products in Australia.

Another observation from scheme participants is that shared responsibility under the NTCRS means that information gathering is fragmented and incomplete. There is a lack of transparency on both sides—it is not publicly revealed how much is being spent by liable parties in meeting the scheme targets, nor how much is being spent by local government and the broader community to deal with the rest of the problem. This seems to be a highly unsatisfactory method for dealing with a serious and rapidly growing environmental problem like e-waste. The liable parties and co-regulators do provide statistical information, but little is known about quantities handled outside the scheme. Privacy concerns and other personal factors cause many disused electronic products to be hoarded by households and businesses, whilst many others still go to landfills, or get dumped illegally (including material left at charity collection points). Another significant proportion is taken up by illegal trade to developing countries.[41] Unfortunately, the information systems that could provide better data on these missing streams of e-waste are weak. The 2009 National Waste Policy sought to address information gaps by establishing a comprehensive National Waste Report every three years. The first National Waste Report in 2010 provided a useful start,[42] but no follow-up reports have yet been issued, and the scope would need to be expanded to provide a better focus on e-waste. The Commonwealth's National Pollutant Inventory also provides a good framework for information of this type but is also too limited in scope, as much of its data is self-reported by industry with little or no verification.[43] Export data for e-waste from the shipping records for containerised international trade is also notoriously unreliable.[44] Another potentially useful information source would be the sales and product life-span data held by the manufacturers, importers and retailers, but they are understandably cautious about providing sensitive information that may be regarded as commercial-in-confidence.

5.   PRODUCT STEWARDSHIP AND THE ROLE OF ENVIRONMENTAL TAXATION

The National Waste Policy placed significant emphasis upon *product stewardship* and *extended producer responsibility*. These expressions are often conflated but they have quite different practical effects. Product stewardship is an expression that can be traced back to the Responsible Care Code developed by Canadian Chemical Producers Association, to embody a commitment by chemical manufacturers to exercise 'care' with respect to the health and environmental impacts of their products throughout their full life cycles.[45] That commitment stopped short of an undertaking of 'responsibility' for those impacts.[46] Thus in the USA (and Australia), product stewardship is commonly understood to involve shared responsibility for funding and operation, shared between all parties in the supply chain including government, industry and the community. By contrast 'extended producer responsibility' ('EPR') is a more demanding concept originating in Europe, which seeks to impose individual responsibility upon the product's manufacturer. Professor Thomas Lindhqvist, of Lund University, has described EPR as:[47]

> an environment protection strategy to reach an environmental objective of a decreased environmental impact of a product, by making the manufacturer of a product responsible for the entire life-cycle of the product and especially for the take-back, recycling and final disposal of the product.

In Europe, e-waste management programmes have been specifically promoted since 2002 by the EU Directive on Waste Electrical and Electronic Equipment (WEEE), which requires producers of waste electrical and electronic equipment to finance the collection and processing of end-of-life electrical and electronic products.[48] WEEE was supplemented by a directive for reduction in the use of hazardous substances in electrical products and a later directive on eco-design for energy related products.[49] The Australian NTCRS is broadly modelled on WEEE, but the scope of products covered is more limited and its recycling targets are considerably lower than the strongest EU schemes. Specific national schemes implemented under WEEE vary significantly across the EU. Whilst some EU countries have achieved collection rates above 60%, the average across all EU countries is only about 35%. This is still much better than Australia, which currently collects only about 9% of the total e-waste,[50] and was recently described as still 'in its infancy' in managing e-waste.[51] The weakness of the Australian scheme is difficult to understand, as there is extensive experience to call upon from more advanced regimes in the EU, Japan, Canada and the United States.[52]

Even in the more advanced countries, very few genuine EPR schemes have been established to date. Under political pressure from the manufacturers, most governments have shied away from individual producer responsibility and settled for collective stewardship approaches administered by an industry body.[53] This compromise undermines one of the most important objectives of EPR, the incentive for producers to change product designs to minimise external impacts.[54] The existing range of product stewardship schemes are thus failing to meet their most central aim, to ensure that external costs are properly managed.[55] Product stewardship and EPR schemes are both conceptually derived from the polluter-pays principle, which aims to internalise external impacts to the greatest extent feasible.[56] Environmental taxes and charges are often invoked as one of the most cost-effective mechanisms for internalisation.[57] They also provide the advantage of raising revenue for rectifying the relevant environmental harm—which stewardship schemes largely ignore. Environmental taxes are also one of the few mechanisms capable of harmonising environmental standards across jurisdictions, which is a highly relevant consideration in the global electronics industry. This can be achieved by using a tax or charge to compensate for lower environmental standards and subsidies in particular countries.[58] Environmental taxation has been endorsed by recent policy reviews in Australia and the UK.[59] Whilst carbon pricing has proven politically difficult in Australia owing to its impact on the resources sector, a similar approach to a problem arising mostly from imported goods should be far less controversial.

The Australian NTCRS was preceded by a Decision Regulatory Impact Statement process ('Decision RIS') completed in October 2009, which recommended the establishment of a co-regulated industry driven approach. In fact, the Decision RIS process found that a co-regulatory model was not the highest ranked option according to a cost–benefit analysis of all options. Interestingly, the most cost-efficient option was a mandatory Commonwealth levy to support a Government-run subsidy scheme to fund appropriate e-waste collection and recycling activities.[60] The reason given in the Decision RIS for rejecting a Commonwealth levy was speculation that this could be in conflict with the outcome of the Henry Review of the Australian Taxation System, which was in progress at that time.[61] In particular, it was suggested by the authors of the Decision RIS that one of the outcomes of the Henry Review would be that 'The Australian Government is expected to move away from specific levies to greater reliance upon broad based taxes'.[62] This appears to be a misguided view on both the role of the Decision RIS and the outcome of the Henry Review, which was completed in December 2009, but not released until May 2010.[63] The Henry Review provided numerous recommendations on tax reform, but was not a statement of government policy, and most importantly, it did not reject the use of specific levies to address environmental problems at all. To the contrary, it stated:[64]

> There is a strong case for governments to use policy instruments, such as taxation and regulation, to address market failures. Where some activities result in unintended costs being imposed on others (spill over costs), there may be a role for a tax or regulatory fee. A 'public bad' is an extreme form of negative spill over where the same 'bad' imposes costs on everyone.

The Henry Review also strongly endorsed the polluter-pays principle and the merits of using environmental taxes as a cost-recovery mechanism:[65]

> Cost recovery taxes should be levied on the parties who are best able to reduce the external costs of an activity. This is normally, but not necessarily, the parties whose activities impose costs on others.

In the context of e-waste, the external spill over costs are proportional to the toxicity of the material components and the ease of dismantling and recycling of a product, which are matters primarily within the control of manufacturers. As most of the relevant products are manufactured overseas, the role of Australian regulation in driving product design changes is very limited. The experience from Europe is that stewardship schemes like NTCRS that impose collective responsibility do not drive improvements in product design, and thus other regulatory interventions are necessary on that point.[66] Another important factor is consumer behaviour in disposing of electronic products. Regulation could be implemented to encourage better disposal patterns, such as bans on e-waste going into garbage, but these remedies may be difficult to enforce. Market-based instruments are strongly indicated in situations where a market failure occurs and direct regulation is difficult. The Henry Review noted that approaches implementing the polluter-pays principle are preferable on both efficiency and equity grounds. These can include environmental taxes, permit-trading schemes, tax concessions and establishment of private property rights, with the choice of instrument based upon maximising the net benefit to society.[67]

Many policy discussions in this area become distracted, and even defeated, at this point by attempting to identify who is the most appropriate 'polluter' and to quantify precisely what amount of environmental cost has been incurred. E-waste is a multi-faceted problem with numerous causes and many undefinable costs. From a practical point of view, the more immediate problem is to provide sufficient funding to ensure the diversion of all e-waste from landfills in an ecologically responsible manner. The Henry Review recognises that it is appropriate in such circumstances to depart from theoretical design principles and simply impose the tax burden upon those best able to ameliorate the harm. Manufacturers, importers and consumers of electronic goods are clearly the most appropriate parties to bear the burden of an environmental charge in this case. It is significant to note that the dominant players in electronics are large and profitable corporations, like Apple, Microsoft, IBM, Samsung and Google, who are all ranked in the top 20 corporations worldwide based on market capitalisation.[68]

The Decision RIS found that a Commonwealth Government levy would be the most cost-effective option. Such a levy could be applied to all sales of electronic products and thus easily administered in similar fashion to the Australian Goods and Services Tax system (and perhaps as part of that system). The rate could be set to recover enough revenue to ensure that 100% of e-waste is diverted from landfills, and recycled in an environmentally responsible manner. The best way to apply those funds is beyond the scope of this chapter, but this could be managed through an 'E-waste Reduction Fund' using an auction process similar to the Australian Government Emissions Reduction Fund, which is the centrepiece of its action to reduce greenhouse emissions.[69] This new Commonwealth levy could either supplement or fully replace the current NTCRS, and it would extend to all electronic products, not just televisions and computers. Funding could be made available to enhance the roles of all current players in the e-waste commodity chain, including local government, charities and commercial operators.

6. CONCLUSIONS

This chapter has reviewed the design and effectiveness of the NTCRS scheme for e-waste management in Australia against the principles of extended producer responsibility. The NTCRS requires manufacturers and importers of certain products to fund collection and recycling of a prescribed proportion of the relevant end-of-life products. Whilst the NTCRS improves upon the outdated landfill-oriented framework at State and Territory level, it fails to impose individual responsibility upon manufacturers of electronic products for the ultimate life cycle impacts of all of their products, and thus little or no mechanism for driving improvements in product design that would minimise e-waste hazards and maximise recovery of valuable material resources.[70] This weakness is difficult for national governments to overcome in an industry dominated by transnational corporations. A more effective approach would be to apply environmental taxation principles to ensure that sufficient funding is available to properly manage all e-waste impacts at a local level, by contrast with the limited coverage of the NTCRS. Thus it is recommended that Australia should introduce a national levy upon all electronic products to create an 'E-waste Reduction Fund' that would enable to more comprehensively deal with the growing environmental impacts of electronic waste.

NOTES

1. This paper is based upon a presentation made to the *16th Global Conference on Environmental Taxation*, University of Technology Sydney, Australia, 23–26 September 2015.
2. Five knowledge-intensive services industries and five high-technology manufacturing industries represented 29% of world gross domestic product in 2014; see National Science Board, Science and Engineering Indicators 2016, p. 6–4, available at: <http://www.nsf.gov/statistics/2016/nsb20161/uploads/1/9/chapter-6.pdf>.
3. Baldé, C.P., Wang, F., Kuehr, R., Huisman, J., 2015. The global e-waste monitor—2014, United Nations University, IAS-SCYCLE, Bonn, Germany. See also Nnorom, I.C. and Osibanjo, O., 2008. Overview of electronic waste (e-waste) management practices and legislations, and their poor application in developing countries. *Resources, Conservation and Recycling*, 52, 843–858.
4. Above note 3, Baldé et al.
5. Above note 3, Baldé et al., at 62.
6. PricewaterhouseCoopers and Hyder Consulting, 2009. Decision Regulatory Impact Statement: Televisions and Computers (Environment Protection and Heritage Council, October).
7. Australian Government, 2014. National Television and Computer Recycling Scheme Outcomes 2012–13 (Department of Environment, February).
8. Frazzoli, C., Mantovani, A. and Orisakwe, O.E., 2011. Electronic waste and human health, in Nriagu, J.O. (editor) *Encyclopaedia of Environmental Health*. Amsterdam: Elsevier, 2011. See also Sthiannopkao, S. and Wong, M.H., 2013. Handling e-waste in developed and developing countries: initiatives, practices, and consequences. *Science of the Total Environment*, 463, 1147–1153.
9. Kama, K., 2015. Circling the economy: resource-making and marketization in EU electronic waste policy, 47.1 Area 16–23.
10. Golev, A. and Corder, G., 2014. Global systems for industrial ecology and recycling of metals in Australia: Research report. Prepared for Wealth from Waste Cluster, by the Centre for Social Responsibility in Mining, Sustainable Minerals Institute, The University of Queensland, Brisbane.
11. Doran, M., 2014. Researchers worried precious metals lost in e-waste recycling. ABC News 10 June 2014 <http://www.abc.net.au/news/2013-06-13/researchers-worried-precious-metals-lost-in-e-waste-recycling/4750774>.
12. Environment Protection and Heritage Council, 2009. Decision Regulatory Impact Statement: Televisions and Computers (PWC/Hyder, October).
13. UNEP, 2011. International Resource Panel Recycling Rates of Metals—a status report.
14. Chen, W. and Graedel, T.E., 2012. Anthropogenic cycles of the elements: a critical review. *Environmental Science and Technology*, 46, 8574–8586.
15. Ibid.
16. Mudd, G.M., 2012. The environmental sustainability of mining in Australia: key mega-trends and looming constraints. *Resources Policy*, 35, 98–115.

17. In Victoria, the landfill levy has been used to contribute to the funding of its Environment Protection Authority.
18. State of Victoria, 2015. Managing e-waste in Victoria; Starting the conversation (Department of Environment, Land, Water and Planning, August).
19. For example, the statutory authority Sustainability Victoria was established in 2005 to facilitate and promote statewide waste management strategies and planning <http://www.sustainability.vic.gov.au/who-we-are>.
20. The Federal Government famously established its constitutional power to override State laws on environmental grounds in the 1983 Tasmanian Dams case; see *The Commonwealth v Tasmania* [1983] HCA 21; (1983) 158 CLR 1.
21. United Nations, 1989. Basel Convention on the Control of Transboundary Movements of Hazardous Wastes and Their Disposal, 22 March, 28 I.L.M. 657, 1673 U.N.T.S. 57 <http://www.basel.int/text/con-e.pdf> [hereinafter the Basel Convention]. *The Hazardous Waste (Regulation of Exports and Imports) Act 1989* (Cth) was enacted to implement these obligations, as well as various guidelines for transfer of hazardous waste between States and Territories, see National Environment Protection Council, 2010. National Environment Protection (Movement of Controlled Waste Between States and Territories) Measure; Vol. F2012C00780.
22. Commonwealth Environment Protection Agency, 1992. National Waste Minimisation and Recycling Strategy. Dept of Environment Sport and Territories.
23. Productivity Commission, 2006. Waste Management, Report no. 38, Canberra.
24. Above note 23, at Recommendation 10.3.
25. The Senate Standing Committee on Environment, Communications and the Arts, 2008. Report on Management of Australia's Waste Streams (including consideration of the Drink Container Recycling Bill 2008, September).
26. Above note 25, at 2–4.
27. Australian Government, 2009. National Waste Policy; Less Waste More Resources (Environment Protection and Heritage Council), at 3.
28. Above note 27, Outcome 8, at 8.
29. National Environment and Heritage Council, 1999. Used packaging materials— National Environment Protection Measure (July 1999), subsequently replaced by the *Australian Packaging Covenant* established under National Environment Protection (Used Packaging Materials) Measure 2011, F2011L02093.
30. *Product Stewardship (Televisions and Computers) Regulations 2011* (Cth).
31. Ibid., Division 2.1.
32. Australian Government, 2014. National Television and Computer Recycling Scheme Outcomes 2012–13 (Department of Environment, February) and Australian Government, 2015. National Television and Computer Recycling Scheme Outcomes 2013–14 (Department of Environment, June 2015).
33. The Wealth from Waste Cluster consists of the University of Technology Sydney, Monash University, The University of Queensland, Swinburne University of Technology and Yale University (USA). Further details of this project can be found at the project website <http://wealthfromwaste.net/> and the Monash University team's website <http://artsonline.monash.edu.au/wfw/>.
34. The five co-regulators under the scheme in 2013–2014 were: Australian and New Zealand Recycling Platform Limited (ANZRP), DHL Supply Chain (Australia) Pty Ltd, Ecycle Solutions Pty Ltd, Electronics Product Stewardship (Australasia) (EPSA) and Reverse E-waste.
35. Australian Government, 2015. National Television and Computer Recycling Scheme— Changes to the Scheme (Department of Environment, Factsheet).
36. A report by Wright-Rawtec, which informed much of the scheme design, had fore-shadowed that the changing technology of televisions owing to the transition away from bulky analogue CRT models to digital units, with larger but flatter LCD and plasma screens would have a significant effect on collection requirements; see Wright Corporate Strategies and Rawtec, 2010. A study of Australia's current and future e-waste

recycling infrastructure capacity and needs <http://www.environment.gov.au/protection/national-waste-policy/publications/australias-current-and-future-ewaste-recycling-infrastructure-capacity-and-needs>.

37. *Product Stewardship (Televisions and Computers) Regulations 2011* (Cth), Reg 3.06.
38. For example, see Ecycle Solutions Annual Report 2014, 5.
39. Standards Australia, 2013. AS/NZS 5377:2013 Collection, storage, transport and treatment of end-of-life electrical and electronic equipment.
40. Above note 21, at Article 4, para 8.
41. Boudier, F. and Bensebaa, F., 2011. Hazardous waste management and corporate social responsibility: illegal trade of electrical and electronic waste. *Business and Society Review*, 116(1), 29–53.
42. Australian Government, 2010. National Waste Report 2010 (Environment Protection and Heritage Council).
43. National Environment Protection Council, 1998. National Environment Protection (National Pollutant Inventory) Measure 1998—F2008C00620. The NPI database is available at: <http://www.npi.gov.au/>.
44. Birnbauer, W., Russel, M. and Hudson, P., 2005. Ports wide open to drug trafficking. *The Age*, 5 June 2005 <http://www.theage.com.au/news/National/Ports-wide-open-to-drug-trafficking/2005/06/04/1117825104828.html>.
45. Lewis, H., 2005. Defining product stewardship and sustainability in the Australian packaging industry. *Environmental Science and Policy*, 8:1, 45–55.
46. Ibid., 49.
47. Lindhqvist, T., 2000. Extended producer responsibility in Cleaner Production. IIIEE Dissertation 2000:2 (International Institute for Industrial Environmental Economics, Lund University).
48. European Parliament, 2003. Directive 2002/96/EC of the European Parliament and of the Council of 27 January 2003 on waste electrical and electronic equipment (WEEE), subsequently replaced by Directive 2012/19/EU of the European Parliament and of the Council of 4 July 2012 on waste electrical and electronic equipment (WEEE).
49. European Parliament, 2003. Directive 2002/95/EC Restriction of Hazardous Substances; and European Parliament, 2009. Directive 2009/125/EC, which established a framework for the setting of eco-design requirements for energy-related products (Ecodesign Directive).
50. Baldé et al., note 3 above.
51. The Economist Intelligence Unit, 2014. Global e-waste systems; insights for Australia from other developed countries (February 2015).
52. Organisation for Economic Co-operation and Development, 2014. The state of play on extended producer responsibility (EPR): opportunities and challenges (Issues paper for Global Forum on Environment: Promoting Sustainable Materials Management through Extended Producer Responsibility, at Tokyo, 17–19 June 2014).
53. Tojo, N., 2003. EPR programs: individual vs. collective responsibility (IIEE Reports 2003:8). Above note 52.
54. Ibid., 66–69.
55. Huisman, J., 2013. Too big to fail, too academic to function; producer responsibility in the global financial and e-waste crises. *Journal of Industrial Ecology*, 17:2, 172–174.
56. Organisation for Economic Co-operation and Development, 1996. Pollution prevention and control extended producer responsibility in the OECD Area Phase 1 Report (OCDE/GD(96) 48, Paris 1996.
57. Pigou, A.C., 2013. *The Economics of Welfare*. Palgrave Macmillan (originally published 1938).
58. Hunter, D., Salzman, J. and Zaelke, D., 2002. *International Environmental Law and Policy* (2nd edn). New York: Foundation Press, 412.
59. Garnaut, R., 2011. *The Garnaut Review 2011: Australia in the Global Response to Climate Change*. Cambridge University Press. Henry Review Panel, 2009. Australia's future tax system, Report to the Treasurer. Mirrlees, J. and Adam, S., 2011. *Tax*

    by Design: The Mirrlees Review. Oxford University Press <http://www.ifs.org.uk/publications/5353>.

60. PricewaterhouseCoopers and Hyder Consulting, 2009. Decision Regulatory Impact Statement: Televisions and Computers (Environment Protection and Heritage Council, October).

61. The Australian Government announced a comprehensive review of Australia's tax system in the 2008–2009 Budget, to be chaired by Treasury Secretary Dr Ken Henry, with Terms of Reference described at: <http://taxreview.treasury.gov.au/content/Content.aspx?doc=html/reference.htm>.

62. Above note 60, at para 9.10, at 169.

63. Commonwealth of Australia, 2009. Australia's future tax system; Report to the Treasurer, December 2009.

64. Ibid., 336.

65. Ibid., 339.

66. Above note 54.

67. Above note 63, at 344–347.

68. Financial Times Global 500 Rankings <http://www.ft.com/indepth/ft500> (accessed 2 February 2016).

69. Implemented under the *Carbon Farming Initiative Amendment Act 2014* (Cth) <https://www.environment.gov.au/climate-change/emissions-reduction-fund/about>.

70. Tojo, N., above note 53. See also Lindhqvist, T., 2000. Extended producer responsibility in cleaner production: policy principle to promote environmental improvements of product systems, No. 2. Lund University.

9. The *ad unit* and *ad valorem* tax burden shifting and its impact on Pigovian taxation in the European Union Member States

Danuse Nerudova and Marian Dobranschi

1. INTRODUCTION

The chapter is concerned with the process of tax shifting of the indirect taxation imposed on transport fuels and the interaction with the Pigovian principle that underlines corrective levies such as environmental taxation. In order to emphasize the potential threats to environmental taxation, this study relies on both theoretical and empirical analysis of the market reaction to the modifications of corrective taxation rates.

While the theoretical part focuses on the debate regarding the process of tax shifting, the empirical research is based on analyzing the impact of *ad valorem* and *ad unit* taxes on transport fuel retail prices, aiming to determine the size of tax burden shifting, considering this process as the main trigger driving tax incidence. Consequently, the chapter tries to establish a connection between tax shifting and its impact on the fundamental rationale of corrective taxation. The starting point relies on the analysis of excise duties as an instrument of choice, which we assume to be the appropriate proxy for environmental taxation. The most important similarity is that environmental taxation bears the same characteristics as excise duties for commodities such as alcohol, cigarettes and transport fuels. The main purpose of levying these selective taxes is to discourage individuals from the consumption of harmful goods in order to decrease the associated negative externalities; however, nowadays these fiscal instruments represent a tool for raising revenues to the public budget. The rationale behind fossil fuel excise tax (mainly gasoline and diesel excise duty) is to preserve oil resources, decrease pollution and protect the environment. Therefore, we understand environmental taxation as an excise duty-wise corrective tax.

In order to produce a solid background for empirical analysis, the research reviews previous papers that have assessed the impact of excise duties on retail prices, observing in particular the process of tax burden shifting. The main scope of empirical analysis is to identify whether the tax burden is shifted more than fully in the case of indirect taxes on fuels, in order to point out the potential threat to the efficiency of environmental taxation. The tax burden can be shifted forward or backward depending on the sensitivity of supply and demand to price changes. Our research aims to identify whether overshifting occurs, indeed whether the increase in retail prices is higher than that in excise duty.

The first part of the chapter covers the review of literature regarding tax shifting and the second part provides empirical analysis employing panel data analysis. In comparison with the current literature, our chapter represents the first study to establish a connection between potential overshifting of the tax burden in the case of indirect taxation on transport fuels and the effects on the Pigovian principle that underlies the corrective taxation. Even though there are studies primarily aimed at the issue of overshifting in the case of unleaded gasoline and diesel, their assessment ignored the impact of overshifting on the rationale that governs the Pigovian environmental taxation.

2. LITERATURE REVIEW

The literature identifies two opposite directions that determine how the tax burden is shifted in the taxation theory—backward shifting, where the tax burden is transferred through a purchase transaction, and forward shifting, where the tax burden is shifted through sale transaction, also known as onward shifting.

The issue of tax shifting has been analyzed in detail by various studies, which point out the difference between the concepts of shifting and tax incidence. One important view argues that the shifting of tax is the process and tax incidence is the result, where the changes in the distribution of wealth are the final effect.[1] Therefore, the debate regarding the incidence depends on the investigation of tax shifting. The true tax incidence can only be identified when it is possible to determine how and why the tax is shifted. Therefore the tax incidence varies according to different forms of demand inelasticity. The demand may be assumed to be inelastic in the sense of being constant, meaning that it always remains the same or it may be assumed to be inelastic in the sense that any attempted increase completely distorts the initial demand.[2]

The idea of iso-elastic or constant demand is an analogy of invariable or inelastic demand. In the case of invariable demand, a tax introduction will raise the price with the amount of the tax, and the final consumer will bear the full tax burden. The incidence of the tax is considered as the result of the shifting process, and the true economic issue stays in the nature of this process.[3] The literature underlines that, through the process of shifting, the initial tax payer, or the statutory incidence established by law, manages to escape the tax burden.[4] Other research papers analyze the process of tax shifting in the conjectural variations of oligopoly settings.[5] The concept of conjectural variations refers to the pattern of how companies interact between themselves and how tax incidence can be measured.

Generally, it is considered that overshifting occurs owing to market power and strategic behavior between companies.[6] In a situation when the company shifts the tax burden forward by increasing the price level, the demand for its products will decrease, thus overshifting appears as a method to compensate for the revenue loss from the decreased demand as an effect of tax imposition. The process of overshifting occurs most often if the demand elasticity with regard to price fluctuation is relatively inelastic. Analyzing the different impact of *ad valorem* and *ad unit* taxation impact on welfare, another study[7] considers that, in an imperfect competitive economy, it is not the presence of profits *per se* that leads to allocation distortions but rather the pricing policy that supports these profits. The same conclusion has been reached in an early paper, where the author[8] states that an excise tax may increase profits if the demand elasticity (e.g. slope of demand) is sufficiently low. In conclusion, the literature considers that 'taxes tend to be borne by inelastic suppliers or demanders'.[9] Hence, the tax burden is supported by those who cannot easily adjust in response to price increases.

The theoretical literature focusing on the forward shifting of taxation is scarce and becomes even more limited when we concentrate on the empirical analysis that analyzes the overshifting of the tax burden. However, there are research papers that analyze the tax shifting of excise duties that cover relatively large numbers of commodities.

The process of tax shifting was analyzed taking into account various tax instruments. One research paper[10] analyzes the tax overshifting in nineteenth-century Prussia, focusing mainly on the milling and slaughter tax. The results obtained in this research show that overshifting occurred, creating notable distortions; these levies were most regressive in those times. Concerned with the same issue, another study performed an extensive empirical analysis on sales tax shifting in retail prices in the US, covering commodities prices from more than 155 US cities for the period 1982–1990.[11] The results obtained show that in most cases the tax burden was one-for-one shifted to final consumers. In some cases, owing to the imperfect competitive markets, the overshifting of sales tax burden was identified. The literature[12] also focused on the comparison between *ad valorem* and *ad unit* taxation. This comparison was empirically applied using the data regarding the European cigarette industry. The results obtained show that, in countries where there is a greater reliance on *ad valorem* taxes, full shifting of the tax burden and overshifting of specific taxation appears. The main conclusion is connected with an earlier paper,[13] where in the case of specific (i.e. unit) taxation, overshifting is more likely to occur with a greater impact on prices than *ad valorem* tax. This chapter underlines some notable theoretical concerns and special attention should be paid to the interdependence between overshifting and the regressive impact of taxes. The excise duty on tobacco was analyzed in the literature, with the objective of calculating the amount of tax shift in the case of cigarette consumption of occasional and daily smokers.[14] The authors[15] found that the burden of taxation was shifted at high rates, above 100%, onto non-daily smokers in comparison to addicted smokers.

Another study[16] analyzed the shifting of excise duties increase on alcohol beverages in the last quarter of 1997 in various US cities. The findings of this chapter conclude that, in the case of beer, spirits and wine tax, overshifting occurs. An important contribution to the literature was made by a study focused on the impact of excise duty increase on alcohol in Alaska.[17] This research found that in all cases of excise tax rate increase, the tax burden was overshifted toward end-consumers. The analysis of the process of tax shifting was made for both perfect competitive and imperfect markets. In the case of perfectly competitive markets with constant marginal costs, the results showed that taxes were shifted one-for-one to the final price, meaning that there was a full shifting of tax burden. On the other hand, in the case of imperfect competition, owing to the market structure and demand conditions, the tax burden was overshifted every time the state increased the excise tax for alcohol with 1 cent ranging from 1 to 4 cents on prices faced by end-consumers.[18] In a more recent study,[19] the research focused on the shifting of tax for six examples of excise tax increase on alcohol in Denmark. The results of this study were consistent with those in an earlier paper,[20] where overshifting of the tax burden was also identified. The literature considers that the process of overshifting strictly depends on factors such as the elasticity of demand function, the relative slopes of the marginal cost, the number of companies and their market power, and also the cost of entry.[21] If the demand curve is sufficiently convex then overshifting will occur and the main assumption that supports this argument is that the demand curve is steeper than the marginal revenue curve. Therefore, if the individual demand curve is linear, it is easily shown that the market demand curve is convex, and overshifting of tax burden will take place. The results obtained by Bergman and Hansen[22] showed that, in the period 1997–2005, with six episodes of tax increase on alcoholic beverages, the tax burden was either fully or overshifted toward end-consumers.

In the case of the fuel market, it is important to mention the contribution of a study[23] that analyzed excise tax incidence in the retail gasoline market for all 50 US states. The authors assumed a perfect competition model where the tax burden is fully shifted to consumers. In highly urbanized cities the authors identified the overshifting of excise duty on gasoline. Approaching from a different angle the issue of tax burden shifting, the literature underlines that there is a high potential for introducing a tax swap mechanism between payroll taxation and environmental levies.[24] Another empirical paper[25] performed a detailed analysis on fuel tax incidence, mainly on diesel and gasoline in the US market. Using a 20 year span of data from more than 23 states, the authors concluded that the excise duties for transport fuel were fully or 'potentially' more than fully shifted to final consumers.

In an earlier paper,[26] the incidence of both federal and state gasoline taxes was analyzed in the US. The results show that the federal state taxes imposed on gasoline consumption are equally supported by consumers and wholesalers. Compared with federal excise duty, the state gasoline tax burden falls primarily on consumers, to whom the tax burden tends to be overshifted. The latest study[27] on tax burden shifting analyzed the rate of pass-through in the case of state diesel taxes and used changes in tax collection regime as a primary explanatory factor. The authors found that the pass-through rate was higher if the point of tax collection was moved to the supplier level. Additionally, the rate of pass-through tended to increase when the state decided that the tax should be remitted by the distributor compared with when it was remitted by the retailer. They concluded that the tax burden pass-through rate rises as the tax collection is moved up the supply chain. In comparison with the above-mentioned study,[28] an earlier paper[29] found that the excise duties for transport fuel were fully or 'potentially' more than fully shifted to final consumers.

3.   DATA AND METHODOLOGY

The panel data analysis is based on the data provided by European Commission Oil Bulletin that includes weekly data on the retail price of unleaded gasoline and diesel and also the package of indirect taxation applied to these commodities. The data for crude oil price are based on Spot Price Europe Brent provided by US Energy Information Administration (US EIA). Our empirical analysis is based on 21 European Union countries: Austria, Belgium, Czech Republic, Denmark, Estonia, Germany, Greece, Finland, France, Hungary, Ireland, Italy, Luxembourg, Netherlands, Poland, Portugal, Spain, Slovenia, Slovakia, Sweden and the UK, for the period between 2005 and 2014. In order to estimate the tax burden shifting we follow the model used in research papers that analyzes the *ad valorem* and specific taxation under imperfect competition[30] and the model proposed by previous empirical research on tax burden shifting in the case of tobacco taxation.[31] In this multiple variable regression, the dependent variable represents the average weekly before-tax and after-tax retail price of transport fuels (e.g. unleaded gasoline and diesel) and the independent variable represents the excise duty rate and the Value Added Tax (VAT) rate for each fuel. To this independent variable, we add also as a control variable—the weekly price of crude oil as one of the most important determinants of transport fuels retail price.

The dependent variable represents the real tax-inclusive and tax-exclusive retail price of fuels (e.g. gasoline and diesel). The independent variables are the excise duties and the price of crude oil, which serve as the main factors that determine the retail price of fuels in the analyzed countries. Our methodology follows the model proposed by previous papers that analyzed excise duty on gasoline shifting[32] and the impact of *ad valorem* and per unit taxes on retail prices.[33] Our research is based on two important assumptions. Firstly, we assume that there is no tax evasion in the case of a fuel excise duty. Secondly, to eliminate the problem of endogeneity, we assume that the state increases the excise tax rate to reduce pollution, regardless of the fuel price fluctuations.

Regressing the tax-inclusive and tax-exclusive prices of fuels to the tax rates (e.g. excise duties and VAT), the obtained coefficient represents the share of the tax burden that is borne by the final consumers. Based on this, we can interpret the results of the analysis as follows. If the obtained coefficient for excise duty impact on the price of fuels is equal to one, then there is a full shifting of the tax burden, through prices, towards end-consumers. If the obtained coefficient is less than one, then the tax burden is shared between sellers and buyers. Finally, if the obtained coefficient is higher than one, then the tax burden is overshifted towards the final consumers. We expect the tax burden applied on the consumption of fuels (e.g. gasoline and diesel) to be overshifted. One explanation of our expectation is the fact that a new tax rate increase will diminish the demand in the long run by increasing the prices; as a consequence, the retailers will increase the price by more than the tax rate to compensate for future losses owing to lower demand. Another explanation for tax burden overshifting is the highly concentrated markets of fuel retailers, where the industry is dominated by a few large players that are price makers and, in the context of a tax increase, tend to behave like a monopolist.

The estimation equations can be described as follows:

$$beftaxprice_{i,t}^g = \alpha_{i,t} + \beta_1(crude_{i,t}) + \beta_2(excise_{i,t}^g) + \beta_3(VAT_{i,t}^g) +$$
$$\beta_4(Interaction_{i,t}^g) + \delta_{i,t} + \varepsilon_{i,t} \tag{1}$$

$$aftertaxprice_{i,t}^g = \alpha_{i,t} + \beta_1(crude_{i,t}) + \beta_2(excise_{i,t}^g) + \beta_3(VAT_{i,t}^g) +$$
$$\beta_4(Interaction_{i,t}^g,1) + \delta_{i,t} + \varepsilon_{i,t} \tag{2}$$

$$beftaxprice_{i,t}^d = \alpha_{i,t} + \beta_1(crude_{i,t}) + \beta_2(excise_{i,t}^d) + \beta_3(VAT_{i,t}^d) +$$
$$\beta_4(Interaction_{i,t}^d) + \delta_{i,t} + \varepsilon_{i,t} \tag{3}$$

$$aftertaxprice_{i,t}^d = \alpha_{i,t} + \beta_1(crude_{i,t}) + \beta_2(excise_{i,t}^d) + \beta_3(VAT_{i,t}^d) +$$
$$\beta_4(Interaction_{i,t}^d) + \delta_{i,t} + \varepsilon_{i,t} \tag{4}$$

where $beftaxprice_{i,t}^g$ and $aftertaxprice_{i,t}^g$ represent the before- and after-tax retail price of gasoline for 1 liter of unleaded gasoline in country I and time t; $beftaxprice_{i,t}^d$ and $aftertaxprice_{i,t}^d$ represent the before- and after-tax retail price of 1 liter of diesel; $crude_{i,t}$ represents the price of 1 liter of crude oil; $excise_{i,t}^g$, $VAT_{i,t}^g$, $excise_{i,t}^d$ and $VAT_{i,t}^d$ represent the set of indirect taxes that affect both unleaded gasoline and diesel in country I and time t; the fifth independent variable (e.g. $Interaction_{i,t}^g$ and $Interaction_{i,t}^d$)[34] represents the interaction term between excise duty and the VAT that affects the retail price of the transport fuels in country I and time t; $\delta_{i,t}$ represents the country fixed effect; $\alpha_{i,t}$ is the constant; and $\varepsilon_{i,t}$ is the error term. All the variables are expressed in EUR. We decided to estimate the impact of indirect taxation and their interaction term on before- and after-tax retail prices of unleaded gasoline and diesel for comparative reasons. In Table 9.1 we present the descriptive statistics of the variables used for panel data analysis.

Table 9.1   Descriptive statistics used for panel data analysis

Variable	Observed	Mean	Standard deviation	Minimum	Maximum
$Beftaxprice_g$	13,000	0.5749	0.1295	0.2149	1.0575
$Aftertaxprice_g$	13,000	1.2877	0.2359	0.6736	1.8898
$Beftaxprice_d$	13,000	0.6213	0.1440	−3.3991	1.0643
$Aftertaxprice_d$	13,000	1.1952	0.2182	0.6966	1.8152
$Crude$	13,000	0.4030	0.1062	0.1591	0.6068
$Excise_g$	13,000	0.4953	0.1162	0.1748	0.7592
$Excise_d$	13,000	0.3722	0.0959	0.143	4.3708
VAT_g	13,000	0.2015	0.0264	0.15	0.27
VAT_d	13,000	0.2015	0.0264	0.15	0.27
$Interaction_g$	13,000	0.1119	0.0470	0.0172	0.2557
$Interaction_d$	13,000	0.1002	0.0278	0.0262	0.1809

Source: European Commission Oil Bulletin, US EIA.

4.   RESULTS

Once the panel data are verified for stationarity and the hypothesis of unit root is rejected using the Levin Lin Chu test, we estimate Equations (1–4) in order to underline the impact of indirect taxation on the before- and after-tax retail price of unleaded gasoline in 21 EU Member States using as control variable the price of crude oil.

The results obtained in Table 9.2 show that the indirect taxation applied to the unleaded gasoline before and after taxation taken individually has a negative impact, decreasing the price of this commodity. However, the interaction term between excise duty and VAT that affects the retail price of gasoline has a positive impact, increasing both before- and after-tax price. Therefore we can observe that the combined impact of indirect taxation increases the retail price by more than the tax rate, and overshifting of the tax burden is identified. In the case of VAT, the impact of this tax on the before tax is statistically insignificant, becoming statistically significant in the case of after-tax price where the tax has a low negative impact. The impact of the crude oil price (e.g. *Crude*) has a positive impact on both analyzed retail prices of gasoline.

According to the results obtained in Table 9.3, the impact of crude oil price on before- and after-tax retail price of diesel is a positive one, where an increase with one monetary unit of crude oil price will increase the before-tax retail price of diesel by 1.244 monetary units. The impact of

Table 9.2   The impact of indirect taxation and crude oil price on the before- and after-tax retail price of gasoline in 21 EU Member States, between 2005 and 2014, OLS estimation

	$Beftaxprice_g$	$Aftertaxprice_g$
Crude	0.739*** (0.0060)	0.823*** (0.0069)
$Excise_g$	−1.085*** (0.0132)	−0.285*** (0.0153)
VAT_g	0.0191 (0.0811)	−0.280*** (0.0360)
$Interaction_g$	2.865*** (0.0355)	4.165*** (0.0411)
Constant	0.490*** (0.0087)	0.687*** (0.0101)
Observations	13,000	13,000

Note: Standard errors in parentheses; * $p < 0.05$, ** $p < 0.01$, *** $p < 0.001$.

Table 9.3   The results regarding the impact of indirect taxation on the before- and after-tax retail price of diesel in 21 EU countries, between 2005 and 2014, OLS estimation

	$Beftaxprice_d$	$Aftertaxprice_d$
Crude	1.244*** (0.0050)	1.524*** (0.0062)
$Excise_d$	−0.812*** (0.0078)	0.225*** (0.0099)
VAT_d	−0.722*** (0.0420)	−1.310*** (0.0523)
$Interaction_d$	1.744*** (0.0493)	2.319*** (0.0613)
Constant	0.393*** (0.0094)	0.529*** (0.0117)
Observations	13,000	13,000

Note: Standard errors in parentheses; * $p < 0.05$, ** $p < 0.01$, *** $p < 0.001$.

indirect taxes that affect this commodity have a negative impact on the before-tax retail price of diesel if taken individually. However, the interaction term between VAT and excise duty applied to the retail price of diesel has a positive impact, in both cases—before- and after-tax price. This result enables us to conclude that overshifting of tax burden in the case of diesel does occur.

For the reason of comparison we also use the General Method of Moments (GMM) assuming that the full body of the distribution function of the data that influence the retail price of transport fuels is not known.

The results from Table 9.4 show that the price of crude oil as control independent variable has a higher impact on the pre-tax retail price of

Table 9.4   *The GMM regarding the impact of excise duties and the interaction term between VAT and excise duties on the pretax retail price of gasoline and diesel in 21 EU countries, period 2005–2014*

	$Beftaxprice_g$	$Beftaxprice_d$
Excise duty	−0.851*** (0.0242)	−0.105** (0.0383)
Crude oil	1.719*** (0.0115)	1.885*** (0.0130)
Interaction$_g$	2.323*** (0.0577)	
Interaction$_d$		1.535*** (0.5440)
Observations	13,000	13,000

Note: Standard errors in parentheses; * $p < 0.05$, ** $p < 0.01$, *** $p < 0.001$.

transport fuels. In comparison with ordinary least square (OLS) estimation, the GMM estimation shows a slightly lower tax burden overshifting coefficient in the case of interaction term between VAT and excise duty in the case of the before-tax price of diesel. On the other hand, the impact of interaction term on the pre-tax retail price of gasoline is higher in the case of unleaded gasoline. Also the GMM estimation shows a lower negative impact of excise tax and VAT when taken individually on the before-tax retail price of both analyzed transport fuels.

5.   DISCUSSION OF RESULTS

The design and the scope of the excise duties aim to decrease the consumption of harmful commodities and raise revenues to the public budget. Consequently, by raising the price of such commodities, the intent is to internalize the external costs associated with their consumption. Even if it is considered as a detrimental treatment, corrective taxation should be borne exclusively by the final consumer because he is the only one responsible for negative externalities that result from consumption of such commodities. Therefore the supplier is entitled to fully shift the tax burden to end consumers through the price mechanism. However, in case of excise duties there can appear deviations from the rule, owing to factors such as market structure, market power and the availability of substitutes. One significant distortionary reaction of the market represents the process of overshifting the tax burden owing to the interaction between the indirect taxes. In this case the price of taxed goods is increased by more than the amount of the increased tax—that is, the end-consumer not only bears the full cost of taxation but is also paying for the future loss of the supplier from decreased demand as response to increased prices.

In the case of environmental taxation, we assume that the exact social cost of one unit of pollution resulting from fossil fuel burning equals t_x. Following the Pigovian principle of taxing the negative externalities, the tax rate should be equal to t_x. Therefore the external costs will be internalized into private costs and the result will be:

$$MSC = MPC + t_x \qquad (5)$$

where the marginal social cost (MSC) equals the marginal private cost (MPC) plus the external cost represented by the tax rate (t_x) applied to 1 unit of harmful commodity (e.g. 1 liter of gasoline or diesel). This represents the polluter pays principle, which states that the social cost of environmental damage should be fully borne by the polluter. Therefore it is justified to assume that the price should be P, where 1 liter of gasoline produces t_x external costs, and the consumer that chooses to burn this unit of fuel should bear the full price of its activity, meaning $P = p + t_x$, where his marginal private costs equals the marginal social cost. For simplicity of assessment let us ignore the other elements that affect Pigovian taxes, such as social benefit share from producing and consuming 'dirty' goods and the double impact of these taxes on the private equilibrium of harmful commodities supplier as Buchanan and Stubblebine (1967) underline.[35] We decided to focus on one particular process that appears in case of corrective taxation—the overshifting of tax burden in the case of interaction with other distortionary taxation such as VAT.

Suppose that an excise-duty-wise carbon taxation is imposed with tax rate of t_x to a unit of pollution and overshifting takes place. In this case, the price of pollution will be:

$$P = p + (t_x + s) \qquad (6)$$

where P is the final price, p is the price before tax, t_x represents the environmental tax rate and s is the overshifting coefficient owing to the interaction between VAT and excise duty. In this case the marginal social cost of the polluter is exceeded by his marginal private cost which is augmented by the overshifting coefficient. The size of the overshifting coefficient (s) strongly depends on the amount of tax increase, market power and the price elasticity of demand. According to the primary research papers,[36] and a more recent empirical paper[37] on the same issue, the demand elasticity with respect to price in market fuel is relatively inelastic, ranging from -0.14 to -0.3. Consequently, it is facile to infer that overshifting of tax burden could occur. In a world of concentrated fuel market (refineries, wholesalers and retailers), dominated by big companies, the market power is assumed to be $L \neq 0$, where L is the Lerner Index. This inferred conclusion shows the presence of oligopolistic behavior, which is representative for the imperfect competitive markets, where big companies involved in this industry are price makers in comparison with small wholesalers and retailers, which tend to be price takers. Once we admit this oligopoly model for the fuel market, then the assumption that overshifting will occur is easily demonstrated. If overshifting of excise duties for fuel occurs, then the Pigovian principle that underlines corrective taxation is violated. This undesired market reaction does not correspond with the baseline policy which targets the pollution reduction. As shown by empirical analysis, the price of transport fuels tends to increase overall by more than the tax rate affecting the welfare of final consumers. This practice of overshifting represents a concealed form of overcharging of the final consumers.

Overcharging the end-consumers, using the context of tax increases, creates an accentuated damage to consumer welfare that stretches beyond the internalization of external costs. Therefore, overshifting violates both the Pigovian principle of corrective taxation and Pareto optimality in resource distribution. Hence, the supplier's surplus is increased at the expense of consumer's already reduced utility owing to the tax imposition. Overshifting can be seen as a suprataxation of the end-consumers, where the seller can abusively increase his receipts and profits using the context of publicly decided tax increases on selected goods. The violation of the Pigovian principle through overshifting increases the regressivity of environmental taxes, reduces the overall welfare and increases the distortionary costs of corrective taxation beyond the social benefits of pollution reduction. This evidence raises new questions such as: if overshifting is identified, can we assume that the often accused distortionary corrective taxes (e.g. environmental taxes) are regressive because of this market reaction? Is the regressivity of environmental taxation enhanced by overshifting the tax burden?

The limitation of our research is given by the difficulty of gathering the necessary information regarding the price formation at the company level, the market share of each company involved into the transport fuel market and the marginal costs. Owing to the lack of data it is not possible to calculate the Lerner Index and also the optimal markup of the pricing policy. Therefore, we assume that the transport fuel market is a concentrated one with big companies acting as price makers and their behavioral pattern in establishing the price close to a monopolist behavior. This assumption is supported by the previous studies that have proved that the market demand elasticity with respect to price for transport fuels is relatively low.

As a consequence, owing to this fact and coupled with high concentration of markets in this particular industry, where big companies play the role of price makers, an introduction of excise duty is expected to be more than fully shifted onto final consumers. Another limitation of this paper can be the lack of further analysis in a general equilibrium model in order to assess the spill-over effects of overshifting onto households and the entire economy. One pertinent reason is that we exclusively focus on demonstrating that overshifting does occur and produces serious violations of both the Pigovian polluter pays principle and Pareto optimal taxation, which would produce distortions, increasing the cost of such policy beyond the assumed environmental benefits. The research has revealed possible directions for further research, mainly in the area of performing detailed analysis of overshifting impact at a general economy level.

6.   CONCLUSIONS

The research in this chapter is placed between two polar cases—monopoly and perfect competition, such as the imperfect competitive markets of transport fuels. Starting with the assumption that the set of indirect taxes imposed on transport fuels will affect both consumers and suppliers to a certain degree, the research aims to quantify the share of consumer and supplier on the resulting final tax burden. Our chapter is based on the empirical analysis using the data from 21 EU Member States in order to quantify the impact of the indirect taxation on the retail prices of transport fuels. Our results strongly support that the tax burden is shifted by more than 100% owing to the interaction between VAT and excise duty.

The opponents of the Pigovian principle consider these market-based tools to be distortionary and regressive, creating a supplementary excess burden by decreasing the value of labor and capital. The process of overshifting can be associated to the direct decrease of labor return as the commodities become artificially more expensive when the Pigovian principle is exceeded. The outcome from imposing environmental taxation might prove to be opposite from the one initially expected, where overshifting can increase profits at the expense of final consumers owing to the overcharged prices. Seen from a different angle, the correction of one market failure—negative (environmental) externalities, owing to the distorted market reaction—can lead to another market failure—overshifting of the tax burden—and violate the Pigovian principle proposed in the first place.

As a consequence, the design and implementation of a new environmental tax such as carbon taxation should take into consideration the implications of tax burden increase and the negative effects of overshifting toward final consumers. Imposing a carbon tax on transport fuels, which are already affected by excise duty and VAT, could lead to over-taxation.

NOTES

1. Seligman, E.R.A. (1927), *The Shifting and Incidence of Taxation*. Columbia University Press, New York.
2. Seligman, above no. 1.
3. Seligman, above no. 1.
4. Seligman, above no. 1.
5. Katz, M. and H. Rosen (1985), 'Tax analysis in an oligopoly model', *Public Finance Quarterly*, 13 (1): 3–21.
6. Fullerton, D. and G.E. Metcalf (2002), 'Tax incidence'. In *Handbook of Public Economics*, Vol. IV, A.J. Auerbach and M.S. Feldstein (Eds), Elsevier, Amsterdam, pp. 1787–1872.
7. Myles, G.D. (1995), *Public Economics*. Cambridge, Cambridge University Press.
8. Stern, N. (1987), 'The effects of taxation, price control and government contracts in oligopoly', *Journal of Public Economics*, 32 (1): 133–158.
9. Kotlikoff, L.J. and L.H. Summers (1987), 'Tax incidence', Chapter 16 in *Handbook of Public Economics*, Vol. II, A.J. Auerbach and M.S. Feldstein (Eds), Elsevier, Amsterdam, pp. 1043–1092.
10. Spoerer, M. (2008), 'The Laspeyres–Paradox: tax overshifting in nineteenth century Prussia', *Cliometrica, Journal of Historical Economics and Econometric History*, 2(3): 173–193.
11. Besley, T.J. and H. Rosen (1999), 'Sales taxes and prices: an empirical analysis', *National Tax Journal*, 40 (3): 157–178.
12. Delipalla, S. and O. O'Donnell (1998), 'The comparison between ad valorem and specific taxation under imperfect competition: evidence from the European cigarette industry', Studies in Economics, School of Economics, University of Kent.
13. Delipalla, S. and M. Keen (1992), 'The comparison between ad valorem and specific taxation under imperfect competition', *Journal of Public Economics*, 49: 351–367.
14. DeCicca, P., Kenkel, D. and F. Liu (2013), 'Who pays cigarette taxes? The impact of consumer price search', *Review of Economics and Statistics*, 95 (2): 516–529.
15. DeCicca, above no. 14.
16. Young, D.J. and A. Bielinska-Kwapisz (2002), 'Alcohol taxes and beverage prices', *National Tax Journal*, 55 (1): 57–73.
17. Kenkel, D.S. (2005), 'Are alcohol tax hikes fully passed through to prices? Evidence from Alaska', *American Economic Review*, 95 (2): 273–277.
18. Kenkel, above no. 17.
19. Bergman, U.M. and N.L. Hansen (2010), 'Are excise taxes on beverages fully passed through to prices? The Danish evidence'. *Mimeo*.
20. Kenkel, above no. 17.
21. Bergman and Hansen, above no. 19.
22. Bergman and Hansen, above no. 19.
23. Alm, J., Sennoga, E. and M. Skidmore (2008), 'Perfect competition, spatial competition, and tax incidence in the retail gasoline market', Working Paper 05-09, UW-Whitewater, Department of Economics.
24. See for example: Nerudova, D. and M. Dobranschi (2014), 'Double dividend hypothesis: can it occur when tackling carbon emissions?', *Procedia Economics and Finance*, 12: 472–479; Nerudova, D. and M. Dobranschi (2015), 'Double dividend hypothesis: can

it be validated by carbon taxation swap with payroll taxes?', *Inzinerine Ekonomika— Engineering Economics*, 26 (1): 23–32.

25. Marion, J. and E. Muehlegger (2011), 'Fuel tax incidence and supply conditions', *Journal of Public Economics*, 95 (9–10): 1202–1212.

26. Chouinard, H. and J.M. Perloff (2004), 'Incidence of federal and state gasoline taxes', *Economics Letters*, 83: 55–56.

27. Kopczuk, W., Marion, J., Muehlegger, E. and J. Slemrod (2013), 'Do the laws of tax incidence hold? Point of collection and the pass-through of state diesel taxes', NBER Working paper.

28. Kopczuk et al., above no. 27.

29. Marion and Muehlegger, above no. 25.

30. Delipalla and Keen, above no. 13.

31. Kenkel, above no. 17.

32. See for example: Li, S., Linn, J. and E. Muehlegger (2012), 'Gasoline taxes and consumer behavior', Working Paper, Harvard Kennedy School and Kopczuk et al., above no. 27.

33. Carbonnier, C. (2011), 'Shifting on prices of per unit and ad valorem consumption taxes', THEMA Working papers.

34. The interaction term—$Interaction_{i,t}^g = excise_{i,t}^g * VAT_{i,t}^g$—is the combined effect of indirect taxes affecting the retail price of unleaded price of gasoline and the second interaction term—$Interaction_{i,t}^d = excise_{i,t}^d * VAT_{i,t}^d$—represents the combined effect of indirect taxes on the retail price of diesel in analyzed EU countries, for the period 2005–2014.

35. Buchanan, J.M. and W.C. Stubblebine (1962), 'Externality'. In *Classic Papers in Natural Resource Economics*. Palgrave Macmillan, Basingstoke, pp. 138–154.

36. See for example: Dahl, A.C. (1993), 'A survey of energy demand elasticities in support of the development of the NEMS', MPRA Paper, No. 13962, University Library of Munich, Germany; Dahl, A.C. (2012), 'Measuring global gasoline and diesel price and income elasticities', *Energy Policy*, 41: 2–13; Pock, M. (2010), 'Gasoline demand in Europe: new insights', *Energy Economics*, 32 (1): 54–62.

37. Havranek, T., Irsova, Z. and K. Janda (2012), 'Demand for gasoline is more price-inelastic than commonly thought', *Energy Economics*, 34 (1): 201–207.

PART IV

Evaluating instruments that protect the
global atmosphere

10. Carbon trading or carbon tax: Which is the more feasible solution to climate change from the perspective of China?

Mingde Cao

Anthropogenic greenhouse gas (GHG) emissions since the Industrial Revolution in the late 18th century have triggered global temperature increases and disrupted the climate system, an important global commons.[1] As a result, huge adverse impacts have been imposed upon humanity and the ecosystem. From an economic perspective, global warming caused by GHG emissions elicits a disproportionate burden on vulnerable countries and groups. Therefore, internalizing the externality of GHG emissions is necessary from the perspectives of climate change justice.[2] Solutions for internalizing the social costs of carbon are many. Traditional methods still work; command and control will continue to be effective in many areas, for example, energy efficiency standards, emission permits, carbon emission caps, carbon budgets, carbon labeling, and so forth. Meanwhile, market-based approaches will give regulated entities more flexibility, promote low-carbon technologies and reduce the social costs of carbon emission reductions—as has been demonstrated by the Acid Rain Program under the Clean Air Act.[3] Globally, a carbon tax and carbon trading are the main market-based solutions for countries to combat climate disruptions to date. However, the two methods obviously each have their own advantages, and would be compatible, complementing each other in facing the challenge of climate change. Given the fledgling market in China, and especially the present lack of national legislation related to carbon emissions trading, the transparency of information,[4] accuracy of carbon emissions data and other defects related to the carbon emissions trading approach, a carbon scheme would be a more feasible economic incentive for China to cope with climate change. This article will explore how to price carbon through market-based approaches in China, with a focus on comparing the two methods from the perspective of China. Section I will compare the advantages and defects of carbon trading and carbon tax in general. Section II will introduce the pilot programs of carbon trading in seven regions in China and comment on the existing challenges. Section III will analyze the feasibility of a carbon tax in China. Section IV provides a brief conclusion.

I.   THE ADVANTAGES AND DISADVANTAGES OF CARBON TRADING AND A CARBON TAX REGIME

Market-based approaches have been adopted pursuant to the Kyoto Protocol as solutions to climate change issues because of their advantages in dealing with environmental problems. Many developed nations are using or plan to use environmental taxation or carbon trading mechanisms to reduce greenhouse gas emissions in order to implement the Kyoto Protocol.[5] Market-based approaches may be the best solutions to cope with the climate change issues on the global scale.[6]

Traditional forms of a command and control approach focus on a single pollution sector, while market-based approaches can distribute the cost of emission reductions among the sectors economy-wide effectively. However, the kind of market-based approach that should be chosen remains controversial. Some think that the carbon trading approach is the best option to mitigate climate change, while others hold that the carbon tax would be.[7] So which approach is the best choice? What are the advantages and disadvantages of carbon trading or a carbon tax respectively? The answer depends on the context.

1.   The Advantages and Disadvantages of Carbon Trading

1.1   The advantages of carbon trading
Carbon trading became the favorite approach of the decision-makers of environmental policies, since it was successfully used to resolve the acid rain issue in the US.[8] Theoretically, a carbon trading approach has the following advantages for the following players. First, for environmentalists, it is effective in guaranteeing environment quality, because it can lower the emission cap gradually. Second, for industry, carbon trading may create a new market of carbon emission reduction credits, from which the companies with lower cost of emission reductions can profit. Third, for economists, a carbon trading approach can internalize the societal cost imposed by carbon emissions, providing the right incentives to minimize the costs. Fourth, for politicians, a carbon trading approach can relieve them of the need to impose a new tax on fossil fuels. Fifth, as

the other market-based approaches, a carbon trading approach is helpful for companies to reach their emission reduction goals at a lower cost. Sixth, a carbon trading approach can constrain the rent-seeking behavior of environmental protection agencies. Seventh, it is beneficial for allowing the public to show their appetite for environmental protection, and thereby to foster the scale of grassroots support for environmental protection.[9,10] Eighth, a carbon trading approach can enhance the feasibility and enforcement of emissions reduction through the emission cap control and flexibility of its price. In short, carbon trading regimes offer many advantages.

1.2 The disadvantages of the carbon trading approach

A carbon trading approach can also bring many disadvantages. First, it is difficult to set an appropriate emissions cap, because it is almost impossible to set a sound environmental pollution level with present day technology. Second, the emission allowances usually have been distributed to polluters for free, which leads to there being no incentives for companies to innovate. Third, because a carbon trading approach includes offset provisions, it offers no guarantee of actually reaching the emission reduction goals. Fourth, the societal cost of carbon trading remains uncertain. If the cost of carbon emission reduction is too high, the policy-makers will face pressure to raise the emissions cap. Fifth, in comparison with the emissions trading programs in the past, the carbon trading regimes are more complicated, because the carbon trading regimes involve massive emissions sources, while the amounts of emissions sources involved with the old cap and trade regimes were relatively small. For instance, the sulphur dioxide cap and trade system of US was specifically intended for 111 heavy polluters. The carbon trading approach is difficult to implement because it needs to design methods for allocating the carbon emission allowances, and needs to monitor and enforce this sophisticated system. Transaction costs are high. Sixth, some hold that a carbon trading approach has very limited powers to stimulate technological innovations.[11] Seventh, because it is agnostic as to where emissions have their greatest impact (and indeed sometimes incentivizes dumping at specific locations), a carbon trading approach is subject to causing hot spot problems. Therefore, it is inconsistent with environmental justice.[12]

2. The Advantages and Disadvantages of a Carbon Tax

2.1 The advantages of a carbon tax

Carbon taxes likewise offer significant advantages and disadvantages. In practice today, carbon taxes are imposed on oil, coal and natural gas.

In theory, a carbon tax has the following advantages theoretically. First, it can provide price signals of externalities, therefore facilitating corrections of market failure. Second, the rate of a carbon tax is determined according to the societal costs of carbon emissions, which is therefore consistent with the polluter pays principle. Third, a carbon tax can exempt the behaviors of carbon emissions reduction, thereby encouraging enterprises to save energy and reduce carbon emissions. Fourth, a carbon tax can increase revenues for the government, providing income that can be used to fund the research and development of less polluting alternatives. Fifth, a carbon tax rate could be adjusted according to new information about the effectiveness of enforcement and new developments. Sixth, unlike the carbon trading approach, a carbon tax approach does not require the creation of a new agency to implement and enforce it. Therefore, its transaction costs and incidence of rent-seeking are minimized. For these reasons, among others, some countries are using, or considering whether to use, a carbon tax approach to dealing with climate change. For example, Canada has a pilot program in the Province of British Columbia to use carbon tax to combat the causes of global warming.[13]

2.2   The disadvantages of a carbon tax

Although a carbon tax scheme offers many advantages, governments still face some problems when imposing a carbon tax on enterprises. First, a carbon tax faces political obstacles. Nobody likes to see another tax. It simply reflects negatively on the political power instituting it. Imposing or increasing a tax is the option of last resort. Second, it is difficult to set the optimal tax rate. If the tax rate is too high, then the carbon emission reduction will exceed the political commitment and be unduly burdensome for the regulated entities, while, if the tax rate is too low, then the carbon emission reduction will not meet the political commitment, and probably not initiate behavioral change sufficient to meet the challenge. Third, even environmental non-governmental organizations would not like to see the existence of a carbon tax, as they prefer to talk about the benefits and significance of environment protection rather than the costs of it. Fourth, there exists benefit uncertainty of a carbon tax, because the total volume of carbon emissions varies under the carbon tax regime.[14]

II.   PILOT PROGRAMS OF CARBON TRADING IN CHINA AND ITS EXISTING CHALLENGES

In 2009, China committed to a 40–45% carbon intensity reduction per unit of the 2005 GDP by 2020, during the Copenhagen climate change international negotiations.[15] In light of the non-binding international agreement, the Copenhagen Accord, China determined that it would take further actions to achieve this goal. China's State Council first announced plans to establish a carbon trading system in October 2010, and the National Development and Reform Commission (NDRC), which is in charge of the climate change issue, announced the launch of the first group of trial programs of carbon trading in 2011.[16] In its announcement, the NDRC requested that local governments where the trial programs are located consider making regulations and principal rules of carbon trading pilot programs. This also involves assessing and defining their caps of GHG emissions, making rules of allowance allocation, establishing monitoring reporting verification systems, and constructing carbon transaction platforms. The main goal of these carbon trading pilot programs is to reach the carbon intensity reduction goal of 2020 through market-based mechanisms at a lower cost than command and control measures would impose.

NDRC has selected four municipalities, two provinces, and one special economic zone, in what has been dubbed the 4+2+1 programs, as the test ground for the trial implementation of carbon trading, including Beijing, Shanghai, Tianjin, Chongqing, Guangdong, Hubei, and Shenzhen. The seven pilot programs are independent from each other, their designs differing in many aspects. The pilot programs are confronting many challenges, such as lack of national legal base, lack of market maturity,[17] inaccuracy of historical carbon emissions data, and the absence of a national unified market and rules. They offer some meaningful insights.

1. Pilot Programs of Carbon Trading in China

1.1 Cap setting
The cap setting of these programs seems to link the cap to regional carbon-intensity goals (Table 10.1). Therefore, they are subject to adjustment on account of the fact that the actual GDP growth will differ from the expectation of economic increase.[18]

1.2 Emissions coverage
The emissions coverage of the pilot programs vary from place to place. The pilot project in Guangdong covers the industrial sectors of electricity, cement, steel, and petrochemical companies that emitted more than 20,000 tons of carbon emissions or had more than 10,000 tons of coal-energy consumption annually, as well as companies in the commercial sector emitting more than 5000 tons of carbon emissions per year. The Shanghai pilot program covers the electricity, industrial, commercial, and transportation

Table 10.1   Cap setting

Cities or provinces	Cap of GHG emissions, million tons of carbon dioxide equivalent per year (Mt CO_2e/year)
Beijing	70
Shanghai	150
Tianjin	150
Chongqing	100
Guangdong	350
Hubei	120
Shenzhen	30

Note: Shuang Zhen, Survey of the Pilot Programs of C&T System of the Seven Provinces or Cities, 2 J. of China Energy 22, 25(2014).

sectors. Aviation, airports, and ports currently are included under the pilot program of Shanghai. The pilot program in Beijing covers the sectors of electricity, heat, cement, petrochemical and service, with the majority of participants being entities with over 10,000 tons of carbon emissions annually. They have the obligation to control CO_2 emissions, whereas other entities with no less than 2000 tons of coal energy consumption per year may voluntarily join the program.[19] Chongqing's pilot program covers industrial enterprises with annual carbon dioxide emissions exceeding 20,000 tons during 2008–2012 (Table 10.2).[20]

1.3   Allowance allocation
Under these schemes, the allowances are mainly allocated for free based on the criteria of grandfathering, output of production, or a combination of the two. That said, Guangdong, Shenzhen and Hubei have also auctioned a small fraction of their allowances, with floor prices having been fixed by the regulators. These pilot markets are currently separated but will be combined by 2020. Nevertheless, there is not yet a national legal basis for these pilot programs.

1.4   Carbon price
The average price of CO_2/t in the seven markets varies from around $1.5 to $13 in the seven places. The price is volatile in each market. The highest price of carbon dioxide per ton reached $23.6 in Shenzhen CEEX in the year of 2013, while the lowest price for offset credits in Guangdong GZEEX was close to $3 in the same year.[21] The price of carbon per ton in the seven markets on 16 December 2015 is shown in Table 10.3.

Table 10.2 Emissions coverage

Cities or provinces	Entities of coverage	Industries covered	GHG coverage
Beijing	490	Electricity, heat, cement, petrochemical, service	CO_2
Shanghai	191	Electricity, steel, petrochemical, chemical, nonferrous metals, building materials, textile, paper-making, rubber, chemical fiber, aviation, airports, ports, shopping malls, hotels, office buildings, railway stations	CO_2
Tianjin	114	Electricity, cement, steel, petrochemical, chemical, extraction of oil and gas	CO_2
Chongqing	240	Industrial enterprises	$CO_2, CH_4, N_2O,$ HFCs, PFCs, SF_6
Guangdong	242	Electricity, cement, steel, petrochemical	CO_2
Hubei	153	Building materials, chemical, electricity, metallurgy, food and beverages, petroleum, automobile, chemical refinery, medicine, paper making	CO_2
Shenzhen	832	Industrial enterprises, building industry	CO_2

Source: Wenda Tang, Comparative Study of the Allowance Allocation in the Pilot Programs of C&T, J. of Modern Business 281, 285(2014).

1.5 Compliance and penalties

In order to make the regulated entities comply, and enforce their obligation under the pilot programs of carbon trading, the seven places have designed Measuring, Reporting and Verification mechanisms and their own penalties for violations, abbreviated to MRV. The enterprises which are restricted from GHG emissions must firstly measure and report their annual GHG emissions, and then the emissions report will be verified by an independent third party. All of the pilot cities and provinces have formulated the rules for measuring reports and verifications, and most of the pilot cities and provinces have also set the punishment rules for the enterprises that breach the regulations of GHG emissions reduction obligations. Beijing, Shanghai, Shenzhen, Guangdong and Tianjin, which started their pilot

Table 10.3   Carbon price

Cities or provinces	Price of CO_2/t
CBEEX, Beijing	$5.99
SEEX, Shanghai	$1.64
TCX, Tianjin	$3.52
CCETC, Chongqing	No transaction, previous record $1.93, on 1 December 2015
GZEEX, Guangdong	No transaction, previous record $2.35, on 11 December 2015
CHEEX, Hubei	No transaction, previous record $3.55, on 15 December 2015
CEEX, Shenzhen	$5.97

Source: China Carbon Trading Network, http://www.tanjiaoyi.com/tanshichang/.

programs in 2013, have each set a different default penalty provision. The penalties fall into four categories: reducing next year's allowances of the violators, publicizing the compliance status of firms to create social pressure, restricting the violator's access to special funds for energy conservation for two years or other programs for a period of time,[22] and/or fining them three times the average allowance price for any increased difference between a firm's carbon emissions and retired allowances.[23]

2.   The Challenging Issues of a Carbon Trading Market in China

The carbon trading market lacks national legal status. This means that the market does not have sufficient legal guarantees, although the relevant local legislatures or local governments have enacted regulations or administrative rules for these pilot programs. As a result, 'the pilot regulators must operate largely in a politically uncertain environment',[24] and the investors have no security for their profits from this speculation from a long-term perspective. This is the first challenge the trial programs are confronting. The second challenge is the volatile market prices. There is a trend for the price to decline in some markets, possibly because of over-allocated free allowances, according to some criticism. The third challenge of the carbon trading pilots is from the other policies relating to energy conservation, air pollution prevention, carbon intensity reduction, coal consumption, etc. These policies influence carbon trading pilot programs on two levels. At the firm level, a facility under a carbon trading program may forego an opportunity to buy an allowance because an additional ton of carbon emission allowance would put it out of compliance with an energy conservation goal. At the market level, the above-mentioned policies that reduce carbon emissions from the same sources covered by the cap would reduce the demand for allowances and lower the price of allowances. Furthermore, the domestic markets are separated by several sectors, and each market has its own unique design in many respects.[25] This fragmentation will probably impair the establishment of a united national carbon market in the near future.

III. THE FEASIBILITY OF A CARBON TAX

As discussed above, theoretically, carbon trading and a carbon tax each have some advantages and some disadvantages when compared with each other. As Professor Janet E. Milne has pointed out, 'predictability of cost and efficiency lend heft to the carbon tax side, and certainty of result weigh in on the cap-and-trade side, but the issue should not be overstated—the Intergovernmental Panel on Climate Change has found taxes to be both economically effective and environmentally effective'.[26] Moreover, 'either a carbon tax or an economy-wide cap and trade system would create the backbone for a comprehensive program, although neither would necessarily supplant policies targeted toward specific issues . . . the Western Climate Change Initiative in the US and Canada is exploring how a tax may work in concert with a cap-and-trade regime. Policymakers can choose combinations from a large portfolio of options.'[27] Whether a carbon tax or carbon trading regime would be more feasible for coping with climate change should be in accordance with the present reality in China. This author prefers a carbon tax over carbon trading for China based on consideration of the following aspects.

1. Time Framework

Climate change is occurring much faster than experts had originally expected during the IPCC third and fourth Reports. The exigency of global warming demands a rapid response from human society. According to the carbon trading plan of China, the pilot programs of carbon trading should run between 2012 and 2015; the national carbon market will be launched in 2016.[28] The formation of a mandatory unified national carbon market will be from 2021 to 2030. The domestic carbon market in China will link to international carbon markets after 2030. The pace of carbon market building seems sluggish, owing to the nature of making such a complicated market. In contrast, imposition of a carbon tax would be less time consuming and more efficient. For example, the sensitive Individual

Income Tax Act of the PRC has already been amended six times from 1993 to 2011, since it was enacted in 1980. The average time between amendments of the individual income tax law is about three years. Based on this example, it would seem easier and more efficient to levy a carbon tax than to build a unified national carbon trading market, and the timing is critical for the exigent property of climate disruption that does not allow us to delay the proper actions.

2. Environmental Benefits

Hypothetically, the environmental benefit of a carbon trading method is certain, because the emission cap is explicitly limited. On the other hand, a carbon tax cannot determine the emission cap in advance. Therefore, its environmental benefit would be uncertain. In fact, the government would loosen the cap of carbon emissions when faced with political pressure, because the price of emission allowances would increase owing to the decline in the total amount of emissions. This would undermine the environmental benefit of a carbon trading method to some extent. The income from a carbon tax can fund the additional climate change mitigation policies that will be beneficial to offsetting the uncertainty of a carbon tax. Theoretically, like a carbon tax, a carbon trading program also can generate revenues, but in practice, most part of emission allowances in EU Emission Trading Scheme (EU ETS) have been distributed for free at the first and second phase.[29,30] Moreover, the rate of a carbon tax can be adjusted according to the needs of environmental protection, while the political pressure when adjusting the rate of a tax is much less than that against levying a new tax. The carbon tax scheme of British Columbia (BC) has proved the environmental benefits. 'Reports by the provincial government and academic analyses both note that BC's consumption of fossil fuels declined by significantly more than the national average between 2008 and 2012, with the sole exception of aviation fuel, which is the one fossil fuel largely exempt from the tax . . . . In the first four years of the carbon tax, BC's per capita consumption decreased by 17.4 %, while that of the rest of Canada increased by 1.5%.'[31] Owing to a carbon tax of CAD \$25 per ton in 2011 there was 'a 12.5% reduction in gasoline consumption due to the tax, compared to an anticipated 1.8% reduction from a comparable price increase due to market forces'.[32] While the economic growth in BC hasn't been affected by the carbon tax, 'GDP growth in BC in the first four years of the carbon tax was virtually identical to the national average. BC has seen twice the national rate of investment in clean energy and hybrid vehicles, and now enjoys the lowest corporate and individual income taxes in Canada.'[33] In addition, 'economic analysis conducted for the carbon tax review indicates that BC's carbon tax has had, and will continue to have, a small negative impact on gross domestic product (GDP) in the province . . . the exemptions from the carbon tax for the greenhouse sector, which were justified primarily based on concerns over international competitiveness, are likely unnecessary.'[34] Relevant experience shows that a carbon tax is likely to be more efficient and effective than a cap and trade regime.

3. Cost of Administrative Management

Because the core of a carbon tax is the setting of a tax rate and the pool of taxpayers, the design of a carbon tax is relatively simple, and therefore carbon tax is easy to manage. On the contrary, carbon trading is more complex and administratively challenging. Carbon trading usually needs to comply with the following procedures. First, the baselines need to be set for the purpose of establishing a GHG emissions cap. Second, the proposal needs to determine how allowances will be created or distributed either for free or for auction. Free distribution needs to determine which industries receive allowances, while an auction requires a complex system to prevent cheating. Third, a system needs to be devised to prevent the same allowance from being used twice, and sanctions need to be established for polluters who exceed their allowances. Fourth, complicated provisions relating to emission credits, banking and borrowing need to be made in order to avoid too much cost uncertainty. Fifth, offsets are needed for carbon sequestration and similar projects, which are more complicated than credits against a carbon tax liability. Sixth, if carbon trading is involving international emission trading, it will be more complicated. In regard to tax imposition and management, the existing tax collecting agency is capable of taking charge of this issue, while a carbon trading system needs to create a new administrative agency to implement and monitor carbon emissions. Obviously, a carbon tax regime saves administrative costs and resources in comparison with a carbon trading system. Furthermore, with regard to over 10 million small and mid-sized enterprises in China, the management costs for carbon trading would be in excess of the benefit it provides.[35,36,37]

4. Fraud and Corruption

Fraud has the potential to become rampant in carbon trading, which involves a large sum of money in the process of allowances trading. Carbon trading lacks incentives for honesty—as the purchaser will get carbon emission reduction credits from the seller regardless of whether the emission reduction actually occurred. The motive to avoid emissions reduction is more 'evil' than that for evading paying taxes. Unlike the situation under a carbon trading system, the amount of money the tax collector wants is exactly the same as that which the tax payer does not want to pay. Tax fraud is a zero sum game for the two parties, but avoiding GHG emissions reduction is a positive sum game to the two parties. Moreover, the room for corruption from a carbon tax regime is much smaller than that from carbon trading, because a carbon tax cannot lead to a scarcity-defined monopoly. In contrast, carbon trading may lead to the creation of fortunes that can be used for items beyond environmental protection. In the context of China, the situation could be worse regarding a carbon trading regime, owing to there being less transparency of the allocation of carbon allowances, and more frequent abuse of power by bureaucratic agencies.

NDRC is the authority that is in charge of the allocation of carbon allowances and carbon emissions trading at large. This agency is dubbed a mini-State Council, and is a legacy of the planned economy during Chairman Mao's reign. NDRC remains the most powerful ministry in China at present, but it is experiencing the bitterness of the anti-corruption campaigns of recent years. Many believe that the agency faces exceptional levels of scrutiny in anti-corruption following the 18th CPC Congress; as the former deputy minister of the agency and also the head of the National Energy Administration, Tienan Liu, and many other high-level officials from NDRC have experienced the crack-down.[38] As a result, there is reasonable doubt about the honest wielding of power by the agency relating to the carbon emissions market. In contrast, a carbon tax regime would be more transparent than a carbon emissions trading mechanism. The taxpayers, amount of taxes, and the object and scope of taxes are publicly and clearly listed by laws and regulations, so the room for manipulation is limited. For this reason, China has been developing environmental taxation legislation in recent years. The main driving force for the reform from environmental fees to environmental taxes is to overcome the deficiencies in administrative discretion relating to pollutant discharge fees, collection and usage. The author participated in the consultation meeting of the draft of the Environmental Taxation Act of the PRC in June 2015. Unfortunately, the draft is very primitive, and mainly focuses on pollutants, not carbon emissions—even though many air pollutants are relevant to greenhouse gases and climate change. However, the draft of the environmental taxation act releases the signal that the government is considering a taxation mechanism as an option to emulate with environmental issues. A carbon tax would be included in the process of environmental tax legislation in the near future—the door has been opened.

IV. CONCLUSION

As we have seen through our comparison, there is no perfect method of comparison between carbon trading and carbon tax, because the only certainty is the uncertainty of global climate change. However, it might be unreasonable to emphasize the environmental benefits of certainty, because even a well-designed policy ultimately will impose annual costs on the order of tens (and perhaps hundreds) of billions of dollars. So the costs should be accounted for if effective and sensible policies are to be designed and implemented. Meanwhile, the benefits of any policy to reduce GHG emissions are worldwide and for the long run, while the cost of any policy adopted by one country will be confined to its own and immediate account. Therefore, it is more important to focus on the costs rather than the benefits.[39,40]

The Chinese government is also facing uncertainty issues because it cannot get information on the marginal costs of emission reductions from individual enterprises when it makes policy. Under this lack of certainty, what kind of climate change policy should China adopt? At present, there are two different points of view among academics.

Some scholars hold that a carbon tax is not suitable to China's situation. The reasons are as follows. First, the reform of energy pricing does not complete, and does not reach the goal of pricing energy by market, so there is no foundation to adopt a carbon tax approach as an incentive to encourage companies to reduce GHG emissions. Second, imposing a carbon tax would create a drag on the economy of China, although it may lower the emissions of greenhouse gases. Third, a carbon tax cannot resolve the GHG emission issues of China. In contrast, carbon trading conforms to China's interest.[41] The reasons are as follows. First, carbon trading is more consistent with China's interest.[42] China embraces the Clean Development Mechanism provided by the Kyoto Protocol, which adopted a carbon trading approach. Second, a carbon trading mechanism is more flexible than a carbon tax; especially in the aspect of allocating emission allowances. It allows more consideration to the common but differentiated responsibility principle, which was adopted by the United Nations Framework Convention on Climate Change. Given the needs of both industrialized and developing economies, more emission allowances would be distributed to them. Finally, carbon trading is less likely to lead to trade friction in comparison with a carbon tax.

Other scholars insist that a carbon tax would be more consistent with China's interests. The author supports this view based upon the aspects listed as below. First of all, the influence on the economy caused by a carbon tax is exaggerated. Although a carbon tax imposed on products leads to price hikes, and will consequently weaken the competitiveness of

China's export goods, other nations will likewise begin to take corresponding measures to deal with climate change. Under these circumstances, a carbon tax will not have much influence on export goods, because of the corresponding increase in the price of goods from other countries.

Second, a carbon trading mechanism is inconsistent with China's position of international negotiations on climate change. Climate change issues are already affecting the world well beyond the environment and climate arena, and have begun to expand into political, economic and development areas. It will occupy the superior position in energy development and economic competition in the future, so it is an issue of the utilization and allocation of natural resources. From China's stance in international climate change negotiations in recent years, we see that China always tries to avoid setting binding GHG emission reduction target, because it is regarded as a constraint to China's economic growth.[43] If China adopts a nationwide carbon trading program, that would imply that China admits to a binding goal of carbon emission reduction, which obviously contradicts China's national interest.

Moreover, the requirements of pricing carbon by the market of carbon trading are more complex than a carbon tax. First, an optimal emissions cap needs to be set. This is the basis of the carbon trading market. Second, the initial market of carbon trading needs to be established, which is the market of carbon emissions allowances distribution. Third, the secondary market needs to be established as well, namely, the transaction market of carbon emissions allowances. For a carbon tax the core issue is the setting of a tax rate. It is similar to setting the optimal carbon emissions cap in nature. A carbon tax does not need to create an initial market and a secondary market.

In addition, a carbon tax is more consistent with China's interest in international trade. Regarding the impacts on international trade caused by carbon trading and a carbon tax, the former inclines to elicit adverse effects on export, because carbon trading is different among nations, as each nation has its own provisions when it designs its carbon trading market. The best solution is to create a global unified carbon trading regime, but at present, it is unfeasible, as a global carbon trading market involves the distribution of initial allowances among nations. This issue reflects a big gap that would require unimaginable agreements to coordinate among nations. In contrast, a carbon tax has less impact on trade compared with carbon trading, and a carbon tax can be effectively coordinated through a border adjustment tax.

As the worries of climate change mount, combined with the poor performance of the Kyoto Protocol in dealing with global warming, intensive global negotiations will undoubtedly be witnessed in the coming years concerning this frightening issue. China, as the largest emitter in the world, has already committed to peak its emissions by 2030, and obviously will assume a binding goal of carbon emission reductions at some point in time in the near future. Among a variety of solutions related to carbon emissions reduction, market-based approaches are definitely the ideal choice to combat climate change. In comparison with other market-based options, a carbon tax is surely more feasible and more consistent with the political, economic, environmental and national interests of China.[44]

NOTES

1. IPCC Climate Change 2001: The Scientific Basis, J. T. Houghton et al., eds, Cambridge University Press, 2001, 87–90.
2. Nicholas Stem, The Economics of Climate Change: The Stern Review, Cambridge University Press, 2007, 16.
3. Reuven S. Avi-Yonah, David M. Uhlmann, *Combating Global Climate Change: Why a Carbon Tax Is a Better Response to Global Warming Than Cap and Trade*, 28 Stan. Envtl L. J.3, 5(2009).
4. Clayton Munnings, Richard Morgenstern, Zhongmin Wang, Xu Liu, Discussion Paper: Assessing the Design of Three Pilot Programs for Carbon Trading in China, October 2014, Washington, DC, at 17.
5. Yucheng Shi and Hui Wang, *On the Function of Market Mechanism in the Course of Alleviating Greenhouse Gas Discharge*, 5 Presentday L. Sci.89, 89(2008).
6. *Id.*
7. Helmuth Cremer, Philippe de Donder Firouz Gahvari, *Political Sustainability and the Design of Environmental Taxes*, 11 Int'L Tax & Pub. Fin.703, 703(2004). Also see Jonathan Remy Nash, *Framing Effects and Regulatory Choice*, 82 Notre Dame L. Rev.313, 325(2006).
8. Reuven S. Avi-Yonah, David M. Uhlmann, *Combating Global Climate Change: Why a Carbon Tax Is a Better Response to Global Warming Than Cap and Trade*, 28 Stan. Envtl L. J.3, 5(2009).
9. *Id.*
10. Mingde Cao, *Study on Cap and Trade Mechanism*, 4 L. Sci. 100, 103(2004).
11. David M. Driesen, *Sustainable Development and Market Liberalism's Shotgun Wedding: Emissions Trading Under the Kyoto Protocol*, 83 Ind.L. J.21, 51(2008); see also David M. Driesen, Economic Instruments for Sustainable Development in Environmental Law for Sustainability: A Critical Reader 303, Stepan Wood, Benjamin J. Richardson eds, Hart Publishing, 2006.
12. *Id.*
13. David G. Duff, *Tax Policy and Global Warming*, 51 Can. Tax.J. 2063, 2090(2003).
14. Helmuth Cremer, Philippe de Donder Firouz Gahvari, *Political Sustainability and the Design of Environmental Taxes*, 11 Int'L Tax & Pub.Fin.703, 703(2004).
15. Xinhuanet: China and US Announced Their Reduction Goals Subsequently, China's Carbon Intensive Reduction Will Reach 40%–45% by 2020, see http://news.xinhuanet.com/environment/2009-11/27/content_12547116.htm, last visit date, 2016-02-12.
16. The Office of NDRC, Notice of Launching Trial Programs of Carbon Emission Trading, No.(2011) 2601, see http://www.chinastce.org.cn/html/2012/xgzc_0213/526.html, last visit date, 2016-02-12.
17. Clayton Munnings, Richard Morgenstern, Zhongmin Wang, Xu Liu, Discussion Paper: Assessing the Design of Three Pilot Programs for Carbon Trading in China, October 2014, Washington, DC, at 17.
18. *Id.*, at 17.
19. Wenda Tang, *Comparative Study of the Allowance Allocation in the Pilot Programs of C&T*, J. of Modern Business 281, 285(2014).

20. *Id.*
21. China Carbon Trading Network, http://www.tanjiaoyi.com/tanshichang/, last visit date, 2016-02-12.
22. Article 40, Provisional Rules of Carbon Emission Trading of Shanghai 2013, see http://www.chinalawedu.com/falvfagui/22598/wa201311260932053529166.shtml, last visit date, 2016-02-12.
23. Article 75, Provisional Rules of Carbon Emission Trading of Shenzhen 2014, see http://www.chinalawedu.com/falvfagui/22016/ca201404081658407234928.shtml, last visit date, 2016-02-12.
24. Clayton Munnings, Richard Morgenstern, Zhongmin Wang, Xu Liu, Discussion Paper: Assessing the Design of Three Pilot Programs for Carbon Trading in China, October 2014, Washington, DC, at 12.
25. T. Schatzki, R.N. Stavins, Implications of Policy Interactions for California's Climate Policy, Analysis Group, Boston, MA, 2012.
26. Janet E. Milne, *Carbon Taxes in the United States: the Context for the Future*, 10 Ver. J. of Envtl Law 1, 29–30(2008).
27. *Id.*, at 27.
28. Zhoujie Wang, China Plans to Launch National Carbon Market in 2016, see www.cnstock.com, last visit date, 2014-09-02; see http://business.sohu.com/20140902/n403993789.shtml, last visit date, 2016-02-12.
29. http://world.people.com.cn/n/2015/0205/c1002-26511841.html, last visit date, 2016-02-12.
30. Robert N. Stavins, *A Meaningful U.S. Cap and Trade System to Address Climate Change*, 32 Harv. Envtl. L.Rev.293, 350(2008).
31. Harrison, K. (2013), The Political Economy of British Columbia's Carbon Tax, OECD Environment Working Papers, at 18, No. 63, OECD Publishing, see http://dx.doi.org/10.1787/5k3z04gkkhkg-en.
32. *Id.*, at 18.
33. *Id.*, at 19.
34. *Id.*, at 19.
35. Reuven S. Avi-Yonah, David M. Uhlmann, *Combating Global Climate Change: Why a Carbon Tax Is a Better Response to Global Warming Than Cap and Trade*, 28 Stan. EnvtlL. J.3, 38 (2009).
36. *Id.*, at 38.
37. *Id.*, at 39.
38. Observer network: 17 corrupt officials of NDRC have been investigated after 18th CPC Congress makes NDRC 'running leader' of anti-corruption war among ministries of PRC, see http://www.guancha.cn/FaZhi/2014_10_02_272751.shtml, last visit date, 2015-07-26.
39. Robert N. Stavins, *A Meaningful U.S. Cap and Trade System to Address Climate Change*, 32 Harv.Envtl.L.Rev.293, 296(2008).
40. Reuven S. Avi-Yonah, David M. Uhlmann, *Combating Global Climate Change: Why a Carbon Tax Is a Better Response to Global Warming Than Cap and Trade*, 28 Stan. EnvtlL. J.3, 36. (2009).
41. Qiaosheng Wu, Jinhua Cheng, *Policies Study on Global Climate Change*, 9 China Soft Science 14, 19(2003).
42. Yongmin Bian, *The Role of Trade Measure in the Mitigate of Climate Change*, 1 J. of Nanjing U. (Phil. Human. & Soc. Sci.)41, 43(2009).
43. Yucheng Shi, Hui Wang, *On the Function of Market Mechanism in the Course of Alleviating Greenhouse Gas Discharge*, 5 Present Day L. Sci.89, 89(2008). Yucheng Shi, Hui Wang, *On the Function of Market Mechanism in the Course of Alleviating Greenhouse Gas Discharge*, 5 Present Day L. Sci.89, 94(2008).
44. William D. Nordhaus, *Life after Kyoto: Alternative Approaches to Global Warming Policies*, 6 Comparative Economic & Social Systems 17, 25(2009).

11. Regulation of ship-sourced carbon dioxide emissions: The creation of economic instruments

Stathis Palassis

I. INTRODUCTION

The reduction of greenhouse gas emissions and the stabilization of global climate is the greatest challenge we have ever faced.[1] It has become imperative that we safely arrest global warming and thereby stabilize global weather patterns. As we move towards a position in international climate change law of all states becoming responsible for the reduction of their climate change emissions, so must the member states of the International Maritime Organization (IMO). In 1997 the IMO adopted the document 'CO$_2$ Emissions from Ships', recognizing carbon dioxide as the principal greenhouse gas emitted by the international shipping sector and the need for the sector to reduce its emissions.[2] In 2003 the IMO adopted the document 'IMO Policies and Practices related to the Reduction of Greenhouse Gas Emissions from Ships', leading the Organization to adopt Resolution A963.23 directing that three types of measures be adopted for the reduction of the international shipping sector's carbon dioxide emissions: technical, operational and market-based.[3] To date the IMO has successfully adopted technical and operational measures; however the adoption of market-based measures has proven much more difficult, leading the IMO to discontinue its work on market-based economic instruments.

 The subject of this article is the significant obstacles surrounding the distinction drawn between developed and developing states and the major rift that has emerged in the IMO. This division has compromised the ability of the IMO to finalize its work in the area of market-based measures. As a result the Organization has been unable to adopt the economic instruments required concerning the reduction of the carbon dioxide emissions of the international shipping sector. The purpose of this article is to examine the problematic distinction between developed and developing states and the difficulties that this poses in the application of the principle of common but differentiated responsibilities and respective capabilities (CBDRRC) to the economic instruments under consideration by the IMO. The article will commence by discussing the international climate change law principle of CBDRRC that seeks to differentiate between the responsibilities owed by developed and developing states. It will highlight both the unsettled aims and content of the principle as well as the problematic distinction that is made between developed and developing states. The article will then discuss the international law concerning the nationality and registration of ships. It will highlight how the registration of ships in open registries distorts the distinction between developed and developing states. The article will then make critical submissions on the major difficulties that exist for the IMO in adopting appropriate economic instruments, owing in large to the dated and no longer adequate distinctions between developed and developing states.

II. COMMON BUT DIFFERENTIATED RESPONSIBILITIES AND RESPECTIVE CAPABILITIES

The principle of CBDRRC and its conceptualization is highly politically charged. The principle rests on the conceptual premise that notions of fairness and equity need to be introduced into the international environmental law-making process. The origins of the principle can be traced to 1972 and the adoption of the Stockholm Declaration of the United Nations Conference on the Human Environment ('Stockholm Declaration') that recognized that, in integrating environmental safeguards into developmental planning, additional international technical and financial assistance must be made available for developing states.[4] The principle, however, was not popularized until 1992 at the United Nations Conference on Environment and Development (UNCED) in Rio de Janeiro and as such recognizes the special needs and differential treatment of developing states.[5] Despite its lack of adequate legal content and its ambiguous legal status, the CBDRRC principle is clearly part of contemporary international environmental law and policy. Further, it is important to note two additional points about the CBDRRC principle. The first is that all the instruments adopted at the UNCED included the CBDRRC principle.[6] The second is that, since the Stockholm Declaration, similar approaches have been adopted in several multilateral regimes including that of the World Trade Organization as well as in that of the Vienna Convention for the Protection of the Ozone Layer and the associated Montreal Protocol.

(i)   The Multilateral Provisions on CBDRRC

The principle of CBDRRC is part of the international law of sustainable development as it integrates environmental and equity considerations and needs with the more traditional economic developmental factors. As an environmental principle of sustainable development common but differentiated responsibilities (CBDR) is provided for in principles 6 and 7 of the Rio Declaration on Environment and Development ('Rio Declaration').[7]

> The special situation and needs of developing countries, particularly the least developed and those most environmentally vulnerable, shall be given special priority. International actions in the field of environment and development should also address the interests and needs of all countries.[8]

> States shall cooperate in a spirit of global partnership to conserve, protect and restore the health and integrity of the Earth's ecosystem. In view of the different contributions to global environmental degradation, States have common but differentiated responsibilities. The developed countries acknowledge the responsibility that they bear in the international pursuit of sustainable development in view of the pressure their societies place on the global environment and of the technologies and financial resources they command.[9]

It is important to note that these normative provisions are not legally binding as they are contained in a declaratory instrument rather than in a treaty with legally binding obligations. These norms can, however, become legally binding rules of international law either upon their subsequent incorporation into a treaty or if they are supported by the practice of states and customary international law crystallizes around them.[10]

The principle of CBDRRC is also part of international climate change law. As such the principle is a political compromise for all states in coming together to cooperatively combat climate change. The CBDRRC principle has two main components. It first recognizes that all states have a common responsibility to cooperate in combating climate change. It then goes on to differentiate the responsibility of states taking into account differing circumstances and the respective capabilities of states. Differentiation is reflected by factors such as the level of development and historical contribution to the global greenhouse gas emissions and in particular carbon dioxide emissions. As a principle of international climate change law the CBDRRC principle is contained in Article 4 of the United Nations Framework Convention on Climate Change (UNFCCC)[11] and Article 10 of the Kyoto Protocol to the UNFCCC ('Kyoto Protocol').[12]

All Parties, taking into account their common but differentiated responsibilities and their specific national and regional development priorities, objectives and circumstances shall: [f]ormulate, implement, publish and regularly update national and, where appropriate, regional programmes containing measures to mitigate climate change by addressing anthropogenic emissions by sources and removals by sinks of all greenhouse gases not controlled by the Montreal Protocol, and measures to facilitate adequate adaption to climate change.[13]

All Parties, taking into account their common but differentiated responsibilities and their specific national and regional development priorities, objectives and circumstances, without introducing any new commitments for Parties not included in Annex I, but reaffirming existing commitments under Article 4, paragraph 1, of the Convention, and continuing to advance the implementation of these commitments in order to achieve sustainable development, taking into account Article 4, paragraphs 3, 5 and 7, of the Convention, shall: . . .[14]

The CBDRRC principle was implemented into international climate change law through the creation of 'Annex I' and 'Non-Annex I States', the distinction reflecting 1992 levels of economic development measured as per capita gross domestic product (GDP). Annex I comprises member states to the Organisation for Economic Co-operation and Development (OECD) as well as some additional states that were undergoing transition to market economies. It is important to note, however, that the distinction between Annex I and Non-Annex I States does not accurately reflect true greenhouse gas emissions, and probably never has. Further, it is this distinction that has been the troubling aspect of international climate change law. Some states including the United States, which have not ratified the Kyoto Protocol, have argued instead for an increased uniformity in the obligations of states.[15] Yet it is claimed that the inability of the international community to effectively deal with issues surrounding the CBDRRC principle has since the adoption of the Kyoto Protocol led to a loss of momentum in the further development of international climate change law.[16]

(ii)   The Legal Content of CBDRRC

The *raison d'etre* of the CBDRRC principle and its underlying notions of introducing equity into international climate change law are certainly viewed as important by the majority of states. Despite this validity the real aim of the CBDRRC principle to a certain extent continues to elude:

There is still much debate of the conceptual basis of this principle—leading one to question its real aim. Is it to contribute to a fairer world system in which developed States recognize their historical responsibility for past environmental damage, or is simply an expedient means of ensuring the participation of developing States in what are primarily northern concerns?[17]

Irrespective of the differences that may distinguish the motivation of states at a political level there is still a parallel legal reality in which we need to define the principle and its content more extensively. It is obvious that this is the necessary precursor before the CBDRRC principle can be legally implemented into appropriate regulatory regimes.

We know that 'common' signifies the responsibility that all states share in common comprising the obligation to stabilize global climate. This means that states multilaterally cooperate in accepting obligations to reduce their national greenhouse gas emissions. According to the recently completed work of the International Law Association on the matter:

> All States have a common responsibility to cooperate in developing an equitable and effective climate change regime applicable to all, and to work towards the multilaterally agreed global goal.[18]

Despite this recognition much less common ground exists on the relevant criteria for differentiation. 'Respective capabilities' are, however, referred to in the principle as the only basis for differentiation. There is, however, another basis that was recognized in the lead-up to the UNCED and which is based on evidence demonstrating differing contributions to global environmental degradation. It is developed states that through their over exploitation of the earth's resources and unsustainable patterns of production and consumption have primarily led to global environmental degradation and the associated detriment of developing states. This position has of course been stressed in the most by developing states. On this basis there may well be a legal responsibility of developed states to take the lead in combating environmental degradation that can in turn be viewed as an application of the polluter pays principle.[19] However, for most states 'differentiated' signifies differing state obligations based on equity as reflected in terms of a state's per capita GDP. Again according to the International Law Association:

> States have differing historical, current and future contributions to climate change, differing technological, financial and infrastructural capabilities, as well as diverse economic fortunes and other national circumstances, States have differentiated responsibilities to address climate change and its adverse effects. In determining if a State's commitments have been adequately tailored to its differentiated responsibilities, the following shall be taken into account:
> (a) Developed States, in particular the most advanced amongst them, shall take the lead in assessing climate change by adopting more stringent mitigation commitments and in assisting developing States, in particular the

least developed among them, small island developing States, and other vulnerable States, to the extent of their need, in addressing climate change and adapting to its adverse effects.

(b) Developing States in particular the least developed among them, small island developing States, and other vulnerable States shall be subject to less stringent mitigation commitments, and benefit from, *inter alia*, delayed compliance schedules and financial, technological and other assistance.[20]

States' commitments, given their differentiated responsibilities, shall fall along a spectrum of commitments, and these commitments shall evolve over time as their contributions, capabilities, economic fortunes and national circumstances evolve.[21]

Differentiated responsibilities may, for example, be implemented by one or more of the following: first, an exemption from set obligations; second, a lesser level of obligations; and third, a longer period within which to meet set obligations. However, it may appear as an over-simplistic solution to believe that the application of the CBDRRC principle whereby there may merely be an exemption to an obligation, a lesser obligation or a longer compliance period can effectively remedy the unlevel playing field of levels of economic development while being in the best interests of all states. Despite this, differential treatment is evident in its various forms in most international environmental agreements entered into over the last few decades.[22]

However, we then need to address the most critical issues surrounding the application of the principle of CBDRRC and that is the distinction between developed and developing states. There clearly appears to be a less than rigorous methodology involved in international climate change law when in 1992 states were classified as Annex I and Non-Annex I. Given that what is involved is at best a shallow distinction, how do we effectively distinguish between developed and developing states? The distinction and dichotomy of states utilized is problematic to say the least:

The Annex I/Non-Annex I dichotomy represents a static—and subsequently anachronistic—distinction that has proved to be overly simplistic and gives way to extreme positions that trouble constructive negotiations under the UNFCCC. Moving beyond this dichotomy is thus paramount to enable parties to differentiate responsibilities in a way that better reflects the diversification of state groups and country coalitions that negotiate under the UNFCCC, notably among developing countries.[23]

The labels developed and developing clearly are not appropriate particularly when considering the emissions of states such as China and India. The current distinction does not distinguish between the diverse types of states that are included as Non-Annex I, although at the same time the precarious position of small island developing states and other vulnerable states is legitimately identified as in need of assistance. Irrespective, literature on the Annex I/Non-Annex I dichotomy issue uses strong language including words such as 'dysfunctional', 'the regime's greatest weakness' and that '[a]ny move forward is complicated by persistent vagueness and uncertainties of CBDR in the realm of international law'.[24]

III. NATIONALITY OF SHIPS

The problematic distinction between developed and developing states employed in international environmental law has been further exacerbated by the international law concerning the nationality of ships that has significantly distorted the developed/developing state distinction. International law generally allows states the right to determine the manner in which they ascribe nationality to ships. A ship's nationality, and the right to fly that state's flag, is granted upon its registration on the state's Register of Ships. Owing to the fierce competition existing in the international shipping sector, certain states, often developing states, offer alternative, more financially advantageous registration to ship owners irrespective of the nationality of the owners. The ability, however, of ship owners based in developed states to register their ships in developing states does not reflect the 'real' nationality of registered tonnage. This competitive advantage offered through registration has resulted in an inability to accurately gauge the extent of developed state interests involved in the international shipping sector through its distortion of developed/developing state interests and an associated lack of transparency concerning legal and beneficial ownership.

(i) Nationality and the Genuine Link

States ascribe nationality to ships in the same way as they ascribe nationality to their citizens. Nationality is a well-accepted head of state jurisdiction based on the allegiance of a national to his/her state. Nationality allows a state jurisdiction over its citizens who in turn are entitled to a series of rights from the state of nationality. Nationals must, however, also comply with the laws and regulations of their state of nationality. International law has, however, left the granting of nationality to the domestic jurisdiction of states and there is, thus, no generally accepted definition of 'nationality' under international law. States are therefore free to determine the conditions under which they will ascribe and grant nationality to their citizens. In this regard the practice of states regarding the nationality of citizens is identical to the practice followed by international law on the issue of nationality of ships. It has been judicially recognized that '[g]enerally speaking it belongs to every sovereign to decide to whom he will accord the right to fly his flag and to prescribe the rules covering such grants'.[25]

Despite customary international law allowing states to ascribe nationality in any way they wish the International Court of Justice (ICJ) has qualified this right. In *Liechtenstein v. Guatemala*[26] the ICJ was asked to address the question of whether Liechtenstein had the right to raise a claim on behalf of one of its nationals against Guatemala. Nottebohm had been granted citizenship in Liechtenstein while residing there temporarily with his brother. The ICJ had to decide whether the nationality granted by Liechtenstein directly entailed an obligation by Guatemala to recognize its effect and thus Liechtenstein's right to exercise its protection. The Court found that as Nottebohm's actual connections with Liechtenstein were extremely tenuous Liechtenstein did not have a right to raise a claim for his protection. The ICJ thus held for the first time that a state cannot extend its protection to any of its nationals without question:

> Whether the factual connection between Nottebohm and Liechtenstein in the period proceeding, and contemporaneous with and following his naturalization appears to be sufficiently close, so preponderant in relation to any connection which may have existed between him and any other State that is possible to regard the nationality conferred upon him as real and effective, as the exact juridical expression of a social fact of a connection and which existed previously or came into existence thereafter. Naturalization is not a matter to be taken lightly. To seek and to obtain it is not something that happens frequently in the life of a human being. It involves his breaking of a bond of allegiance and his establishment of a new bond of allegiance. It may have far reaching consequences and involve profound changes in the destiny of the individual who obtains it.[27]

(ii)   Open Registries

The nationality of a ship is granted upon its registration on to the Register of Ships of a particular state. Registration is an administrative task and every state maintains its own laws and regulations concerning ship registration and the granting of nationality. Traditionally ships were registered where the owner kept the operating centre of the business signifying the entitlement of a particular ship to fly that state's flag and that the ship came under that state's jurisdiction. The granting of nationality to a registered ship signifies that the ship's external and internal legal relations are governed by the jurisdiction, laws and regulations of the flag-state. A ship while sailing on the high seas is therefore entitled to protection by the flag-state against the acts of any individual group or any third state which threatens the interests of that ship, including piracy. At the same time the legal rights and obligations of the owner and the ship over fiscal matters, manning, labor, social security, construction, pollution prevention and safety regulation are subject to flag-state jurisdiction.

Kasoulides identifies three systems of attribution of nationality to ships: first, closed or regulated registries where the ships are wholly owned by its nationals and manned primarily with national crew; second, a hybrid form where ownership and manning requirements are limited only by require-ments that they include a majority of citizens of the registering body; and third, open registries allowing ships to fly a flag of convenience.[28] Open registries appeared globally after World War II and owing to their financial advantage have been steadily increasing in popularity, representing a con-stantly growing percentage of world tonnage. As the international shipping sector has expanded and competition intensified, owners have tightened running costs. Ships flying under a flag with more favorable registration costs, taxation regimes, safety and environmental regulation, and social security requirements have a definite advantage. Open registries attract those owners seeking alternative registries that offer more benefits than the registries of their own state. Further, open registries apply a lax policy con-cerning the nationality of owners under their flag. Under open registries, owners who do not wish to appear as the real owners can shield behind beneficial ownership and more easily remain unidentified. Open registries have thus generated significant problems in so far as true ownership and management is concerned and have made accountability and responsibility in international law much more difficult.

The International Transport Workers' Federation (ITF) is the inter-national trade union that affiliates with national unions in the different branches of transportation. The ITF was once an influential union with a network in all major maritime states, its actions leading to adoption of col-lective agreements between ship owners and transport workers. It pursued its goals by placing pressure on ship owners, individual companies and governments. It lobbied for the adoption of stricter legislation in matters including crews' wages and their social security as well as safety and living conditions upon ships. The popularity of flags of convenience (FOCs) has, however, threatened the work of the ITF as shipowners can circumvent strict laws and collective agreements by re-registering their ships under an open registry. During the 1980s the ITF aggressively campaigned against the system of open registries, in particular against those states in which there was little or no legislation on matters such as wages and social security and safety and living conditions upon ships, and declared that all ships under open registries were substandard. During the last two decades, however, the ITF has had little success with its campaign against open registries and has recognized the reality of FOCs.

(iii) The Multilateral Position

Around the time of the *Nottebohm* case the International Law Commission (ILC) started work on preparation for the 1958 Law of the Sea Conference. The Conference was faced with two different and competing principles regarding the nationality of ships. First was the general principle of international law allowing each state to set out rules according to which a ship could sail under its flag, and second, whether it should adopt the newly emerged concept of 'genuine link'. The Conference opted for a provision incorporating both of these elements in a rather unsatisfactory fashion into the 1958 Convention on the High Seas (CHS):[29]

> Each state shall affix the conditions for the grant of its nationality to ships, for the registration of ships in its territory, and for the right to fly its flag. Ships have the nationality of the state whose flag they are entitled to fly. There must be a genuine link between the state and the ship; in particular, the state must effectively exercise its jurisdiction and control in administrative, technical and social matters over ships flying its flag.[30]

The 1982 United Nations Convention on the Law of the Sea (UNCLOS)[31] also deals with the issue of the genuine link. Unfortunately, however, it failed to either abolish the requirement for the existence of a genuine link altogether or to define and clarify the content of this requirement. In the UNCLOS the provision requiring a genuine link to exist between a ship and its flag state is totally separate from the provision of the exercise of effective jurisdiction and control by the flag state over ships' administrative, technical and social matters. Following the position of the CHS the UNCLOS provides that:

> Every state shall affix the conditions for the grant of its nationality to ships, for the registration of ships in its territory, and for the right to fly its flag. Ships have the nationality of whose flag they are entitled to fly. There must exist a genuine link between the state and the ship.[32]
>
> Every state shall effectively exercise its jurisdiction and control in administrative, technical and social matters over ships flying its flag.[33]
>
> In particular every state shall:
> (a) Maintain a register of ships containing the names and particulars of ships flying its flag, except those which are excluded from generally accepted international regulations on account of their small size; and
> (b) assure jurisdiction under its internal law over each ship flying its flag and its master, officers and crew in respect of administrative, technical and social matters concerning the ship.[34]

For the first time in international law the UNCLOS introduces into flag state jurisdiction the obligation to ensure safety at sea by taking measures regarding: construction; equipment; seaworthiness; manning; labor conditions; crews' training; and prevention of collisions.[35] However, the approach of the UNCLOS on the legitimacy of open registries is obviously a compromise and balanced position reflecting both maritime and non-maritime interests.

Not surprisingly the debate about the international system of open registries has continued post 1982 and the adoption of the UNCLOS. Issues concerning the continued legitimacy have been extensively considered within the United Nations Conference on Trade and Development (UNCTAD). The UNCTAD is a subsidiary organ of the United Nations General Assembly and was established in 1975 pursuant to a 1964 General Assembly Resolution with its primary function being: '[t]o promote international trade particularly trade between countries at different stages of development'. It is an intergovernmental organization composed of representatives from all United Nations member states who meet in a conference every three to four years to formulate policy guidelines and decide on programs of action.

The UNCTAD has for some time shown an interest in open registries and the FOCs debate and has expressed interest in collection of data regarding beneficial owners as the true managers of the world's tonnage. Beneficial owners are those persons, companies or organizations which gain the pecuniary benefits from the shipping operation. Merchant fleets of states with open registries are beneficially owned by interests based in other states. Discussions of the UNCTAD clearly recognize the need for stricter regulation of the international system of ship registration.

The basic principles upon which ship registration should be based were set out in a 1981 Resolution of the UNCTAD at its committee on shipping.[36] The Resolution provided the basic principles upon which ship registration should be based: the management of ship owning companies and ships; the identification and accountability of ship owners and operators; the equal participation of the state of registration in the capital of ship owning companies; and the manning of ships and other measures essential to ensure proper exercise of jurisdiction and control of the state on a ship flying its flag. The Resolution also recommended that, on the basis of these principles, an international conference should be convened.

The International Conference on Conditions for Registration of Ships thus began its work on 16 July 1984. The international community, however, was divided on the issue of open registries. The different studies undertaken by the UNCTAD during the 1970s and 1980s concluded that open registry fleets have adversely affected international shipping, especially the development and competitiveness of fleets of developing states. The UNCTAD considered that defining the 'genuine link' was of utmost importance, which unfortunately, however, led to the rejection of every proposal. The Conference commenced with the main aim of phasing out open registries, yet the only thing achieved was to legitimize the existing system.

In 1986 the international community adopted the final text of the United Nations Convention on Conditions for Registration of Ships (UNCCROS).[37] The objectives of the Convention are set out as:

> For the purposes of ensuring or, as the case may be, strengthening the genuine link between a state and ships flying its flag, and in order to exercise effectively its jurisdiction and control over such ships with regard to identification and accountability of shipowners and operators as well as with regard to administrative, technical, economic and social matters, a flag state shall apply the provisions contained in this Convention.[38]

The Convention provides that the state of registration will take measures to ensure that the owner or persons accountable for the management and operation of ships would be identifiable. Such information would be kept on the Register as well as on-board ships and must be made available to port state authorities.[39] The Convention then goes on to provide that:

> A state of registration has to comply either with the provisions of paragraphs 1 and 2 of Article 8 (ownership) or with the provisions of paragraphs 1 to 3 of Article 9 (manning), but may comply with both.[40]

Article 8 of the Convention provides for the participation of the flag-state or its nationals in the ownership of ships under its flag. However, the level of participation is left to the flag-state. The Convention merely provides that the said level: 'should be sufficient to permit the flag-state to exercise effectively its jurisdiction and control over ships flying its flag'.[41]

Article 9 of the Convention provides for the 'Manning of Ships'. It imposes on the flag-state a duty to observe the principle according to which a satisfactory part of the officers and crew will be nationals of the flag-state or persons permanently residing there. The flag state must ensure that manning is of a level and competence that will enable the ship to comply with international rules and standards.

IV.   THE IMO AND ECONOMIC INSTRUMENTS

This final section of the article builds on previous discussion on the principle of CBDRRC within international climate change law and the registration of ships under the international law of the sea. Discussion in both of these areas has had a particular focus on the problematic distinction between developed and developing states. In this section it will be demonstrated that, owing in large to the problems surrounding the developed/developing distinction, the IMO is unable to continue its work on economic instruments for the reduction of the carbon dioxide emissions of the international shipping sector. However, we first need to discuss the general position taken by international courts and tribunals in their examination of issues concerning the registration and nationality of international commercial interests concerning the distinction between developed and developing states.

(i)   International Courts and Tribunals on Nationality of Commercial Interests

The matter of genuine link was again judicially addressed by the ICJ in 1960 in its Advisory Opinion in the *IMCO* case.[42] In this case the ICJ had to address the issue of what was meant by the expression 'the largest ship-owning nations'. Membership of the IMO's Maritime Safety Committee required that it would consist of 14 members, representative of states having an important interest in maritime safety of which no less than eight must be 'the largest shipowning nations'. Traditional maritime states, including The Netherlands and the United Kingdom, sought to exclude Panama and Liberia from claiming two of the eight posts. Applying the genuine link doctrine from the *Nottebohm* case they argued that, as the owners of ships under Panama and Liberia registries were not nationals of those states, they must be excluded. The Court held that the concept of the genuine link was irrelevant and refused to examine it. It held that the provision referred to largest registered tonnage and not to beneficially owned tonnage. In effect, after registration, the nationality of the ship is one of the flag under which it flies, and third parties should recognize this without entering into the issue whether a genuine link exists or not between the ship and the flag state.

In its *Advisory Opinion on the Responsibilities and Obligations in the Area*[43] the Seabed Disputes Chamber of the International Tribunal for the Law of the Sea considered whether developing states should have preferential treatment, thereby allowing them less onerous environmental protection obligations than developed states. In this regard it was the opinion of the Chamber that:

> Equality of treatment between developing and developed sponsoring States is consistent with the need to prevent commercial enterprises based in

developed States from setting up companies in developing States, acquiring their nationality ... in the hope of being subjected to less burdensome regulations and controls.[44]

As can be seen, the requirement of a genuine link between the place of registration and nationality of the ownership commercial interests has not been supported by international courts and tribunals. This is probably because of the unimaginable difficulties of having to go behind registration and the granting of nationality in an economic world characterized by the transboundary activities of international commercial interests.

(ii)   The Creation of Economic Instruments

The Marine Environmental Protection Committee (MEPC) of the IMO has been discussing issues surrounding the adoption of economic instruments for the reduction by international shipping of its carbon dioxide emissions since its 58th meeting in 2008. Discussion has focused on a variety of economic instruments including an emissions trading scheme, a global levy on fuel, and other hybrid economic market-based schemes for ships engaged in international trade.[45] However, since the outset of discussions the majority of state delegations have expressed difficulty in incorporating the CBDRRC principle into any rules of the international shipping sector and in particular into any economic instruments that the IMO must adopt.

As reflected in state practice and as an established rule of customary international law, every state can affix its own conditions and requirements for the granting of its nationality to ships. This has tended to be the basis for justifying the common position of Developed Market Economy countries (DMEC) basing their interests in Less Developed countries (LDC).[46] As developed state interests can clearly be based in developing states, it has been demonstrated that open registries allowing owners many financial and other entitlements are a complicating factor owing in large to their blurring the distinction between developed and developing states.

Until the IMO suspended its work in the area there were 10 proposals on economic instruments that were being considered by an Expert Group. The economic instruments under consideration were in essence of two basic types, emissions trading schemes and levies. Either way, whatever economic instruments are ultimately adopted, the IMO will have a difficult time owing to the pricing of carbon needing to reflect the CBDRRC principle. In other words the IMO needs to synthesize into its rules on economic instruments the work of the UNFCCC. This has proven an immensely difficult task for the IMO and a significant rift has emerged between the

Organization's developed and developing state members. At the heart of these difficulties is an underlying and major theoretical conflict between differentiation and uniformity.

Developing states assert their position in what is in essence a three-pronged argument. First, they maintain the view that as a rule of international climate change law the CBDRRC principle needs to be applied to any economic instruments that may be created by the IMO rather than it adopting merely uniform measures which they perceive as economically disadvantageous for themselves. Second, they argue that the IMO is not the appropriate forum within which to create these rules, preferring instead a forum more sympathetic to their needs which could potentially be at the forefront of any measures that may be adopted in the area. Third, they have also questioned whether Annex VI of the International Convention for the Prevention of Pollution by Ships (MARPOL),[47] the principal ship-sourced air pollution multilateral instrument, is the correct regulatory strategy.

Developed states on the other hand maintain the converse position to that put forward by developing states. First, they argue that, owing to the transboundary nature of shipping activities, uniformity of international standards is the correct theoretical premise allowing for the effective regulation of this inherently international industry, which position they claim is of course further supported by the UNCLOS. Second, as a specialized international agency established with the express purpose of regulating the safety and pollution activities of the international shipping sector, the IMO is the appropriate forum within which to create these rules. This is further supported by the UNCLOS, which obligates states to act through the competent international organization in creating international rules protecting the oceans and seas from threats by shipping. Third, they argue that Annex VI of MARPOL is the correct regulatory strategy.

This is no mere *impasse* existing between the member states of the IMO; it is a head-on conflict not easily amenable to reconciliation. Certain developing states, most notably Brazil, China, Cuba and Saudi Arabia, have successfully advocated for a postponement of further work on market-based measures until further agreement is reached between the parties to the UNFCCC. We know, however, from the findings of the Intergovernmental Panel on Climate Change that humanity is facing irreversible changes to global weather patterns with potentially devastating consequences. There is thus an urgency with which we need to act so as to prevent such extensive devastation. This article now makes the following observations.

First, the carbon dioxide emissions from the international shipping sector contribute approximately 2.7% of total global carbon emissions. However, as economies and trade expand so will demands on the international shipping sector, resulting in increases in its carbon dioxide emissions. The IMO has a 'common' responsibility concerning the reduction of the international shipping sector's carbon dioxide emissions that includes responsibility for creating appropriate economic instruments. Furthermore, the IMO must reconcile the issues it faces surrounding the application of the principle of CBDRRC. It has been shown by this article the inherently problematic distinction in the methodology employed within international climate change law concerning the dichotomy of states into the regulatory classification of states as Annex I and Non-Annex I. It is hoped that the current Paris discussions at COP 21 will effectively deal with the developed/developing state dichotomy and the particular position of developing states, especially small island developing states and other vulnerable states to the effects of climatic change and rising sea levels.

Second, in many ways the discussions at COP 21 and the way forward in international climate change law particularly concerning the differentiation of responsibilities between developed and developing states may not be of as great an assistance to the creation of economic instruments by the IMO as one may have hoped. It has been unequivocally demonstrated by this article that the dichotomy between developed and developing and the subsequent classification of states does not accurately distinguish between shipping interests as reflected by registered tonnage. Through open registries allowing interests based in DMECs to register enterprise in LDCs, the dichotomy and classification of states as developed and developing becomes highly distorted. Further, the inability of the register of ships in states with open registries to identify the true beneficial owners of registered tonnage further exacerbates the already inaccurate dichotomy and distinction between developed and developing states.

Third, the legal framework of open registries has facilitated increased profits for the international shipping sector, one of the most fiercely competitive industries in the world. Open registries have been providing their services to shipping interests based in DMECs over the last seven decades. Any expectation of potential reform towards a greater transparency and accountability would be misplaced. All the multilateral initiatives that have been discussed in this article have perpetuated the continued existence of open registries despite any contrary intentions that may have been expressed at earlier stages of diplomatic negotiations. Further, it does not appear that any international court or tribunal, in particular the authoritative ICJ or ITLOS, is prepared to examine any issues beyond what appears in a state's register and it has been unequivocally stated by the ITLOS that there must exist equality of treatment between developed and developing states.

V. CONCLUSION

The article has highlighted the difficulties faced by international climate change law in the application of the principle of CBDRRC because of both an ill-defined meaning and a problematic classification of developed and developing states as Annex I and Non-Annex I states. The article has also highlighted how the registration of ships in open registries and the subsequent granting of nationality have further blurred the distinction between developed and developing states as it is commonplace for interests based in DMECs to register their tonnage in LDCs. The article has thus demonstrated that the CBDRRC principle and open registries that are both directly related to the distinction and subsequent division between developed and developing states are the main obstacles in the IMO's adoption of economic instruments concerning the reduction of the carbon dioxide emissions of the international shipping sector.

The article then went on to discuss the obstacles faced by the IMO in creating appropriate economic instruments concerning the reduction of the carbon dioxide emissions of the international shipping sector. Following this the article made three main submissions. First, the IMO cannot distinguish between developed and developing states, at least for the moment. So it needs to address the common responsibility that states have for the reduction of the carbon dioxide emissions of the international shipping sector and adopt appropriate economic instruments. Second, the IMO is the appropriate forum in which the economic instruments are to be made. This is supported by a direction in the UNCLOS to the competent international organization which is obviously a reference to the IMO. Third, as the *lex specialis* regarding the regulation of the air emissions of the international shipping sector, Annex VI of MARPOL is obviously the correct regulatory strategy for the creation of the economic instruments.

The CBDRRC principle conflicts 'head-on' with the well-established principles of equality of states, reciprocity of obligations and uniformity of international standards. These are all well-enshrined principles reflected in the laws of the IMO. It is thus concluded that owing to the magnitude of the difficulties demonstrated we need to look beyond the distinction drawn between Annex I and Non-Annex I states. Further, given the potential of irreversible climate change, the IMO cannot defer any longer its responsibility for the reduction of the international shipping sector's carbon dioxide emissions and needs to act now in the creation of appropriate economic instruments. There is now an urgency to dramatically cut global climate change emissions and move towards low carbon emission economies. It will be interesting to see how the principle of CBDRRC, reiterated in the new climate change agreement adopted at Paris in December 2015, will be implemented.

NOTES

1. Intergovernmental Panel on Climate Change, Climate Change 2014 Synthesis Report 6-9 (2014), available at http://www.ipcc.ch/reportar5/syr/.
2. International Maritime Organization, *Historical Background on GHG*, http://www.imo.org/OurWork/Environment/PollutionPrevention/AirPollution/Pages/Historic%20Background%20GHG.aspx.
3. International Maritime Organization, *IMO Policies and Practices Related to the Reduction of Greenhouse Gas Emissions from Ships*, Res. A.963(23) (5 Dec., 2003).
4. United Nations Conference on the Human Environment, Stockholm Declaration, 16 June 1972, UN Doc A/CONF.48/14 (1972), principle 12, reprinted in (1972) 11 ILM 1416–1419 [hereinafter Stockholm Declaration].
5. Between 3 and 14 June, 1992 the United Nations Conference on Environment and Development [hereinafter UNCED] was held in Rio de Janeiro, Brazil. It remains the greatest environmental conference of our time attended by over 170 governments and resulting in the adoption of a suite of both legally and non-legally binding multilateral instruments.
6. Duncan French, 'Developing States and International Environmental Law: The Importance of Differentiated Responsibilities' (2000) 49 *Int'l & Comp. L. Q.* 35, 35–36.
7. Rio Declaration on Environment and Development, 1 U.N. Doc. A/CONF.151/26/Rev.1 (12 Aug., 1992) [hereinafter Rio Declaration].
8. *Id.* principle 6.
9. *Id.* principle 7.
10. Stathis Palassis, 'Beyond the Global Summits: Reflecting on the Environmental Principles of Sustainable Development' (2011) 22 *ColoradoJ. of Int'l Env'l L. & Pol.* 41–77.
11. United Nations Framework Convention on Climate Change, 9 May, 1992 1771 U.N.T.S. 107 [hereinafter UNFCCC].
12. Kyoto Protocol to the United Nations Convention on Climate Change, FCCC/CP/1997/C.7/Add1 (11 Dec., 1997) [hereinafter Kyoto Protocol].
13. UNFCCC, article 4(1)(b).
14. Kyoto Protocol, article 10.
15. See generally, Paul G. Harris, 'Common but Differentiated Responsibility: The Kyoto Protocol and United States Policy' (1999) 7 *N.Y.U. Envtl L. J.* 27–48.
16. See generally, Lavanya Rajamani, 'The Principle of Common but Differentiated Responsibility and the Balance of Commitments under the Climate Change Regime' (2000) 9 *Rev. Eur. Community & Int'l Envtl L.* 120–131.
17. Duncan French, 'Developing States and International Environmental Law: The Importance of Differentiated Responsibilities' (2000) 49 *Int'l & Comp L. Q.* 35–60.
18. International Law Association [hereinafter ILA], *Washington Conference (2014): Legal Principles Relating to Climate Change*, Draft Article 5(2), 12.
19. Yoshiro Matsui, 'Some Aspects of the Principle of 'Common but Differentiated Responsibilities'' (2002) 2 *Int'l Env'l Agreements: Pol., L. & Econ's* 151–171, 155.
20. ILA, Draft Article 5(3).
21. ILA, Draft Article 5(4), 12.
22. International Law Association, *Washington Conference (2014): Legal Principles Relating to Climate Change*, citing L. Rajamani, *Differential Treatment in International Environmental Law* (Oxford University Press, Oxford, 2006), 2.

23. Pieter Pauw, Steffen Bauer, Carmen Richerzhagen, Clara Brandi and Hanna Schmole, 'Different Perspectives on Differentiated Responsibilities' *German Development Institute/Deutsches Institut fur Entwicklungspolitik (DIE)*, 6/2014, 28.
24. Pauw et al., 2.
25. The *Muscat Dhows* case 1905 XI R.I.A.A. (Reports of International Arbitral Awards) 83.
26. *Liechtenstein v Guatemala* (The *Nottebohm* Case) [1955] *ICJ Rep* 4.
27. *Id.*, at 24–26.
28. George C. Kasoulides, 'The 1986 United Nations Convention on the Conditions of Registration of Vessels and the Question of Open Registry' (1989) 20 *Ocean Development & International Law* 543–576, at 546.
29. Convention on the High Seas (1958) 450 U.N.T.S. 11 [hereinafter CHS].
30. CHS, article 5(1).
31. United Nations Convention on the Law of the Sea, Dec. 10, 1982, 1833 U.N.T.S. 397 [hereinafter UNCLOS].
32. UNCLOS, article 91(1).
33. UNCLOS, article 94(1).
34. UNCLOS, article 94(2).
35. UNCLOS, articles 94(3) and (4).
36. United Nations Conference on Trade and Development, Resolution 43(S-III).
37. United Nations Convention on Conditions for Registration of Ships, Doc. TD/RS/ CONF/19/Add.1 [hereinafter UNCCROS].
38. UNCCROS, article 1.
39. UNCCROS, article 6.
40. UNCCROS, article 7.
41. UNCCROS, article 8.
42. *IMCO Case* [1960] *ICJ Rep* 150.
43. Request for an Advisory Opinion from Nii Allotey Adunton, Secretary General of the International Seabed Authority, to Judge Tullio Treves, President of the Seabed Disputes Chamber (May 11, 2010).
44. Responsibilities and Obligations of State Sponsoring Persons and Entities with Respect to Activities in the Area Advisory Opinion Feb. 1, 2011, 6, at 159.
45. Marine Env't Prot. Comm., *Marine Environmental Protection Committee (MEPC), 58th Session: 6–10 October 2008*, International Maritime Organization.
46. Mervyn Rowlinson, 'Flags of Convenience: The UNCTAD Case' (1985) 12 *Marit. Pol. & Management* 241–244.
47. International Convention for the Prevention of Pollution by Ships (MARPOL 73) (London), 12 *ILM* (1973), 1319 (Amended by Protocol of 1978); Protocol Relating to the Convention for the Prevention of Pollution from Ships (MARPOL 78) (London).

12. Sectoral allocation patterns in the EU Emission Trading Scheme: Empirical evidence and outlook

Claudia Kettner

1. INTRODUCTION

The EU Emission Trading Scheme (EU ETS) is the most important climate policy instrument in the European Union. Implemented in 2005, the EU ETS was the first international trading system for greenhouse gas emissions and it is still the largest carbon market worldwide: currently the scheme covers more than 11,000 power stations and industrial plants in 31 countries responsible for more than 50% of the EU's CO_2 emissions.

In the first two trading phases, the performance of the EU ETS was, however, characterised by pronounced surplus allocation that translated into low carbon prices.[1] Therefore, for the third trading phase—which covers the period from 2013 to 2020—and beyond, a number of changes to the EU ETS were adopted in the EU's 2008 Climate and Energy Package[2] that should help improve the credibility of the scheme, incentivising low carbon investment. One major modification referred to the change in allocation procedures, giving more weight to the auctioning of allowances as compared with previous trading phases.

Despite these fundamental changes, the third trading phase so far is still characterised by an oversupply of allowances. This situation reflects not only the structural surplus of allowances banked from the second to the third trading phase[3] but also persistent surplus allocation to sectors deemed to be exposed to carbon leakage. This excess supply on the sector level reflects the fact that sectoral production is below the levels anticipated when free allocation was determined. While this can be regarded as a means for alleviating the pressure of carbon prices on exposed sectors in times of an economic slowdown, it also hampers the long-term economic efficiency of the ETS, since the oversupply of allowances translates into a very weak price signal that is not sufficient for inducing low carbon innovation.

This chapter starts out with a description of (sectoral) allocation rules in the EU ETS and their development over time (Section 2). In Section 3, the empirical evidence on the stringency of allocation on sector level is analysed using installation data from the EU Transaction Log, focussing on differences between the second trading phase (2008–2012) and the first two years of the third trading phase (2013 and 2014). This is complemented by a discussion of the potential role of the amendments of allocation rules for the upcoming trading periods with the aim of mitigating (sectoral) surplus allocation in Section 4. The final section concludes.

2.   SECTORAL ALLOCATION IN THE EU ETS

In the first two trading phases, Member States were responsible for allocating allowances to sectors and installations in National Allocation Plans that had to follow certain guidelines defined by the European Commission.[4] Allocation was largely based on grandfathering since the Emission Trading Directive 2003/87/EC[5] limited the share of allowances eligible for auctioning to 5% of the total allocated allowances in Phase 1 and to 10% in Phase 2.

For Phase 3, which covers the period 2013–2020, in contrast, an EU-wide cap[6] and allocation process were established in the New Emission Trading Directive 2009/29/EC.[7] This directive furthermore defines different allocation procedures for three categories of sectors according to their potential exposure to carbon leakage.

A sector is considered to be at risk of carbon leakage if it experiences a certain increase in production cost owing to emission trading or if it is strongly exposed to international trade. More precisely, a sector is defined to be exposed to carbon leakage:

(1)   if the direct and indirect costs of emissions trading (cost intensity) amount to at least 5% of sectoral gross value added, *and* the sector's trade intensity with third countries—that is, the share of exports and imports in the market[8]—exceeds 10% (Article 10a, Paragraph 15); *or*

(2)   if the cost intensity of emissions trading adds up to at least 30% of sectoral gross value added (Article 10a, Paragraph 16a); *or*

(3)   if the sector's trade intensity is at least 30% (Article 10a, Paragraph 16b).

The concrete list of sectors considered to be potentially at risk of carbon leakage based on the above criteria has been published in Commission Decision 2010/2/EU and amended in the Commission Decisions 2011/278/

EU, 2011/745/EU, 2012/498/EU and 2014/9/EU for the years 2013 and 2014.[9] For the period 2015–2019 an updated list of exposed sectors has been published in Commission Decision 2014/746/EU.[10]

In the years 2013 and 2014, 146 (sub)sectors were identified to be at risk of carbon leakage based on the indicators laid out above. Some 132 (sub)sectors qualified on the basis of the trade intensity criterion, and 14 on the cost intensity or the combined criterion. The latter 14 (sub)sectors accounted, however, for almost 60% of allocations. Overall, sectors constituting 97% of the industrial emissions covered by the EU ETS were considered to be at risk of carbon leakage in the years 2013 and 2014. For the period 2015–2019, again, virtually all sectors qualify for preferential allocation owing to potential leakage.[11]

Sectors considered to be potentially exposed to carbon leakage will receive up to 100% free allocation until 2020.[12] The power sector, in contrast, has already been facing full auctioning since 2013.[13] All other sectors received a share of 80% of free allocation in 2013 that will be linearly reduced to 30% in 2020.

Both the initial carbon leakage list and the updated list for the period 2015–2019 are based on an assumed carbon price of €30. While this assumption seems plausible for the period until 2014 given economic growth rates expected in 2008 and the associated scarcity of certificates, the use of a €30 carbon price for the period until 2030 is questionable owing to persistently low carbon prices.[14] Nevertheless the European Commission argued in Decision 2014/746/EU[15] that it was justified in using this price in the assessment of carbon leakage as 'the carbon price will in the future be more strongly driven by mid- and long-term emission reductions', as for example defined in the EU's 2030 climate and energy policy framework.[16]

3.   DEVELOPMENT OF ALLOCATION PATTERNS AT SECTOR LEVEL

3.1   Database and Methodological Approach

For the empirical analysis of sectoral allocation patterns, data on free allocation and emissions on installation level from the EU Transaction Log (EUTL)[17] is used. The EUTL currently covers more than 11,000 installations in the EU-28 and the EFTA countries Iceland, Norway and Liechtenstein.[18] As of autumn 2015, allocation and emissions data are available for the period 2005–2014. For the analysis a sample of 9000 installations, for which both data on allocation and emissions are available for the individual years, is used.

The comparison of free allocation and emissions is based on the indicators put forward by Kettner et al.:[19] the sector's gross surplus and gross shortage as the sum of all allowance surpluses and respective shortages of the installations included in the sector; and the sector's allowance net surplus and shortage as the balance of the gross surplus and the gross shortage if the balance is positive (negative), that is, if the gross surplus exceeds (is below) the shortage.

3.2 Development of Free Allocation over Time

Figure 12.1 contrasts sectoral free allocation in the second trading phase and in the first two years of the third trading phase.[20] In Phase 2, free allocation in the EU ETS amounted to 1900 Mt for the sample of installations; in the third trading phase, the number of free allowances has been reduced by more than 55% to 840 Mt.

The combustion sector[21] is the largest ETS sector in terms of allocation: in the second trading phase, about 1250 million of free allowances (corresponding to 65% of total ETS allocation) were distributed to this sector. In the third trading phase, the sector's free allocation has been reduced by more than 70% to 340 Mt in line with the new allocation principles.[22]

In addition to the combustion sector, the sectors 'cement and lime',

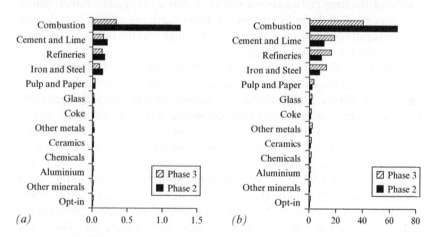

Source: EUTL (2015), 'European Union Transaction Log', http://ec.europa.eu/ environment/ets/welcome.do, accessed 11 November 2015; own illustration.

Figure 12.1 Average annual free allocation in the EU ETS at sector level: (a) free sectoral allocation in Gt CO$_2$e; (b) sectoral share in free EU allocation in per cent

'refineries' and 'iron and steel' hold significant shares in EU ETS allocation. In the second trading phase, 210 Mt of allowances were assigned to 'cement and lime'; the allocation to 'refineries' and 'iron and steel' amounted to 170 Mt and 140 Mt respectively. For these three sectors, free allocation was reduced by only 18–23% since they qualified for preferential treatment as potentially being exposed to carbon leakage.[23] Overall, these four largest sectors accounted for 93% of (free) EU ETS allocation in the second trading phase and for 88% of free allocation in the current, third trading period.

3.3   Free Allocation Versus Verified Emissions at Sector Level

In this section, the free allocation is compared with verified emissions in Phases 2 and 3. In the second trading phase, all ETS sectors except for the combustion sector showed a, partly pronounced, surplus of allowances (see Figure 12.2a). As a percentage of sectoral allocation, the surplus ranged from 6% ('refineries') to 42% ('iron and steel'). In absolute terms, the sector 'iron and steel' also showed the largest surplus (70 Mt), followed by 'cement and lime' (52 Mt). In the combustion sector, emissions exceeded free allocation, however, by approximately 10% (121 Mt).

The oversupply of allowances in the second trading phase only partly reflected the fall of emissions owing to reduced economic activity in the course of the financial and economic crisis, but also depicts a rather 'generous' allocation to the industrial sectors included in the scheme that showed an oversupply of allowances even in 2008, which was the only year in Phase 2 to be characterised by a stringent cap.[24]

In the first years of the third trading phase, 2013 and 2014, in contrast, verified emissions exceeded free allocation in eight out of the 13 ETS sectors (see Figure 12.2b). Besides the combustion sector, which generally faces a higher share of auctioning compared with the industrial sectors (see above), opt-in installations[25] as well as the sectors 'refineries' and 'non-ferrous metals' showed the highest percentage shortage of allowances. In absolute terms, emissions exceeded free allocation by 892 Mt in the combustion sector, while the second largest shortage accrued to the sector 'refineries' with 22 Mt. In the period 2013/2014, five sectors still exhibited a net surplus of free allocation over verified emissions: 'aluminium', 'ceramics', 'pulp and paper', 'iron and steel' and 'cement and lime'. The largest percentage net surplus showed for 'iron and steel' with 27% and 'pulp and paper' with 16%. In absolute terms the highest net surpluses can again be found for 'iron and steel' with 37 Mt followed by 'cement and lime' with 20 Mt. Moreover, in all sectors at least some installations received more free allowances than they eventually needed: in sectors with a net shortage of free allowances, gross surplus allocation ranged between

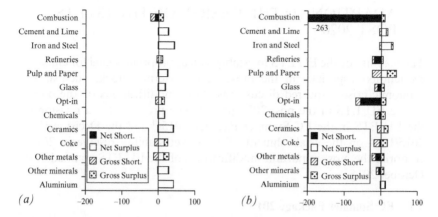

Source: EUTL (2015), 'European Union Transaction Log', http://ec.europa.eu/
environment/ets/welcome.do, accessed 11 November 2015; own illustration.

Figure 12.2   *Average annual sectoral free allocation and emissions in the*
            EU ETS in percentage of free allocation: (a) Phase 2
            (2008–2012); (b) Phase 3 (2013–2014)

4 and 16% of sectoral allocation and amounted to 42 Mt for the total EU
ETS. In contrast, also in sectors with a net surplus of allowances, some
installations were short in free allocation resulting in gross shortages of
between 2 and 25%. Overall, allocation disparities within sectors as indicated by gross shortage and surplus in Figure 12.2 have increased in the
third trading phase as compared with the second.

The excess supply on the sector level reflects that sectoral production is
lower than anticipated for the third trading period when free allocation was
determined. While this reduced the pressure of carbon prices on sectors in
times of an economic slowdown, the long-term economic efficiency of the
EU ETS is hampered, since the oversupply of allowances implies a very
weak price signal inadequate for incentivising low-carbon innovation. This
issue is even more precarious given the surplus allowances transferred by
the industrial sectors from the second to the third trading phase.[26] While the
general price signal established by the EU ETS is very weak—with prices
between €2.6 and €8.6 in the third trading phase[27]—installations endowed
with surplus allocation are confronted with even lower incentives for emission reduction: opposed to economic theory that stresses the opportunity
costs of holding free allowances,[28] installations covered by the EU ETS in
practice did not perceive an adequate price signal from free allocation as long
as they were able to cover verified emissions with their existing allocation.[29]

4.   ADAPTION TO THE DESIGN OF THE EU ETS POST 2020

The inability of the EU ETS to establish an appropriate signal for emission reductions—especially in the presence of external shocks such as the economic crisis—spurred discussions about modifications of the design of the EU ETS in the post-2020 period. The proposal for a revision of the EU ETS in the EC Summer Package 2015[30] and the Decision (EU) 2015/1814 on the establishment of a market stability reserve in 2018[31] comprise the most important modifications of the EU ETS planned as of October 2015.

4.1   EC Summer Package 2015

In July 2015, the European Commission published a legislative proposal for a revision of the EU ETS in the fourth trading phase in line with the 2030 climate and energy policy framework of October 2014.[32] This proposal includes the following major changes to the current design of the emissions trading scheme:

(1) *A change of the linear annual reduction factor:* up to 2030, the EU aims for a reduction of greenhouse gas emissions of 40% compared with the level of 1990. Just as for the period until 2020, this overall target will be split between the EU ETS and the non-ETS sectors. While in the non-ETS sectors emissions will have to be cut by 30% compared with 2005, for the ETS sectors a reduction requirement of 43% compared with 2005 will apply.[33] This implies an increase of the annual linear reduction factor by which the cap of the EU ETS will be reduced to 2.2% as compared with 1.74% in the third trading phase (2013–2020).

(2) *A fixed share of auctioned allowances in total allocation:* post 2020, emission allowances again will partly be allocated free of charge on the basis of sector-specific benchmarks and partly be auctioned. The Commission Proposal suggests fixing the percentage of allowances to be auctioned in the period until 2030 at 57% of total allocation. This share corresponds to the average proportion of allowances auctioned in the third trading phase. Sectors potentially exposed to carbon leakage shall receive up to 100% free allocation, while the power allocation to the power sector will be largely based on auctioning[34] and the other sectors continue to receive up to 30% free allocation.

(3) *New criteria for the assessment of carbon leakage:* revised criteria for the assessment of carbon leakage shall apply beyond 2020 according to the Commission's proposal. The assessment of carbon leakage will

be based on trade and CO_2 intensity (as compared with trade and cost intensity in the third trading phase; see Section 2). In Phase 4, a sector will be considered to be at risk of carbon leakage if its trade intensity with third countries[35] multiplied by the sector's carbon intensity[36] exceeds a value of 0.2. If sectors receive a score that is higher than 0.18, they may also be included in the list of exposed sectors on the basis of a qualitative appraisal of the sectoral potentials for the reduction of emissions or electricity consumption, the market characteristics and profit margins.

(4) *Support for sectors at risk of carbon leakage owing to indirect cost increases:* according to the Commission (sub)sectors that are exposed to carbon leakage owing to significant indirect carbon costs, that is, higher electricity costs resulting from a pass-through of carbon prices, should receive financial support by the Member States.

(5) *Update of benchmarks to reflect technological advances:* the benchmark values that determine the effective level of the installations' free allocation in sectors exposed to carbon leakage will be updated in order to reflect technological progress since 2008. The (sub)sectoral benchmark values defined in 2007/2008 shall generally be decreased by 1% for each year between 2008 and the middle of the relevant ETS trading period.

(6) *Implementation of an Innovation Fund and a Modernisation Fund:* as successor of the NER300 Program, an Innovation Fund will be installed in order to support innovation in the fields of renewable energy and CCS as well as low-carbon innovation in emission-intensive industries. A total of 400 million of allowances will be used for financing the fund.[37] In addition, a Modernisation Fund will be set up to support the transition to a low carbon emission system in Member States in which the GDP per capita in 2013 was below 60% of the EU average.[38] Some 2% of the total EU ETS allowances in the period 2021–2030, that is, 310 million, will be used to finance this fund.

(7) A more frequent alignment of allocation to production data is planned.

4.2   Establishment of a Market Stability Reserve

In October 2015, the European Parliament and Council decided that a market stability reserve (MSR) will be established that will start operation in 2019.[39] The key objective of the MSR is to deal with surplus allocation that accumulated during the second and third trading phase and will be transferred to the subsequent trading period.[40] Allowances will be placed in or released from the MSR, depending on the number of allowances in the market not needed for compliance ('the number of allowances in circulation'): each year 12% of the circulating allowances shall be placed in the MSR via a reduction of the volume of allowances to be auctioned, if the amount of circulating allowances amounts to at least 100 million. In contrast, 100 million allowances are to be released from the MSR if the number of circulating allowances falls below 400 million; if the number of allowances in the MSR is below 100 million, all allowances should be released from the reserve. Moreover, if measures in the event of excessive price fluctuations (Article 29a of Directive 2009/29/EC) are adopted, 100 million allowances shall be released from the MSR even if the number of circulating allowances exceeds 400 million.

Some 900 million allowances whose auctioning had been postponed from the beginning to the end of the third trading phase ('backloading', Commission Regulation (EU) 176/2014[41]) will not be auctioned in 2019 or 2020 but placed in the MSR. In addition, unused allowances from the New Entrants Reserve[42] as well as allowances that will not have been distributed owing to installation closures will also be placed in the reserve.

5.   CONCLUSIONS

Despite fundamental changes of allocation principles, in the third trading period some ETS sectors still see overallocation, and owing to the transfer of allowances from Phase 2, a massive excess supply of allowances is found for the EU ETS in total.

Evidence on the sector level shows that the current practice of benchmark-based free allocation on the sector level is not adequate: on the one hand, the level of free allocation is fixed in advance based on production volumes that are not updated and the sector-specific benchmark. On the other hand, one criterion for the assessment of a sector's potential to be considered to be exposed to carbon leakage is cost intensity that is calculated assuming a carbon price of €30 throughout the third trading phase, which is leading to an overestimation of the carbon leakage potential and in turn to an exaggerated share of free allocation.

The decision to prepone the establishment of the MSR and to place the backloaded allowances in it will help reduce the excess supply of allowances in the market. The comparably small share of allowances of 12% that are to be shifted in the reserve in case there is more than 100 million circulating allowances implies, however, that there will only be a gradual reduction of the structural surplus of allowances in Phase 4.

The revision of the allocation mechanisms for free allowances as proposed by the European Commission in summer 2015[43] would generally have the potential for increasing the incentives for emission abatement generated by the EU ETS. This will, however, strongly depend on the implementation of the more frequent alignment of free allocation to production levels that is not specified in the current proposal. Moreover, if the new assessment criteria limit the number of (sub)sectors that are considered to be at risk of carbon leakage to 50, as suggested in the Commission Proposal (compared with more than 160 in the second trading phase), this might contribute to reinforcing the carbon price signal.

NOTES

1. In Phase 1 (2005–2007) oversupply reflected incomplete information in the allocation process; in Phase 2 (2008–2012) it resulted from a drop in emissions in the course of the economic and financial crisis.
2. COM/2008/30, Communication from the Commission: 20 20 by 2020—Europe's climate change opportunity, Brussels.
3. Kettner, C. (2015), 'The EU Emission Trading Scheme: First Evidence on Phase 3', in Kreiser, L., et al. (eds), *Critical Issues in Environmental Taxation Vol. XV*, Northampton, MA: Edward Elgar, pp. 63–75.
4. An overview is provided in Kettner, C., A. Köppl and S. Schleicher (2010), 'The EU Emissions Trading Scheme—Insights from the First Trading Years with a Focus on Price Volatility', in Dias Soares, C., et al. (eds), *Critical Issues in Environmental Taxation Vol. VIII*, Oxford: Oxford University Press, pp. 205–225.
5. Directive 2003/87/EC of the European Parliament and of the Council of 13 October 2003 Establishing a Scheme for Greenhouse Gas Emission Allowance Trading within the Community and Amending Council Directive 96/61/EC.
6. The cap of the EU ETS will be reduced linearly by 1.74% (38 Mt CO_2e) per annum in the third trading phase, thereby achieving an emission reduction in ETS sectors of 21% in 2020 compared to 2005 levels.
7. Directive 2009/29/EC of the European Parliament and of the Council of 23 April 2009 Amending Directive 2003/87/EC so as to Improve and Extend the Greenhouse Gas Emission Allowance Trading Scheme of the Community.
8. Defined as sector turnover plus imports.
9. Commission Decision 2010/2/EU of 24 December 2009 Determining, pursuant to Directive 2003/87/EC of the European Parliament and of the Council, a List of Sectors and Subsectors Which Are Deemed to Be Exposed to a Significant Risk of Carbon Leakage; Commission Decision 2011/278/EU of 27 April 2011 determining transitional Union-wide rules for harmonised free allocation of emission allowances pursuant to Article 10a of Directive 2003/87/EC of the European Parliament and of the Council; Commission Decision 2011/745/EU of 11 November 2011 Amending Decisions 2010/2/ EU and 2011/278/EU as Regards the Sectors and Subsectors Which Are Deemed to Be Exposed to a Significant Risk of Carbon Leakage; Commission Decision 2012/498/ EU of 17 August 2012 Amending Decisions 2010/2/EU and 2011/278/EU as Regards the Sectors and Subsectors Which Are Deemed to Be Exposed to a Significant Risk of Carbon Leakage; Commission Decision 2014/9/EU of 18 December 2013 Amending Decisions 2010/2/EU and 2011/278/EU as Regards the Sectors and Subsectors Which Are Deemed to Be Exposed to a Significant Risk of Carbon Leakage.
10. Commission Decision 2014/746/EU of 27 October 2014 determining, pursuant to Directive 2003/87/EC of the European Parliament and of the Council, a list of sectors

and subsectors that are deemed to be exposed to a significant risk of carbon leakage, for the period 2015–2019.

11. Despite minor changes in the calculations, such as updated emission factors for electricity in the calculation of the indirect carbon costs. SWD(2015)135 final, Impact Assessment accompanying the document Proposal for a Directive of the European Parliament and of the Council amending Directive 2003/87/EC to enhance cost-effective emission reductions and low-carbon investments, Brussels.

12. The level of free allocation will, however, be reduced in line with the linear reduction of the total cap by 1.74% per annum.

13. Exceptions for highly efficient co-generation and district heating as well as for some New Member States are, however, provided for.

14. As of October 2015 carbon prices are in the range of €8.

15. Above n. 10.

16. COM/2014/15, A policy framework for climate and energy in the period from 2020 to 2030, Brussels.

17. EUTL (2015), 'European Union Transaction Log', http://ec.europa.eu/environment/ets/welcome.do, accessed 11 November 2015.

18. The EFTA countries joined the EU ETS in 2008.

19. Kettner, C., A. Köppl, S. Schleicher and G. Thenius (2008), 'Stringency and Distribution in the EU Emissions Trading Scheme: First Evidence', *Climate Policy*, **8** (1), 41–61.

20. Between the first and the second trading phase, sectoral allocation had been roughly constant (see Kettner et al., above n. 4).

21. According to Directive 2009/29/EC, the combustion sector covers 'combustion of fuels in installations with a total rated thermal input exceeding 20 MW'—that is, mostly power and heat generation but also combustion activities related to other economic activities.

22. This corresponds to a 40% share in total free allocation in the third trading phase.

23. 'Refineries' met the combined cost and trade intensity criterion (as defined in Article 10a(15) of the emissions trading directive); the subsectors 'cement' and 'lime' met the cost intensity criterion as set out in point (a) of Article 10a(16) and the sector 'iron and steel' qualifies under both Article 10a(15) and Article 10a(16b). See Commission Decision 2010/2/EU, above n. 9, and European Commission (2014), Detailed data on direct and indirect costs, and trade, for all assessed sectors, http://ec.europa.eu/clima/policies/ets/cap/leakage/docs/carbon_leakage_detailed_info_en.pdf, accessed 11 November 2015.

24. Kettner, C., D. Kletzan-Slamanig and A. Köppl (2015), 'The EU Emission Trading Scheme. Sectoral Allocation Patterns and Factors Determining Emission Changes', *Journal of Environmental Economics and Policy*, **4** (1), 1–14.

25. The high shortage of 56% might reflect the fact that opt-in installations comprise mainly small-scale combustion activities below the threshold of a total rated thermal input exceeding 20 MW for mandatory inclusion in the EU ETS.

26. Kettner, above n. 3; SWD(2014)331/F1, Impact assessment accompanying the document Commission Decision determining, pursuant to Directive 2003/87/EC of the European Parliament and the Council, a list of sectors and subsectors which are deemed to be exposed to a significant risk of carbon leakage for the period 2015–2019, Brussels.

27. EEX Spot Prices, https://www.eex.com/en/market-data/emission-allowances/spot-market/ecarbix#!/2015/11/10.

28. The opportunity cost of holding certificates can be defined as the 'revenue forgone by refraining from selling the allowances and by employing them in producing output' (Woerdman, E., S. Clò and A. Arcuri (2008), 'Emissions Trading and the Polluter-Pays Principle: Do Polluters Pay under Grandfathering?', in Faure, M. and M. Peeters (eds), *Climate Change and European Emissions Trading. Lessons for Theory and Practice*, Cheltenham: Edward Elgar, pp. 128–150).

29. Sandoff, A. and G. Schaad (2009), 'Does EU ETS Lead to Emission Reductions through Trade? The Case of the Swedish Emissions Trading Sector Participants', *Energy Policy*,

37 (10), 3967–3977; Jaraite, J., F. Convery and C. Di Maria (2010), 'Transaction Costs for Firms in the EU ETS: Lessons from Ireland', *Climate Policy*, **10** (2), 190–215.

30. COM/2015/337, Proposal for a Directive of the European Parliament and of the Council amending Directive 2003/87/EC to enhance cost-effective emission reductions and low-carbon investments, Brussels.

31. Decision (EU) 2015/1814 of 6 October 2015 concerning the establishment and operation of a market stability reserve for the Union greenhouse gas emission trading scheme and amending Directive 2003/87/EC.

32. COM/2014/15, above n. 16.

33. Sectoral emission reduction requirements are defined as changes vis-à-vis 2005, since a distinction between emissions from ETS and non-ETS sectors is possible only since the first emissions trading year.

34. Just as in the second trading phase exceptions apply for highly efficient co-generation and district heating as well as for some New Member States.

35. The trade intensity is again defined as 'the ratio between the total value of exports to third countries plus the value of imports from third countries and the total market size for the European Economic Area (annual turnover plus total imports from third countries)' (COM/2015/337, above n. 30).

36. The emission intensity is defined as greenhouse gas emissions per gross value added and measured in kg CO_2 per €.

37. In addition, 50 million of unallocated allowances from the third trading phase will be dedicated to the Innovation Fund for projects starting before 2021.

38. The countries eligible for support from the modernisation funds are hence Bulgaria, Croatia, the Czech Republic, Estonia, Hungary, Latvia, Lithuania, Poland, Romania and Slovakia.

39. In the initial Commission proposal (COM/2014/20, Proposal for a decision of the European parliament and of the council concerning the establishment and operation of a market stability reserve for the Union greenhouse gas emission trading scheme and amending Directive 2003/87/EC, Brussels) the market stability reserve was supposed to start operation not until 2021, the first year of the fourth emission trading period.

40. See Kettner (above n. 3) for a detailed analysis of surplus allowances in the EU ETS.

41. Commission Regulation (EU) 176/2014 of 25 February 2014 Amending Regulation (EU) 1031/2010 in Particular to Determine the Volumes of Greenhouse Gas Emission Allowances to Be Auctioned in 2013–20.

42. Some 5% of the total number of allowances for the third trading phase have been set aside for new installations eligible for free allocation (Article 10a(7)).

43. COM/2015/337, above n. 30.

13. Paris: The dilemmas of international climate change negotiations and the role of linked Emissions Trading Schemes in the post-2020 regime

Elena de Lemos Pinto Aydos[1]

> If not us, then who? If not now, then when? If not here, then where?
> (Philippines Climate Commissioner, Naderev Saño's speech at COP18 in Doha)

I. INTRODUCTION

In 1994, a near-universal assembly of countries under the auspices of the United Nations Framework Convention on Climate Change (UNFCCC)[2] recognised that the increasing concentration of greenhouse gases (GHG) in the atmosphere from anthropogenic sources is causing climate change and its adverse effects are a common concern for humankind. Parties agreed for the first time in 2009 that the increase in global temperature should be below 2°C above pre-industrial temperature.[3] Paradoxically, the same nations have failed for over a decade to achieve an effective, legally binding agreement to reduce global GHG emissions.

A new paradigm of international cooperation is now being shaped, based on universal—but not uniform—participation, reflecting national circumstances. Complementing the multilateral platform, there is a proliferation of regional approaches to climate change mitigation and adaptation. It is therefore the right moment to reflect on the decade-long impasse of international negotiations under the auspices of the UNFCCC, in order to understand the challenges and opportunities that have materialised in this process.

This paper focuses on two important factors that undermined efforts to adopt legally binding commitments by all major emitters under the first commitment period of the Kyoto Protocol.[4] Firstly, strict divisions between the developed and developing countries were formalised by the

Kyoto Protocol. Secondly, there were common concerns that led governments from the key polluter countries to the conclusion that adhering to a legally binding agreement was irrational.[5] Based on the lessons from the historical analysis that follows, I identify a key role for the linking of Emissions Trading Schemes (ETS) within the new framework for international cooperation under the Paris Agreement.

II. HISTORY OF INTERNATIONAL COOPERATION FOR CLIMATE CHANGE MITIGATION

Based on the findings of the IPCC's first assessment report,[6] the United Nations General Assembly commenced negotiations to form a framework convention. The UNFCCC acknowledges that the Earth's changing climate and its adverse effects are a common concern for humankind and recognises that the increasing concentration of GHG in the atmosphere from anthropogenic sources is causing climate change.[7]

The Parties to the UNFCCC only agreed for the first time in 2009 that the increase in global temperature should be below 2°C above pre-industrial temperature.[8] Following the IPCC's Fourth Assessment Report (AR4), indicating that a stabilisation target of 450 parts per million (ppm) CO_2-e was necessary in order to limit the global temperature rise to 2°C above pre-industrial levels, this has been adopted as a suitable goal.[9]

The UNFCCC specifically notes that 'the largest share of historical and current global emissions of greenhouse gases has originated in developed countries' (Preamble), which was the case at the time. Parties agreed to protect the climate system in accordance with responsibilities and capacities, where developed countries are expected to take the lead.[10]

1. The Kyoto Protocol

In 1997 the Conference of the Parties (COP) adopted the first Protocol under the auspices of the UNFCCC, known as the Kyoto Protocol. The Kyoto Protocol required ratification by at least 55 Parties to the UNFCCC, accounting for 55 per cent of total GHG emissions for 1990 of Parties included in Annex I. It did not enter into force until 16 February 2005, largely owing to the withdrawal of the US.[11]

In fact, the implementation of the Kyoto Protocol only became possible after the ratification of the Protocol by Russia, which accounted for 17 per cent of Annex I emissions. Despite being a fossil fuel exporter, Russia agreed to ratify the Protocol in exchange for European Union (EU) support for the country to join the World Trade Organization (WTO)[12] negotiated at the EU–Russia Summit of 21 May 2004.[13]

Under the Kyoto Protocol, a list of 37 OECD countries and the European Community (Annex B countries) committed for the first time to maintain national systems for the estimation of anthropogenic emissions (arts 5–8) and to collectively reduce emissions of specified GHG by at least 5 per cent below 1990 levels in the first commitment period, from 2008 to 2012.

Individual legally binding targets were quantified as a percentage of each country's emissions in 1990 (art 3). Reduction targets were converted into 'assigned amounts units' (AAUs). At the end of the compliance period, Annex B countries committed to hold a sufficient number of AAUs in their national registries to cover their actual emissions.

The Kyoto Protocol encouraged developed counties to implement a range of policies and measures in accordance with national circumstances, including the application of domestic market instruments (art 2). Furthermore, it introduced three market-based mechanisms supplemental to domestic action, known as 'flexibility mechanisms', which included the trading of AAUs amongst Annex B countries (Emissions Trading), crediting of removal units to Annex B countries that adopt additional activities related to land use, land-use change and forestry, joint implementation and the clean development mechanism (CDM).

The Kyoto Protocol has the undisputable historical relevance of being the first international agreement in which some Parties to the UNFCCC committed to quantifiable emission reduction targets to mitigate climate change. Nevertheless, its counter effect was to formalise a structure of uneven carbon policy between developed and developing countries.

Indeed, while many developed countries adopted binding emissions reduction targets, the effectiveness of the Treaty was compromised by the US refusal to ratify the Protocol, followed by Canada's withdrawal in 2011. Moreover, emerging countries, such as China and Brazil, never committed—and were not expected to do so—to legally binding emission reductions.

The rigid distinction between developed and developing countries under the Kyoto Protocol, referred by Leal-Arcas[14] as 'collective irresponsibility', increased the challenges of reaching an agreement for a second Kyoto period. Hochstetler and Viola claim that 'since Kyoto, the emerging powers have occupied an awkward position in this divide, and negotiations over post-Kyoto arrangements have struggled over their role'.[15]

The history of negotiations for a post-Kyoto climate regime confirms the impacts that the common but differentiated responsibility under the

Kyoto Protocol had on the negotiations of an international cooperation model. Some important developments in this process are discussed below.

2. Post-Kyoto Climate Negotiations

The post-2012 climate change regime negotiations followed a twofold approach. While the Ad Hoc Working Group on Further Commitments for Annex I Parties under the Kyoto Protocol (AWG-KP) focused on negotiating a second commitment period to the protocol,[16] a subsidiary body known as the Ad Hoc Working Group on Long-term Cooperative Action (AWG-LCA) was established to address other forms of long-term cooperation.[17]

At COP13 parties to the UNFCCC agreed on a two-year road map ('Bali Road Map') for negotiations on post-Kyoto commitments.[18] A 'Bali Action Plan' was put in place, creating high expectations of reaching a post-Kyoto agreement at COP15 to be held in Copenhagen, 2009.

The very much anticipated legally binding agreement on emissions reduction commitments was not reached, which was generally understood as a diplomatic fiasco. Still, COP15 resulted in the conclusion of the Copenhagen Accord, a political (non-legally binding) instrument in which governments agreed that global warming should be limited to no more than 2°C.[19] Developed and developing countries pledged to implement mitigation action through the adoption of voluntary commitments, which became official under the Cancun Agreements.[20]

In the week prior to COP15 representatives of BASIC countries negotiated for the first time a collective strategy, which included 'non-negotiable terms' of a new round of Kyoto based commitments for the Annex I countries and additional financing for developing countries.[21] Under the Copenhagen Accord, developed countries committed to finance mitigation and adaptation in developing countries, which was expected to mobilise approximately US$30 billion for the period 2010–2012, reaching US$100 billion a year by 2020.[22]

Following COP15 and in preparation for COP16 in Cancun, BASIC countries submitted voluntary commitments. Brazil adopted a voluntary target for emission reductions of 36.1–38.9 per cent compared with business as usual by 2020.[23] South Africa adopted a target of 34 per cent reductions compared with business as usual emissions by 2020 and 42 per cent by 2025.

China adopted a different measure for setting voluntary targets, stating that it would lower its carbon dioxide emissions per unit of GDP between 40 and 45 per cent by 2020 compared with the 2005 level, increase the share of non-fossil fuels in primary energy consumption to around 15 per cent by

2020 and increase forest coverage by 40 million hectares and forest stock volume by 1.3 billion cubic metres by 2020 from the 2005 levels. Similarly to China, India stated that it would reduce the emissions-intensity of its GDP between 20 and 25 per cent by 2020 in comparison to the 2005 level. Russia adopted voluntary conditional targets of emission reductions ranging between 15 and 25 per cent below 1990 levels.

At COP16 governments adopted the Cancun Agreements, based on the outcome of the work of the AWG-LCA. The Cancun Agreements consolidate and extend the Copenhagen Accord, reaffirming that all Parties to the UNFCCC should cooperate, on the basis of equity and in accordance with common but differentiated responsibilities and respective capabilities.[24]

The Cancun Agreements endorsed the long-term goal of reducing global GHG emissions so as to hold the increase in global average temperature below 2°C above preindustrial levels, recognising the need to consider strengthening the long-term global goal to a global average temperature rise of not more than 1.5°C.[25] Parties agreed to make efforts to achieve the peaking of global and national GHG emissions as soon as possible, recognising that the time frame for peaking will be longer in developing countries.[26]

Governments committed to enhance mitigation through, amongst other measures, further refining and adopting the REDD+ mechanism to incentivise emission reductions from deforestation and forest degradation in developing countries.[27] The 'Cancun Adaptation Framework' was established with the objective of enhancing action on adaptation, under which developed countries agreed to provide support to particularly vulnerable developing countries.[28]

A 'Green Climate Fund' was established to support developing countries' climate change responses, which was further developed at COP19 in Warsaw.[29] While social and economic development and poverty eradication were declared to be the first and overriding priorities of developing countries,[30] they were urged to increase the ambition of their emission reduction targets and to make voluntary commitments, translated into Nationally Appropriate Mitigation Actions. Governments agreed to work towards a global goal for reducing emissions by 2050 to be negotiated at COP17, in Durban.[31]

At Durban COP17, under the auspices of the AWG-KP, a decision was reached to commence the second commitment period of the Kyoto Protocol on 1 January 2013.[32] Annex B countries were invited to convert their Kyoto targets into 'quantified emission limitation or reduction objectives' for the second commitment period under the Kyoto Protocol by May 2012 for consideration by the AWG-KP.[33]

Parties acknowledged the gap between mitigation pledges by 2020 and aggregate emission pathways consistent with having a likely chance of holding the increase in global average temperature below 2 or 1.5°C above pre-industrial levels.[34] A subsidiary body known as the 'Ad Hoc Working Group on the Durban Platform for Enhanced Action' (ADP) was established, aiming to develop a Protocol, another legal instrument or an agreed outcome with legal force under the UNFCCC applicable to all Parties.[35] The AWG-LCA was extended for only one more year.[36]

3. The Doha Amendment to the Kyoto Protocol

At COP18 Parties approved the Doha Amendment to the Kyoto Protocol, providing for a second legally binding commitment period starting on 1 January 2013 and ending on 31 December 2020.[37] The amendment will enter into force once it is ratified by at least three-quarters of the Parties to the Kyoto Protocol, that is, 144 countries. At the time of writing, the Amendment is yet to be ratified. Still, countries have agreed to abide by their commitments on a voluntary basis.

The environmental effectiveness of the Doha Amendment is questionable owing to the refusal of five key OECD countries to commit to a second commitment period under the Kyoto Protocol. The US, Canada, Russia, Japan and New Zealand expressed concerns with regards to the perpetuation of the division between developed and developing countries and 'free-riding' issues.[38] A more comprehensive agreement between developed and industrialised developing countries was agreed to at COP21 in Paris.

4. The Road to Paris

Negotiations for further international cooperation took place under the auspices of the ADP. At Doha, the ADP was tasked with two streams of work. The first workstream concentrated on negotiating a protocol, another legal instrument or an agreed outcome with legal force under the Convention applicable to all Parties, to be adopted at COP21 in Paris, 2015 and enter into force from 2020. The second workstream focused on ways to raise global ambition before 2020 to accelerate the response to climate change.[39]

At COP19 the ADP was requested to accelerate its work towards a climate change agreement that would include commitments from developed and developing countries.[40] Parties advanced negotiations on the elements for a draft negotiating text of the 2015 agreement.[41]

The draft explicitly rejected the 'binary approach' adopted under the Kyoto as it is 'not consistent with the current and evolving situation of the world and cannot be used as the basis for the 2015 agreement'.[42] The common but differentiated responsibility principle was still present in this framework, although it was no longer interpreted as the strict divide of responsibilities between developed and developing countries. The work of the ADP has been completed at COP21, with the adoption of the Paris Agreement, as further discussed below.

III.   HISTORICAL ANALYSIS OF COUNTRIES' KEY CONCERNS

It has been repeatedly stated that incentives to 'free-ride' exceed incentives for countries to enter into a comprehensive legally binding agreement for global emission reductions.[43] Strategies adopted by a few key Parties at negotiations under the auspices of the UNFCCC in the past decade arguably have been guided by the understanding that 'unilateral action to address climate change is thus irrational, and an actor's best option is to shirk, doing nothing while others address the problem'.[44] Two basic concerns have been a constant at the negotiation rounds:[45]

(1)   Why should one commit to legally binding emissions reductions, when one's actions alone will not be sufficient to achieve meaningful global emissions reductions?

(2)   Why should one commit to legally binding emissions reductions, when others will not?

I suggest that regional cooperation offers an effective answer to both concerns. Within this framework, the linking of independent ETSs has an important role to play in cooperation for climate change mitigation.

1.   Why Should One Commit to Legally Binding Emissions Reductions, When One's Actions Alone Will be Insufficient to Achieve Meaningful Global Emissions Reductions?

The climate system is characterised as a common pool resource, or a common.[46] As such, it is often pointed out that, unless all countries take action, meaningful emissions reductions may not be achieved. Strictly speaking, this is not the case.

When it comes to climate change, a few polluters can impact the volume of global GHG emissions on their own or in small groupings.[47] Indeed, the behaviour of a few developed and industrialised developing countries—major GHG emitters such as China, the US and the EU (as a single entity) who together were responsible for 55 per cent of the total global CO_2 in

2012—could be effective in achieving a meaningful global GHG emissions reduction.[48]

In point of fact, strong agreements between China, the US, the EU (as a single entity), India, the Russian Federation and Japan—either as a block or in a fragmented approach—would cover approximately 70 per cent of the global CO_2 emissions from fossil fuel use and cement.[49] Next in line would be the remaining high per capita emitting countries, such as Australia, Saudi Arabia, Canada and South Korea.[50]

At a first glance, this approach may seem to be conflicting with the objectives of the UNFCCC in achieving multilateral climate change mitigation. Yet the apparent partiality towards regionalism over multilateralism only exists at a superficial level.

When one looks at the EU support for Russia's WTO accession in 2004, it was an early example of the role that bilateral agreements can play in facilitating cooperation for climate change mitigation. Similarly, prior to the Paris Agreement, a bilateral agreement between the US and China, historical antagonists in the negotiations for global GHG reductions, set a valuable precedent. On 11 November 2014 the US and China announced a bilateral agreement to cooperate for the development of clean energy and to achieve emission reductions beyond current voluntary commitments.[51]

The two largest polluters in the world (around 40 per cent of global GHG emissions) demonstrated that bilateral agreements can assist with deepening commitments from major emitters, while mitigating concerns with 'free rider' behaviour. In terms of the expectations pre-COP21, a successful multilateral process would have meant that developed and developing countries—with special provisions for the least developed countries—agreed to commit and contribute towards global emission reductions. This goal was finally met at COP21.

The adoption of the Paris Agreement at COP21 signals that the Parties have acknowledged that limiting the temperature increase to 2°C is no longer conceivable without emissions reduction commitments from all heavily industrialised developing countries. Application of the agreement by all Parties, however, was never expected to be uniform. The other 180 or so developing countries who are Parties to the UNFCCC and contribute very little to global GHG emissions will accept different levels of mitigation action.

2.   Why Should One Commit to Legally Binding Emissions Reductions, When Others Will Not?

The refusal of the US to sign the Kyoto Protocol illustrates this point. In July 1997, just before COP3 in Kyoto, the Senate resolved—with

95–0 votes—that the US 'should not be a signatory to any protocol to, or other agreement regarding, the United Nations Framework Convention on Climate Change of 1992, at negotiations in Kyoto in December 1997' as long as such an agreement 'specifically exempts all Developing Country Parties from any new commitments in such negotiation process for the post-2000 period'.[52]

The concern is relevant only in relation to those industrialised countries mentioned above who have not yet committed to legally binding reduction targets, rather than the whole group of developing countries. The fears expressed by the US Senate were particularly confirmed by the exponential increase in emissions from China in the past decade.

Still, Hochstetler and Viola[53] point out at the failure of the strategy, stating that the US 'has tried to insist on legal obligations for the emerging powers, making that a condition of its own participation as early as 1997, but has not been willing or able to compel them to join'. A much more sensitive strategy has been recently put in place by the US, which has taken it upon itself to directly negotiate with China an unprecedented bilateral agreement for cooperation on emission reductions. Details of this agreement are discussed below.

A different approach to the same issue was the adoption of conditional commitments by a few governments in order to push others to participate or increase emission reduction targets.[54] The EU, Australia and New Zealand as well as developing countries such as China and India are amongst the list of countries pursuing this approach.

History shows that conditional targets have failed to incentivise a universal multilateral agreement and in some cases led to a reverse situation, of a country deciding no longer to pursue legally binding targets, as was the case of New Zealand. In August 2009 New Zealand announced emission reductions between 10 and 20 per cent below 1990 levels by 2020, conditional on the existence of a comprehensive legally binding global agreement that would limit the temperature rise to not more than 2°C, in which developed countries would make comparable efforts to those of New Zealand and major emitting developing countries would take action according to their respective capabilities.

As a comprehensive legally binding agreement for the post-2012 was not negotiated by COP18, New Zealand announced that it would not participate in the second commitment period under the Kyoto Protocol.[55] In other words, concerns with free riding behaviour framed the New Zealand policy, which was not effective in increasing international collaboration.[56]

IV. THE ROLE OF MARKET-BASED INSTRUMENTS IN PROMOTING COOPERATION BETWEEN DEVELOPED AND DEVELOPING COUNTRIES: THE CASE OF THE CDM

Converging interests can assist with negotiations for the development of clean energy, technology transfer and linking of independent carbon pricing schemes.[57] There are obvious economic advantages to major emitters who agree, for instance, to invest in renewable energy, pushing down the cost of technology innovation as a result of the scale of investment.

Historically, market-based instruments can have a key role in incentivising cooperation between developed and developing countries. This is illustrated by Brazil's participation in the negotiations for the first commitment period of the Kyoto Protocol.

Brazil was the first country to sign the UNFCCC and succeeded in ratifying it in 1994. During negotiations for the Kyoto Protocol, Brazil initially proposed the creation of a Clean Development Fund to assist developing countries, based on the rationale of historic responsibility. The fund would be composed by fines paid by developed countries that failed to comply with reduction commitments. The proposal was rejected by developed countries.[58]

It was through collaboration with the US in 1997 that the Clean Development Fund was transformed into what became the CDM under the Kyoto Protocol, a market-based instrument capable of attracting investment from developed to developing countries.[59]

Hochstetler and Viola[60] suggest that after the US withdrew from the Kyoto Protocol in 2001, 'Brazil helped pull together the alliance between the European Union, Japan, and emerging countries that made the final agreements possible', attributing it to the successful negotiation of the CDM.[61] Brazil ratified the Kyoto Protocol in 2002.

As its deforestation rates were very high, Brazil resisted the inclusion of the forestry sector in CDM.[62] However, once the CDM was adopted, investment flows were directed to China and India, while Brazil benefited from fewer opportunities.[63] Local governments in the Amazon area heavily criticised the Federal government for blocking a market-based mechanism that would bring investment in the forest conservation sector.[64] From this point, Brazil became engaged in the development of a new market instrument to promote abatement in the forestry sector, reducing emissions from deforestation and forest degradation (REDD+), endorsed by the Cancun Agreement.[65]

The project-based focus of CDM has been criticised[66] and new market mechanisms have been negotiated under the auspices of the ADP. A new market-based 'mechanism' is established under the Paris Agreement, to operate under the guidance and authority of the COP in order to enhance cost-effectiveness of mitigation, as further explained below.[67]

V.   LINKING EMISSIONS TRADING SCHEMES IN THE POST-2020 REGIME

At the COP21, the Parties to the UNFCCC reached a historical agreement, known as the Paris Agreement.[68] According to the Paris Agreement, 195 countries will communicate their intended nationally determined contribution,[69] with the exception of least developed countries and small island developing states, which will communicate their strategies, plans and actions for low GHG development.[70] Developed countries have also agreed to finance at least US$100 billion per year, to meet the needs and priorities of developing countries.[71]

The new model for international cooperation is based on fragmented action that reflects national circumstances, with leadership expected to be taken by Parties with the greatest responsibility and highest capacity.[72] Thus, the common but differentiated responsibility principle has been reframed in a way that ensures universal participation while respecting local differences.

Multilateral negotiation processes can be complex and, at the time of writing, the Paris Agreement is yet to be signed and ratified by the Parties. The Paris Agreement will be open for signature from 22 April 2016 to 21 April 2017. The agreement only enters into force on the thirtieth day after the date on which at least 55 countries, accounting for at least 55 per cent of global emissions, have deposited their instruments of ratification.[73]

This process may be lengthy and could take up to several years. Meanwhile, the history of international cooperation under the UNFCCC demonstrates that further regional cooperation through the development and linking of market instruments—such as ETSs, carbon offset markets and carbon taxes—would be essential to increase key industrialised countries' ambitions.

The Paris Agreement establishes a market 'mechanism' to contribute to the mitigation of greenhouse gas emissions and support sustainable development and encourages Parties to engage on a voluntary basis in 'cooperative approaches that involve the use of internationally transferred mitigation outcomes'.[74] Despite the vague language, the Paris Agreement clearly recommends countries to cooperate by linking independent market-based instruments, such as ETSs.

The linking of independent ETSs facilitates the setting of an international carbon price and, where certain conditions are met, reduces the cost of mitigation for major emitters, including developed and developing countries, increasing the political viability and intensity of international cooperation for emission reductions. De Sépibus[75] argues that, for developed countries, 'an important part of the financial support needed by developing countries could and should be delivered through the carbon market'. In terms of political acceptability, the OECD[76] states that 'at the international level, any income transfers required to encourage large developing countries to join in may be more acceptable to the electorates of developed countries if they take place indirectly, through permit allocation, rather than through direct income transfers'.

The success of such approach would greatly hinge on the adoption of internationally acceptable rules for measurement, reporting and verification. A multilateral process to institute common accounting standards to ensure the environmental integrity of carbon markets, facilitating the robust functioning of international carbon markets and avoiding double counting of offset credits, is now very much needed.

Therefore, this is a strategic moment for the multilateral platform, under the auspices of the UNFCCC, to deliver a framework for the accounting, recording and tracking of international units, facilitating future links between domestic schemes adopted by major emitters (minimising free riding concerns) and between major emitters and least developed countries (providing financial assistance). Based on the previous experience with the international negotiations under the UNFCCC, a framework supporting the linking of independent market-based instruments would provide the vital balance between centralisation and flexibility, which was lacking in the past.

VI. CONCLUSION

The paper focused on two elements which, amongst others, contributed to the deadlock at Copenhagen. The first was the interpretation and application of the principle of common but differentiated responsibility under the Kyoto Protocol, strictly dividing obligations between developed and developing countries. The second was concerns with free riding and the exclusive focus on a multilateral approach, leaving bilateral and plurilateral agreements in the periphery of the UNFCCC.

An alternative model of international cooperation is being formed, based on the complementarity of regional and multilateral approaches. Within this model, regional agreements can incentivise major emitters to collaborate with each other. Financial assistance for transition towards low-carbon economies in developing countries is likely to be better accepted by developed countries where economic interests converge, for instance through the implementation and linking of market-based instruments such as ETSs. While the multilateral framework being formed under the Paris Agreement facilitates regional integration, bilateral and plurilateral agreements provide the levels of trust and legitimacy necessary to further deepen multilateral commitments.

Linking ETSs will enhance coordination towards an international climate policy framework post-2020 and is likely to attract large developing countries, such as China, which will be interested in internationally linking their domestic schemes. The setting of an international carbon price via linking ETSs is a key element in reducing global emissions at reduced cost. Within this structure, there is a demand for harmonised rules for monitoring, reporting and verification standards amongst others, ensuring environmental integrity to the system.

NOTES

1. I have benefited greatly from the feedback and discussions with Diego Werneck Arguelhes, Daniel Vargas, Kellen Trilha, Evan Rosevear and Pedro Cantisano. The errors remain my own.
2. *United Nations Framework Convention on Climate Change*, opened for signature 9 May 1992, 1771 UNTS 107 (entered into force 21 March 1994) ('*UNFCCC*').
3. Conference of the Parties, United Nations Framework Convention on Climate Change, *Report of the Conference of the Parties on Its Fifteenth Session, Held in Copenhagen from 7 to 19 December 2009—Addendum—Part Two: Action taken by the Conference of the Parties at Its Fifteenth Session*, UN Doc FCCC/CP/2009/11/Add. 1 (30 March 2010) ('*COP 15*') para 1.
4. The analysis is not intended to exhaust the topic. There are several other factors and hidden interests, both in the domestic context of each Party as well as from an international political economy perspective, which have contributed to the incapacity of Parties to reach a centralised multilateral agreement under the UNFCCC.
5. Scott Barret, 'Self-enforcing International Environmental Agreements' (1994) 46 *Oxford Economic Papers* 878; Robert Stavins, 'The Problem of the Commons: Still Unsettled after 100 Years' (2011) 101 *American Economic Review* 81.
6. Intergovernmental Panel on Climate Change, 'Climate Change: The IPCC Scientific Assessment ' (Intergovernmental Panel on Climate Change, 1990).
7. *UNFCCC*.
8. *COP 15*, para 1.
9. Intergovernmental Panel on Climate Change, 'Climate Change 2007: Synthesis Report' (2007).
10. *UNFCCC*, art 3.
11. Rosemary Lyster et al., *Environmental and Planning Law in New South Wales* (The Federation Press, 3rd edn, 2012), 244.
12. *Marrakesh Agreement Establishing the World Trade Organization*, opened for signature 15 April 1994, 1867 UNTS 3 (entered into force 1 January 1995). The WTO is a multilateral trading system counting a total of 160 members in 2014.
13. Wybe Douma, 'The European Union, Russia and the Kyoto Protocol' in Marjan Peeters

and K. Deketelaere (eds), *EU Climate Change Policy: The Challenge of New Regulatory Initiatives* (Edward Elgar, 2006), 51; Peter Baker, 'Russia Backs Kyoto to Get on Path to Join WTO', *The Washington Post* (Moscow), 22 May 2004 <http://www.washington-post.com/wp-dyn/articles/A46416-2004May21.html>.

14. Rafael Leal-Arcas, *Climate Change and International Trade* (Edward Elgar, 2013).

15. Kathryn Hochstetler and Eduardo Viola, 'Brazil and the Politics of Climate Change: Beyond the Global Commons' (2012) 21(5) *Environmental Politics* 753, 757.

16. Conference of the Parties, United Nations Framework Convention on Climate Change, *Report of the Conference of the Parties Serving as the Meeting of the Parties to the Kyoto Protocol on Its First Session, Held at Montreal from 28 November to 10 December 2005—Addendum —Part Two: Action Taken by the Conference of the Parties Serving as the Meeting of the Parties to the Kyoto Protocol at Its First Session,* UN Doc FCCC/KP/CMP/2005/8/Add. 1 (30 March 2006) para 2.

17. Conference of the Parties, United Nations Framework Convention on Climate Change, *Report of the Conference of the Parties on Its Thirteenth Session, Held in Bali from 3 to 15 December 2007—Addendum—Part Two: Action Taken by the Conference of the Parties at Its Thirteenth Session,* UN Doc FCCC/CP/2007/6/Add. 1 (14 March 2008), para 2.

18. *Ibid.*, para 1.

19. *COP 15.*

20. Conference of the Parties, United Nations Framework Convention on Climate Change, *Report of the Conference of the Parties on Its Sixteenth Session, Held in Cancun from 29 November to 10 December 2010—Addendum—Part Two: Action Taken by the Conference of the Parties at Its Sixteenth Session,* UN Doc FCCC/CP/2010/7/Add. 1 (15 March 2011) ('*COP 16*').

21. Hochstetler and Viola, above n 15, 766.

22. *COP 15*, paras 1, 4, 5, 8.

23. *Law 12.187/2009, Instituting the National Policy on Climate Change* (Brazil) 29 December 2009 art 12 provides that the target of 36.1–38.9 per cent emission reductions compared with business as usual by 2020 are mandatory under Brazilian domestic legislation. Nevertheless, Brazil has failed to commit to mandatory targets internationally.

24. *COP 16*, paras 1, 2.

25. *Ibid.*, paras 4, 5; Intergovernmental Panel on Climate Change, above n 9.

26. *COP 16*, para 6.

27. *Ibid.*, paras 68–79.

28. *Ibid.*, para 18.

29. Conference of the Parties, United Nations Framework Convention on Climate Change, *Report of the Conference of the Parties on Its Nineteenth Session, Held in Warsaw from 11 to 23 November 2013—Addendum—Part Two: Action Taken by the Conference of the Parties at Its Nineteenth Session,* UN Doc FCCC/CP/2013/10/Add. 1 (31 January 2014).

30. *COP 16*, para 102.

31. *Ibid.*, para 5.

32. Conference of the Parties, United Nations Framework Convention on Climate Change, *Report of the Conference of the Parties on Its Seventeenth Session, Held in Durban from 28 November to 11 December 2011—Addendum—Part Two: Action Taken by the Conference of the Parties at Its Seventeenth Session,* UN Doc FCCC/CP/2011/9/Add. 1 (15 March 2012) ('*COP 17*') 1/CMP7 para 1.

33. *Ibid.*, para 4.

34. *Ibid.*, 1/CP17 Preamble.

35. *Ibid.*, para 2.

36. *Ibid.*, para 1.

37. Conference of the Parties, United Nations Framework Convention on Climate Change, *Report of the Conference of the Parties Serving as the Meeting of the Parties to the Kyoto Protocol on Its Eighth Session, Held in Doha from 26 November to 8 December 2012—Addendum—Part Two: Action Taken by the Conference of the Parties Serving as the*

Meeting of the Parties to the Kyoto Protocol at its Eighth Session, UN Doc FCCC/KP/CMP/2012/13/Add. 1 (28 February 2013) ('*COP 18*') 1/CMP 8 para 4.

38. Nastassia Astrasheuskaya, 'Russia will Not Cut Emissions under Extended Kyoto Climate Pact' (2012) *Reuters* <http://www.reuters.com/article/2012/09/13/us-russia-kyoto-idUSBRE88C0QZ20120913>.

39. United Nations Framework Convention on Climate Change, *The Doha Climate Gateway* <http://unfccc.int/key_steps/doha_climate_gateway/items/7389.php>.

40. *COP 18* para 1.

41. Ad Hoc Working Group on the Durban Platform for Enhanced Action, *Parties' views and proposals on the elements for a draft negotiating text*. ADP.2014.6. Non Paper.

42. *Ibid*.

43. Barret, above n 5; Stavins, above n 5; OECD, *The Economics of Climate Change Mitigation: Policies and Options for Global Action Beyond 2012* (2009); Ross Garnaut, 'Garnaut Climate Change Review Update: Progress Towards Effective Global Action on Climate Change' (Commonwealth of Australia, 2011), 8; Intergovernmental Panel on Climate Change, 'Climate Change 2013: The Physical Science Basis—Summary for Policymakers' (2013) <http://www.ipcc.ch/>.

44. Hochstetler and Viola, above n 15, 754.

45. This list is not exhaustive. See, e.g., Richard Stewart, Michael Oppenheimer and Bryce Rudyk, 'Building Blocks for Global Climate Protection' (2013) 32 *Environmental Law Journal* 341; Nicholas Stern, *The Economics of Climate Change: The Stern Review* (Cambridge, 2006); Ross Garnaut, *The Garnaut Climate Change Review: Final Report* (Cambridge University Press, 2008); The Global Commission on the Economy and Climate, 'The New Climate Economy: Better Growth, Better Climate' (2014); Sustainable Development Solutions Network and Institute for Sustainable Development and International Relations, 'Pathways to Deep Decarbonization' (2014).

46. Garret Hardin, 'The Tragedy of the Commons' (1968) 162 *Science* 1243.

47. Hochstetler and Viola, above n 15, 754.

48. Jos Olivier et al., 'Trends in Global CO_2 Emissions' (PBL Netherlands Environmental Assessment Agency, 2013).

49. *Ibid*.

50. *Ibid*., 18.

51. The White House, 'Fact Sheet: US–China Joint Announcement on Climate Change and Clean Energy Cooperation' (2014) <http://www.whitehouse.gov/the-press-office/2014/11/11/fact-sheet-us-china-joint-announcement-climate-change-and-clean-energy-c>. As part of the agreement, the US announced a new reduction target of 26–28 per cent below 2005 levels by 2025 and China committed to peak CO_2 emissions by 2030 or earlier and to increase the non-fossil fuel share of all energy to around 20 per cent by 2030.

52. Byrd-Hagel Resolution, S Res 98, 105th Congress (1997). The Resolution was sponsored by Senator Robert Byrd (D-WV) and Senator Chuck Hagel (R-NE) and passed by the Senate by 95–0.

53. Hochstetler and Viola, above n 15, 756.

54. Karsten Neuhoff, *Climate Policy after Copenhagen: The Role of Carbon Pricing* (Cambridge University, 2011), 137.

55. New Zealand Government Ministry for the Environment, 'Statement Made by New Zealand Ambassador for Climate Change, Dr Adrian Macey, to the United Nations Climate Change Negotiating Session on 10 August 2009 in Bonn, Germany' (2009) <http://www.mfe.govt.nz/issues/climate/emissions-target-2020/statement-nz-ambassador.html>.

56. Neuhoff, above n 54, 117, 137.

57. Fabiano de Andrade Correa, 'The Integration of Sustainable Development in Trade Agreements of the European Union' in David Kleimann (ed.), *EU Preferential Trade Agreements: Commerce, Foreign Policy, and Development Aspects* (European University Institute, 2013), 143.

58. Eduardo Viola, 'A Evolução do Papel do Brasil no Regime Internacional de Mudança Climática e na Governabilidade Global' (2004) 6(1) *Cena Internacional: Revista de Análise em Política Internacional* 82, 97.
59. *Ibid.*; Hochstetler and Viola, above n 15, 759.
60. Hochstetler and Viola, above n 15, 759.
61. *Ibid.*, 761.
62. *Ibid.*
63. Wolfgang Sterk, 'New Mechanisms for the Carbon Market? Sectoral Crediting, Sectoral Trading, and Crediting Nationally Appropriate Mitigation Actions' (Wuppertal Institute for Climate, Environment and Energy, 2010), 3.
64. Hochstetler and Viola, above n 15, 762.
65. *COP 16*, paras 68–79.
66. Sterk, above n 63.
67. Conference of the Parties, United Nations Framework Convention on Climate Change, *Adoption of the Paris Agreement, Annex* UN Doc FCCC/CP/2015/L9/Rev. 1 (12 December 2015) (Paris Agreement), art 6.
68. Paris Agreement.
69. Paris Agreement, art 4.2.
70. Paris Agreement, art 4.4, 4.6. The INDCs will differ amongst countries. While developed countries must commit to economy-wide absolute emission reduction targets, developing countries are only encouraged to move towards economy-wide absolute emission reduction targets.
71. Conference of the Parties, United Nations Framework Convention on Climate Change, *Adoption of the Paris Agreement*, UN Doc FCCC/CP/2015/L9/Rev. 1 (12 December 2015) para 54.
72. *Ibid.* Also see Centre for European Policy Studies, 'Submission to the UNFCCC on FVA and NMM' (2012) <www.ceps.eu> 3.
73. The final review of this chapter was completed on 11 February 2016.
74. Paris Agreement, art 6.2, 6.4.
75. Joëlle de Sépibus, Wolfgang Sterk and Andreas Tuerk, 'Top-down, Bottom-up or In-between: How Can a UNFCCC Framework for Market-Based Approaches Ensure Environmental Integrity and Market Coherence?' (NCCR Trade Regulation, 2012).
76. OECD, above n 43, 62.

14. Just ETS? Social justice and recent reforms in EU and US carbon markets

Achim Lerch and Sven Rudolph

1. INTRODUCTION

Besides environmental effectiveness and economic efficiency, social justice plays a key role in sustainable climate policy. Social justice was a founding principle of sustainable development[1] and recent empirical research has proven the appreciation that people in various countries show for an equitable approach to climate policy.[2] In addition, current energy transformation debates have raised questions on a fair burden sharing, especially because even an efficient policy mix is expected to increase overall costs.[3]

While still not the dominating force, carbon pricing has become more popular,[4] and most certainly, in order to keep compliance costs to a minimum, market-based instruments must lead the way. Recently, cap-and-trade schemes have spread across the world, and while still notable design differences exist, linking domestic schemes continues to be a relevant supplement to global climate action.[5] The EU still operates the flagship supra-national carbon market, but US regions are picking up with cross-state schemes. The EU Emissions Trading System (EU ETS) and the Regional Greenhouse Gas Initiative (RGGI), are of particular interest as, after heavy critique, they have undergone fundamental constructive reforms. Still, carbon market design has considerable justice implications, which, other than environmental and economic issues, have been widely neglected in research and policy.

Hence, we ask: what are thorough social justice criteria for carbon market design? To what extent do early schemes on both sides of the Atlantic fulfill these criteria? And have recent reforms made these schemes more socially just? We answer the questions by using normative concepts from modern climate justice theory in order to derive criteria for socially just carbon markets. We then apply them to carbon market design in the EU and the US. We mainly argue that, as a socially just design is basically possible, justice criteria must be considered thoroughly in carbon market design. So far, even after improvements by recent reforms, existing EU and US markets only partly fulfill ambitious social justice criteria, but further improvements are possible.

2. WHAT'S JUST IN CARBON MARKET DESIGN?

2.1 Social Justice Concepts

The concept of social justice has been controversially debated for hundreds of years, but still opinions differ on whether or not social justice can be defined in abstract terms and how it can be applied to climate policy. Some scholars still believe social justice to be a concept of competing claims and case-by-case negotiations. Yet even competing claims can be logically discriminated against, and priorities can be defined on social justice grounds without ethically discriminating against individuals.[6] Global warming, in turn, represents one of mankind's most pressing challenges with immediate social justice implications: climate change strongly influences the livelihood of current and future generations; historic and geographical responsibilities have so far not been sufficiently considered in distributional decisions; and carbon markets even distribute implicit private property rights to the common good of our atmosphere. Hence, defining social justice and thoroughly considering respective criteria for climate policy and carbon market design seems feasible and highly desirable.

With climate policy and carbon market design in mind, the following social justice concepts apply:[7] first, the concepts of procedural justice and result-based distributional justice can be differentiated. Procedural justice implies that only procedures and rules of social processes can be just, while result-based justice refers to fair outcomes of social processes. Some authors claim that the concept of result-based justice implies presumptuousness and overbearance with respect to the availability and manageability of knowledge; it would dictate an abstract distributional result independent of its genesis.[8] However, using some notion of the concept of result-based distributional justice is indispensable already on theoretical grounds. In addition to that, economic psychology studies show that individuals base their economic decisions on result-based concepts of fairness rather than on procedures alone.[9]

The concept of result-based distributional justice can be further differentiated into justice in transfer and acquisition, justice within allocation and redistributive justice.[10] Justice in transfer and acquisition demands that an effort is compensated by an equivalent service, a requirement inherently fulfilled by market transactions. Justice within allocation, in contrast, asks for a fair distribution of goods according to individual claims. Redistributive justice refers to a fair outcome of redistributive procedures subsequent to market allocations.

Acceptance of the latter two concepts, however, raises the question of what the criteria for (re-)distribution should be. Welfare-based justice calls for a fair distribution to be based on individuals' needs, while desert-based justice requires a fair distribution to be based on each individual's contribution to the production of a good. Desert-based justice is thus faced with at least two serious problems: first, effort can be measured either in input or in output terms; second, with respect to natural resources, even if the appropriation of natural resources by humans can be justified by the fact that it requires human labor in addition to nature's services, still, a relevant part of the service is provided by nature. A combination of desert-based and welfare-based justice implicitly proposed by Karl Marx—'from each according to his ability, to each according to his needs'[11]—however, does not set proper economic incentives. John Rawls, in turn, proposed a more promising combination of the two concepts, which we discuss later in this paper.[12]

Yet does a fair distribution necessarily imply an equal distribution? In the 'why equality' debate egalitarianism is strongly challenged, and inviolable standards such as human dignity are proposed as alternatives.[13] However, while equality should not be considered the sole criterion for social justice and as it has to be accompanied by minimum standards, e.g. for human dignity, anyway, preferring equality to inequality seems theoretically adequate[14] and empirically justified.[15] Yet even if equality is accepted, the 'equality of what' question arises. Reference points proposed in the literature are, for example, preferences and talents not under individual control (Amartya Sen), basic rights (Robert Nozick), or income (Herman Daly). While a naïve notion of equality in terms of equal welfare for everybody is obviously inadequate, John Rawls (1971) called for equality in terms of rights and freedom as well as chances and opportunities. He accepts inequalities only for income and capital, if, and only if, first, they provide the highest benefit to the poorest—compared with a situation of equality, in which the poorest benefit less—and, second, if offices and positions are equally open to everybody (difference principle).

Last, the Brundtland Report defined sustainable development by emphasizing that both the needs of the current and those of future generations should be taken into account.[16] While intra-generational justice refers to the distribution within one current generation—e.g. on the national (rich vs poor citizens) or international (industrialized vs developing countries) level—inter-generational justice accounts for distributional issues between the present and future generations.

This variety of social justice aspects certainly makes deriving concrete design recommendations for carbon markets quite a challenge. However, as questions on economically efficient and environmentally effective climate policy cap-and-trade schemes have been discussed in detail before[17] and social justice remains the blind spot of sustainable carbon market design,[18] significant scientific and policy progress can be expected from applying social justice concepts to carbon market design.[19]

2.2 Social Justice in Carbon Market Design

To begin with, result-based distributional justice calls for a close look at the actual carbon market design in practice. It is obvious that establishing a fair climate policy and carbon market negotiation procedure alone, e.g. under the United Nations or democratically elected national governments, is not sufficient. We have to thoroughly consider the program outcome, in this case the detailed carbon market design itself.

A socially just carbon market should hence cover all pollutants and polluters and make participation mandatory for all emitting sources. The polluter-pays principle reflects desert-based justice and allows for the taking into account of historic responsibilities for climate change. If only selected greenhouse gases (GHG) were covered, first, emitters of covered gases would be disadvantaged compared with those emitting non-covered gases, which would both violate the intra-generational justice and the equality criteria. Second, exemptions would leave some pollutants unregulated, which might hurt future generations' rights and might even violate the polluter-pays-principle. Excluding some GHG would only be justifiable if the reliability of monitoring is questionable or if monitoring costs are prohibitive. Exempting selected polluters would have the same detrimental effects on social justice as excluding certain pollutants. Obligatory participation alone would guarantee compliance with reduction targets and the complete emission cost payment by all relevant polluters thus complying with inter-generational justice, the polluter-pays principle, and the equality criterion. As a design consequence, social justice suggests an upstream carbon market, which covers emissions at the level of entry into the economy (e.g. fossil fuel producers or importers), instead of a downstream scheme, which covers pollutants at the actual point of emissions (e.g. factories, utilities). Only the former is usually capable of accounting for almost 100% of total emissions, while the latter often only covers around 50%. In addition, carbon dioxide equivalents (CO_2eq) can facilitate the inclusion of all GHG.

Socially just carbon markets should have absolute volume caps in line with the 2°C target in order to comply with inter-generational justice. As global warming is determined by GHG concentrations in the atmosphere, absolute emission amounts matter. Hence, in order to protect future generations from excessive global warming burdens, absolute volume targets and caps are indispensable. Intensity targets (e.g. emissions per product or per unit GDP), in contrast, allow absolute emissions to increase even with low emission rates when total production output increases. Concerning a number target, while an exact global climate policy goal is difficult to justify, scientific evidence—and even the political will at the Paris COP 21—supports a maximum temperature increase of no more than 2°C.[20] With some probability this would at least protect future generations from the worst consequences of global warming. As a consequence, industrialized countries would have to reduce their emissions by 25–40% by 2020 and by 80–95% by 2050 compared with 1990 levels. The Budget Approach estimates only 600 million tons of additional CO_2eq emissions to be acceptable between 2010 and 2050 in order to achieve this target.[21] Equality arguments would then call for equal per capita emission rights. If, in turn, the polluter-pays principle is applied consequently, industrialized countries' historic responsibility might lead to even more generous emission right endowments for developing countries. In this case, however, a starting year for the calculation of historic responsibilities has to be thoroughly justified. Based on either of these ideas, national socially just carbon caps could be calculated. However, as the distributional consequences of such an approach would be sudden and dramatic, intra-generational justice calls for a more moderate transitional approach such as Contraction and Convergence.[22] Following this, over a specified period of time, the total number of emissions allowances would contract from the status quo level to the target level and, at the same time, the distribution of emission rights would converge from the status quo to equal per capita rights. Anyway, it has to be kept in mind that even dramatic re-distributional burdens could be alleviated by well-targeted revenues spending.

The initial allocation of emissions allowances should be done by auctioning, because only then would the design comply with the polluter-pays-principle, with result-based justice in transfer and acquisition, and with result-based justice in allocation. Mutual compensation for efforts would be provided, the resulting distribution would follow individual claims, and polluters would have to fully pay resource use costs. In addition, major parts of the scarcity rents created by the cap remain with the government and can be used for multiple purposes. In free allocation schemes, in turn, the scarcity rents cap are transferred to polluters, who realize windfall profits if they can pass on opportunity costs to consumers.

The exact design of revenue spending decides to what extent the proceed-recycling complies with inter- and intra-generational justice as well as with the equality criterion. First, revenues can be used for lowering distortion-ary taxes, create a double dividend, and increase overall efficiency,[23] thus mainly serving national intra-generational justice. Second, investing rev-enues in additional climate mitigation measures would primarily promote inter-generational justice, because future global warming burdens would be further reduced. Third, using revenues for adaptation measures or damage compensation in countries or regions that suffer most from climate change would mainly foster international intra-generational justice. Fourth, com-pensating low-income households for higher energy costs or even cush-ioning cost increases for selected industries in order to prevent carbon leakage would cater to national intra-generational justice. Fifth, the Sky Trust proposal suggests reimbursing revenues to citizens on an equal per capita basis;[24] this follows the principle of equal entitlements to natural resource use and would also serve international intra-generational justice. In general, full auctioning combined with a well-designed re-distributional scheme addresses social justice issues most adequately.

While banking—the saving of early reduction credits for later use— might foster inter-generational justice, borrowing—the present use of future reductions—may be in violation of this criterion; offsets, anyway, might even serve social justice. Both borrowing and banking reduce com-pliance costs and thus serve intra-generational justice. However, compen-sating for present emissions by borrowing allowances from prospective future emission reductions, which then do not really take place, increases atmospheric GHG concentrations and hurts future generations. Banking, on the other hand, could additionally profit future generations if banked allowances are not used in the future. While bad offsets violate several social justice criteria, high quality offsets may serve inter-generational as well as intra-generational justice, because of compliance cost reductions as well as money, technology, and know-how transfers. Quantity limits are then dispensable for the same reasons, and the polluter-pays-principle fully applies anyway.

Following the equality principle, equal and easy access to the market should be granted to all emitters in order not to disadvantage specific groups or individuals. Market interventions should be used only with utmost care. Increasing the amount of allowances in the case that allowance prices hit a certain level (safety valves) can jeopardize inter-generational justice and also violates the polluter-pays principle as well as result-based justice in transfer and acquisition. At first glance, price ceilings protect present generations from excessive cost burdens and hence serve national intra-generational justice, and price floors seem to guarantee revenues usable for re-distributional measures even in the case of a lack of scarcity. However, price corridors with upper and lower price limits prevent the market from exhibiting the real resource scarcity and from making the polluter fully pay; hence, they interfere with inter-generational justice, the polluter-pays principle, and result-based justice in transfer and acquisition. In order to lower the cost burden for current generations, a stringent cap combined with a redistribution of auction revenues to poor households or international linkages of domestic carbon markets would be preferable. Compliance periods should be short, because this allows for short-term control over reduction achievements. They should also provide opportunities for immediate penalties and ex-post emission compensation in the case of non-compliance. This would significantly foster inter-generational justice. Trading periods, in turn, can be long, if supplemented by a short-term submission requirement for major parts of used emissions rights.

Reliable monitoring and quenching penalties are a necessary component of inter-generationally just carbon markets; they would also make polluters fully pay, and comply with result-based justice in transfer and acquisition. In emission markets, authorities have to check whether emitters can compensate for each and every unit of emissions by an emission allowance. Only this guarantees that emissions at one point are compensated for by emission reductions at another point, which then leads to compliance with the overall cap. Continuous emissions monitoring is preferable, while verified self-reporting can also be made sufficiently reliable. Both have to be combined with dependable emission allowance tracking. In the case of non-compliance, severe penalties punish polluters for breaching the rules ex post; ex ante, such penalties discourage emitters from non-compliance. This safeguards future generations, makes polluters fully pay, and complies with result-based justice in transfer and acquisition. Equality demands identical fine levels for all non-complying polluters. The above-mentioned social justice criteria also call for ex post compensation of allowance shortages.

Protective measures such as border (tax) adjustments are reasonable from an intra-generational international and inter-generational justice point of view as well as from an equality perspective. Ambitious domestic carbon markets may suffer from leakage, if competitors do not use comparably stringent policies. Leakage can be prevented by either creating an ambitious common carbon market amongst all major competitors, by protecting ambitious countries by border (tax) adjustments, or by making domestic carbon markets less stringent. The first alternative is obviously the most desirable from a social justice perspective—although politically the most difficult. For the same obvious reasons the last alternative is clearly unacceptable. On the grounds of equality, inter-generational justice, international intra-generational justice, and the polluter-pays-principle, border (tax) adjustment is certainly the second best option, because it levels the playing field for emitters in ambitious countries.

Against the background of these concrete design recommendations, we now ask to what extent current carbon markets in the EU and the US comply with social justice criteria?

3. HOW FAIR ARE CURRENT CARBON MARKETS?

3.1 EU Greenhouse Gas Emissions Trading Scheme

The EU ETS, still the biggest carbon market in the world, started operation in 2005, but has since been significantly revised when moving from Phase I (2005–2007), via Phases II (2008–2012) and III (2013–2020) to the planning stage of Phase IV (2021–2028).[25]

The EU ETS complies fully with the social justice criteria for bindingness, but only partly for coverage, although recent reforms have broadened the latter. It is a mandatory scheme that mainly covers CO_2 emissions from big stationary emitters such as utilities and energy intensive industries downstream. While air transport from, to, and within the EU should have been included from 2012 onwards, owing to international controversies, only flights within the EU are covered so far. Other major emitting sectors such as ground transport and households, however, are deliberately excluded from addition. In addition, the EU ETS covered CO_2 only in the first two phases (2005–2007, 2008–2012), but since 2013 additional GHG such as N_2O and PFCs can be included. Still, major pollutants such as methane remain unregulated under the EU ETS, so that overall the EU ETS continues to only comprise around 45% of EU GHG emissions. Nevertheless, while the social justice criterion for coverage is not fully fulfilled by the EU ETS alone, it has to be taken into account that additional, even partly market-based policy instruments such as energy taxes and energy efficiency standards cover major parts of the non-ETS sectors. Reasons for limited coverage under the EU ETS might be problems of measuring or respective EU or national targets and regulation under different schemes such as eco taxes or energy standards. Still, significant social justice problems remain as not all pollutants and polluters are treated on an equal basis, cost burdens are not shared fairly within the present generation, future generations may face unnecessary burdens, and not all polluters pay their fair share of using natural resources.

The EU ETS increasingly complies with social justice criteria for the cap size, but still lags behind the necessities. While the annual absolute volume cap was 2298.5 million metric tons of CO_2 in Phase I, allowing an increase of emissions by 8.3% compared with the actual emissions in 2005, in Phase II, the annual emissions budget was only 2086.5 million tons, representing a 5.9% decrease in allowed emissions compared with 2005.[26] In Phase III, a European cap replaces the National Allocation Plans of the first two phases. In addition, starting with average total emissions from 2008–2012, the EU cap is being reduced by 1.74% annually, which adds up to a 21% reduction by 2020 compared with 2005 emissions. The aviation cap is at a constant 210 million tons until 2020. After 2020, the total allowance amount is intended to decrease by 2.2% in order to achieve a 43% emission reduction by 2030 compared with 2005 levels. As a short-term measure against low carbon prices the EU has been holding back of 900 million tons of CO_2 allowances from the years 2014–2016; these allowances will be transferred to the Market Stability Reserve, available from 2019 onwards. Hence, there is a significant improvement in terms of allowed emissions from Phases I to IV, improving also the compliance with social justice criteria. Still, considering the reduction necessity for industrialized countries (25–40% by 2020, 80–90% by 2050), it remains questionable if the EU ETS effort is big enough to help the EU to fulfill its share of responsibility for achieving the 2°C target.

The social justice criteria for the validity of emission rights and the initial allocation are increasingly fulfilled after recent reforms, but still many flaws persist. Using CO_2 equivalents, one EU allowance authorizes polluters to emit 1 ton of CO_2eq in a given year. While in Phases I and II, 95 and 90% of all allowances had to be handed out for free, from Phase III onwards utilities have to buy all of their emission rights, with the exception of low GDP member states, which can provide 60% for free. The share of free allocation to energy intensive industries is supposed to decrease steadily from 80% in 2013 to 30% in 2020 and 0% in 2027; however, major exemptions for industries under the threat of carbon leakage have been granted so far, allowing 100% free allocations even beyond 2020. The aviation sector must only buy 15% of its emission allowances. New entrants receive allowances for free from a special reserve, while in the case of facility shut-downs allowances have to be returned. Banking and borrowing within compliance phases are unlimited. However, across compliance phases, banking was not allowed from Phases I to II, but was allowed for the following phases; cross-period borrowing remains prohibited. Limitations on offset credit use have become more stringent over time. While there were not limits in Phase I, since Phase II credits from nuclear and land use have been excluded. Since the start of Phase III, in addition, new credits are only accepted from projects in Least Developed Countries, industrial gas credits are excluded, and since 2015 no credits from the

Kyoto I period are accepted. Also, since Phase II, the use of credits must not exceed 50% of total EU reductions between 2008 and 2020 (approximately 1.6 billion tons). From Phase IV onwards, any international credits will be excluded. Hence, while social justice criteria are increasingly met in Phases III and IV, in particular the continuous use of free allocations remains questionable.

Auctioning off major parts of EU allowances allows the use of revenues for social justice purposes, but EU regulations only earmark 50% of these revenues to energy and climate policy use, leaving the rest up to member states' decisions. This leaves a lot of leeway to national member states. While many south-eastern European countries only use the earmarked 50% for climate-change-related spending, Germany established the Special Energy and Climate Fund, which transfers almost 100% of the revenues to national and international climate financing; France dedicates almost 100% to retrofitting social housing; and Finland invests 100% climate action in development cooperation.[27] This variety of revenue utilization makes an assessment difficult. However, while energy efficiency programs also lower energy costs for current generations and development aid might help vulnerable regions, intra-generational justice could be more directly targeted, e.g. by cost compensations for poor households or adaptation measures in most vulnerable areas.[28] This is particularly true, as environmental and economic goals are already targeted by capping emissions and generating carbon prices.

The EU ETS market design complies with social justice criteria to a large extent. The allowance market is equally open to all covered facilities and interested parties. Allowances can be bought from two major auctions, EEX in Leipzig and ICE in London, in a non-discriminatory procedure. While compliance periods are 1 year, trading periods have been steadily increased from 3 via 5 to 8 years, trying to increase the long-term planning reliability for abatement investment. For price control, the EU decided on a Market Stability Reserve from 2019 onwards for addressing market imbalances, where measures such as cap reductions or international linkages would be preferable from the social justice perspective.[29]

The EU ETS monitoring scheme complies entirely with the respective social justice criteria. All installations have to file annual emission reports according to harmonized EU rules. Reports are verified by accredited verifiers. If allowed emissions are exceeded, facilities have to cover excess emissions and pay a penalty of 100 Euro per ton from Phase III (40 Euro in Phase I and II). Also, the names of facilities not meeting their obligations are published.

Overall, while having started poorly, after the recent reforms the EU ETS complies with major social justice criteria. Still, much leeway for improvements exist, especially in the areas of coverage, cap size, initial allocation, revenue spending, and price control.

3.2   The Regional Greenhouse Gas Initiative

RGGI was the first large-scale, multi-state carbon market in the US and started in 2009. It now covers nine North-eastern states' CO_2 emissions. Already in Phase I (2009–2014), RGGI underwent a fundamental reform before entering Phase II (2015–2020).[30]

RGGI fulfills social justice criteria for bindingness but only partly for coverage. RGGI is mandatory for all participating sources, but it only covers CO_2 emissions from combustion in big utilities (>25 MW) downstream. While industry emissions are of minor relevance (e.g. in New York State, e.g. they comprise only 7% of all energy-related CO_2 emissions), RGGI still neither covers emissions from other sectors such as transport or households nor does it include non-CO_2 GHG emissions. Again, other policies might step in and there are problems of measurement, but still similar social justice problems as in the case of the EU ETS remain.

RGGI increasingly fulfills the social justice requirement after the 2014 reform. While the cap was initially set at a generous constant 188 million US tons of CO_2 per year from 2009 to 2014 (4% above average 2002–2004 emissions) and a reduction path of 2.5% per year in Phase II, the tremendous oversupply led to a cap reduction by more than 50% in 2014. For 2014 the cap was set at 91 million US tons and it then enters the yearly reduction dynamics of 2.5% until 2020, resulting in a total emission reduction of more than two-thirds compared with 2002–2004 emissions, a period when RGGI region emissions already did not significantly exceed 1990 levels.

Social justice criteria for the initial allocation of allowances and allowance validity are largely fulfilled in the RGGI case. While RGGI rules only oblige participating states to auction off at least 25% of all allowances, the actual average auction rate is higher than 90%. New entrants have to buy all of their allowances, and there are no specific rules for returning unused allowances in the case of facility shut-downs. Banking is unlimited within and across compliance periods; however, Phase II caps were adjusted for Phase I banked allowances in the 2014 reform. Borrowing is prohibited. Offset use is limited to 3.3% of facility emissions and to additional and sustainable CH_4, SF_3, and CO_2 project credits from agriculture, forestry, waste treatment, and building energy efficiency within the US. While the early program allowed the use of Kyoto credits if allowance prices exceed US$10, since the 2014 reform no such credits are accepted.

Revenue spending so far focusses on climate action and budget consolidation, thus mainly serving inter-generational justice. The auctioning rules oblige participating states to invest all revenues from the 25% mandatory auctioning share into climate and energy measures. However, the real auction share of approximately 90% leaves a lot of leeway to participating states. Around two-thirds of all revenues are used for climate and energy programs, 15% go to the support of disadvantaged communities, and 15% to budget consolidation. While obviously the focus is on inter-generational justice, efficiency programs and cost compensation also serve intra-generational national justice.

RGGI's market design also increasingly complies with social justice criteria, but is still flawed with market intervention mechanisms. The allowance market is equally open to all covered entities and interested parties. Allowances can be bought from non-discriminator state auctions and several secondary markets such as the Chicago Climate Futures Exchange. Control periods are 3 years, after which 100% of emissions have to be covered by allowances, but in addition, after the first 2 years of each control period 50% of needed allowances must be held in stock, providing extra safety in terms of compliance. For price control, RGGI implemented a floor price of US$1.89, which has increased annually by 2.5%. In addition, the 2014 reform implemented a Cost Containment Reserve (CCR) populated with 10 million allowances taken from the overall budget and refilled only if necessary. CCR allowances are auctioned if the carbon price exceeds US$4 (2014), 6 (2015), 8 (2016), or 10 (2017); after 2017 trigger prices increase by 2.5% per year. While the CCR replaces earlier price ceilings, still, better options for limiting price fluctuation, such as international linkages, are available.

RGGI's monitoring scheme complies entirely with the respective social justice criteria. Emissions data is continuously provided by the US Environmental Protection Agency based on 1995 Clean Air Act rules. Allowances, emissions, and transfers are recorded in the CO_2 Allowance Tracking System, which is even open to the public. In the case of non-compliance, fines of up to US$25,000 apply in addition to a 3-for-1 excess emissions coverage requirement.

Overall, RGGI also complies with major social justice criteria. In particular, the 2014 reform accomplished major improvements. Still, coverage, revenue use, and market design could be improved.

4. CONCLUSIONS

We are convinced that social justice, being a founding principle of sustainable development and becoming more and more important owing to carbon pricing driven energy price increases, has to play a key role in the design of sufficiently ambitious and politically feasible carbon pricing schemes. Carbon pricing itself also should be the main pillar in sustainable climate policy not only because it provides emission reductions at lowest cost to society and thus minimizes the burden to current generations, but also because considering social justice issues in carbon pricing design is possible. However, research and policy have not adequately considered social justice in carbon pricing design.

Here, as a first step, we have provided a framework for designing socially just carbon markets and for evaluating existing programs on social justice grounds. We have derived concrete design recommendations from rather general and sometimes even vague social justice concepts; we have shown that carbon pricing can easily serve social justice purposes if well designed; and we have evaluated early EU and US markets, the EU ETS and the RGGI, on these grounds. Such markets started poorly, but after recent reforms, in addition to becoming more environmentally effective and economically efficient, they increasingly comply with social justice criteria. Still, of course, both programs can be improved. The key design elements for improvements are coverage, cap size, the initial allocation, revenue spending, and price control mechanisms.

As more carbon markets have emerged recently e.g. in California, China, Japan, New Zealand, and South Korea, evaluating those from a social justice perspective is certainly a promising endeavor for future research. The same is true for expected design proposals in Canadian provinces, other US states, and maybe even Australia. Still, California's Cap-and-Trade Program seems to be particularly interesting, as much thought has been spent on designing auction proceed investment plans (http://www.arb.ca.gov/cc/capandtrade/auctionproceeds/auctionproceeds.htm distribution), one of the key design elements for targeting social justice in carbon markets. Also, as linking domestic carbon markets can be considered an important complement to global climate policy, the social justice implications of such linkages is a worthwhile subject for further studies with, for example, the already established California–Québec link as an empirical example. Not least, adjusting and applying our evaluation framework to carbon taxation might further strengthen the case for sustainable market-based climate policy. This is precisely because, despite critical voices, carbon pricing can be designed in such a way to effectively foster social justice in climate policy.

NOTES

1. WCED (1987), *Our Common Future*, Oxford: Oxford University Press.
2. Schleich, J. et al. (2014), 'Citizens' perceptions of justice in international climate policy', *Climate Policy*; DOI: 10.1080/14693062.2014.979129.
3. Heindl, P., R. Schüßler and A. Löschel (2014), 'Ist die Energiewende sozial gerecht?' *Wirtschaftsdienst*; DOI: 10.1007/s10273-014-1705-7.
4. World Bank (2015), *State and Trends of Carbon Pricing*, Washington DC.
5. Ranson, M. and R.N. Stavins (2015), 'Linkage of greenhouse gas emissions trading systems', *Climate Policy*; DOI: 10.1080/14693062.2014.997658.
6. Ott, K. and R. Döring (2004), *Theorie und Praxis starker Nachhaltigkeit*, Marburg: Metropolis.
7. Helmstädter, E. (1997), 'Über die Gerechtigkeit gerechter Regeln', in M. Held (ed.), *Normative Grundfragen der Ökonomik*, Frankfurt: Campus; Krebs, A. (ed.) (2000), *Gleichheit oder Gerechtigkeit*, Frankfurt: Suhrkamp; Lerch, A. (2003), *Individualismus, Ökonomik und Naturerhalt—Zu den normativen Grundlagen der Ökologischen Ökonomik*, Marburg: Metropolis.
8. Hayek, F.A. von (1996), *Die Anmaßung von Wissen*, Tübingen: Mohr; Nozick, R. (1974), *Anarchie, Staat, Utopia, Moderne*, München: Verlags Gesellschaft.
9. Kahneman, D., J.L. Knetsch, and R. Thaler (1986), 'Fairness as a Constraint on Profit Seeking', *American Economic Review* 75, 728–741.
10. Above n. 7.
11. Marx, K. (1972), *Kritik des Gothaer Programms*, in K. Marx, F. Engels, *Werke Vol. 19*, Berlin.
12. Rawls, J. (1971), *A Theory of Justice*, Cambridge, MA: Harvard University Press.
13. Above n. 6.
14. Above n. 6.
15. Above n. 2.
16. Above n. 1.
17. Fankhauser, S. and C. Hepburn (2010), 'Designing carbon markets Part I+II', *Energy Policy* 38, 4363–4370, 4381–4387.
18. Rudolph, S. et al. (2012), 'Towards sustainable carbon markets', in Kreiser, L. et al. (eds), *Carbon Pricing, Growth and the Environment*, Cheltenham: Edward Elgar, 167–183.
19. Harris, P.G. (2010), *World Ethics and Climate Change*, Edinburgh: Edinburgh University Press; Lerch, A. (2011), 'CO$_2$-Emissionshandel—effizient oder gerecht?' *Zeitschrift für Sozialökonomie* 48, 39–47; Ott, H.E. and W. Sachs (2002), 'The ethics of international emissions trading', in Pinguelli-Rosa, L. and M. Munasinghe (eds), *Ethics, Equity and International Negotiations on Climate Change*, Cheltenham: Edward Elgar, 159–178.
20. IPCC (2014), *Climate Change 2014—Synthesis Report*, Geneva.
21. WBGU (2009), *Solving the Climate Dilemma*, Berlin.
22. Meyer, A. (2000), *Contraction and Convergence*, Totnes: Green Books.
23. Bovenberg, L.A. (1999), 'Green tax reforms and the double dividend', *International Tax and Public Finance* 6, 421–443.
24. Barnes, P. (2001), *Who Owns the Sky?* Washington, DC: Island Press.
25. EU Com (2013), *The EU Emissions Trading System* (EU ETS), Brussels; EU Com (2014), *A Policy Framework for Climate and Energy Policy in the Period 2020 to 2030*, Brussels.
26. Ellerman, A.D. and P.L. Joskow (2008), *The European Union's Emissions Trading System in Perspective*, Cambridge, MA: Pew Center on Global Climate Change (MIT).
27. Germanwatch (2013), *Using EU ETS Auctioning Revenues for Climate Action*, Berlin.
28. Caney, S. and C. Hepburn (2011), 'Carbon trading—Unethical, unjust and ineffective?' Centre for Climate Change Economics and Policy Working Paper No. 59/

Grantham Research Institute on Climate Change and the Environment Working Paper No. 49.
29. Lerch, A. (2015), 'Emissionshandel reloaded', *Ökologisches Wirtschaften* 4/2015, 12.
30. RGGI (2013), *Model Rule—Revised 2013*, New York; Rudolph, S. and A. Lerch (2012), 'Treibhausgas-Emissionshandel in den USA', *Zeitschrift für Umweltpolitik & Umweltrecht*, 35, 421–449.

Index

AB 32 *see* cap-and-trade programs, in California

abalone industry *see* Marine Park protection via market-based instruments (South Australia)

Abalone Industry Association of South Australia 14

absolute volume caps *see* carbon markets and social justice, in EU/US

ACEEE (American Council for an Energy-Efficient Economy) 66

Acre, Brazil *see* REDD+ programs, in Brazil

ad valorem and *ad unit* taxes *see* tax burden shifting and Pigovian principle, in EU

Advisory Opinion on the Responsibilities and Obligations in the Area (ITLOS) 185–186

Africa *see* subsidy reform and renewable energy, in African/Indian Ocean island states

agricultural sector
  water depletion due to fracking 79
  water shortages 95–96, 98
  see also carbon price incentives, in Australian land sector; tax incentives/penalties and water resource protection, in US

air pollution
  due to drought in California 97–98
  due to natural gas emissions 74–76

air transport emissions 227, 228

Amazon forest *see* REDD+ programs, in Brazil

Annex I/Non-Annex I States division 204–209
  see also Emissions Trading Scheme (ETS) linkage and Paris Agreement; IMO economic

instruments and CBDRRC principle

anti-corruption measures 30

aquifer depletion *see* hydraulic fracturing and water resources, in US

Australia
  Agriculture, Food and Fisheries, Ministry of 10–11, 14
  Carbon Credits Act (2011) 36, 37, 38, 41, 42
  Carbon Farming Initiative (CFI) 42–43
  Carbon Pollution Reduction Scheme (2008) 43
  Clean Energy Act (2011) 42
  Climate Change Authority 42
  conditional targets as incentivisation 212
  Direct Action Plan 35, 39
  Emissions Reduction Fund (ERF) grants (2014-2017) 35–36
  Fisheries Management Act (2007) (SA) 5, 8
  Henry Review of the Australian Taxation System 133–135
  Income Tax Assessment Act (1997) 41
  Marine Park Local Advisory Groups (MPLAGs) 6–7
  Marine Parks Act (2007) (SA) 5–6, 8, 9, 10, 14
  National Greenhouse Gas Inventory 35
  National Packaging Covenant (1999) 128
  National Pollutant Inventory 131
  National Waste Minimisation and Recycling Strategy 127
  National Waste Policy 127–128, 131–132

Printed and bound by CPI Group (UK) Ltd, Croydon, CR0 4YY

23/04/2025

14660957-0003